May. 5, 2010

FILES
FROM THE
EDGE

ABOUT THE AUTHOR

Philip J. Imbrogno has researched UFOs and other paranormal phenomena for more than thirty years and is recognized as an authority in the field. A science educator at the secondary and collegiate levels for twenty-eight years, he has been interviewed by the *New York Times* and *Coast to Coast AM*, has appeared on NBC's *Today Show* and *The Oprah Winfrey Show*, and has been featured in documentaries on the History Channel, A&E, Lifetime, and HBO. Imbrogno worked closely with many top UFO investigators, including Dr. J. Allen Hynek and Budd Hopkins. He can be contacted by e-mail at Bel1313@yahoo.com.

FILES
FROM THE
EDGE

A PARANORMAL
INVESTIGATOR'S
EXPLORATIONS
INTO HIGH
STRANGENESS

PHILIP J. IMBROGNO

Lle
We

First Edition
First Printing, 2010

Cover design by Kevin R. Brown
Cover images © iStockphoto.com, except for crystal ball © Photographer's Choice/PunchStock
Interior art by Llewellyn art department

Llewellyn is a registered trademark of Llewellyn Worldwide, Ltd.

Library of Congress Cataloging-in-Publication Data
Imbrogno, Philip J.
    Files from the edge: a paranormal investigator's explorations into high strangeness / Philip J. Imbrogno.—1st ed.
        p. cm.
    Includes bibliographical references and index.
    ISBN 978-0-7387-1881-1
    1. Parapsychology. 2. Supernatural. I. Title.
    BF1031.I43 2010
    130—dc22
                                                        2009053261

Llewellyn Worldwide does not participate in, endorse, or have any authority or responsibility concerning private business transactions between our authors and the public.
    All mail addressed to the author is forwarded but the publisher cannot, unless specifically instructed by the author, give out an address or phone number.
    Any Internet references contained in this work are current at publication time, but the publisher cannot guarantee that a specific location will continue to be maintained. Please refer to the publisher's website for links to authors' websites and other sources.

Llewellyn Publications
A Division of Llewellyn Worldwide, Ltd.
2143 Wooddale Drive
Woodbury, MN 55125-2989, U.S.A.
www.llewellyn.com

Printed in the United States of America

To Dr. J. Allen Hynek, who will be remembered
as a Galileo of the twentieth century. He paved the way
for new worlds that await our exploration.

ALSO BY PHILIP J. IMBROGNO

Night Siege: The Hudson Valley UFO Sightings

Celtic Mysteries in New England:
Windows to Another Dimension in America's Northeast

Interdimensional Universe:
The New Science of UFOs, Paranormal Phenomena,
and Otherdimensional Beings

FORTHCOMING BY PHILIP J. IMBROGNO

Ultraterrestrial Contact: A Paranormal Investigator's
Explorations into the Hidden Abduction Epidemic

CONTENTS

PREFACE

When picking up a book for the first time, most people have a tendency to skip the introduction or preface and go right to the main chapters and look for what they consider the important information. They may also look to see how the author is presenting the material and what the "angle" is. I hope you will read this preface before you scan through the chapters because it is an introduction to who I am and my true feelings about the topics in the books I write. In order for my readers to understand my work in the field of the paranormal, I strongly recommend that my previous books be read first; they include: *Night Siege: The Hudson Valley UFO Sightings*, *Contact of the 5th Kind*, *Celtic Mysteries: Windows to Another Dimension in America's Northeast*, and *Interdimensional Universe: The New Science of UFOs, Paranormal Phenomena, and Otherdimensional Beings*.

I have been a science educator for the past twenty-eight years with undergraduate and graduate degrees in astronomy, earth science, and chemistry. When investigating paranormal phenomenon, I try to use my scientific background as much as possible, but since we are dealing with forces and dimensional states of the universe that are very hard to perceive, the scientific method breaks down and for the most part cannot be used in this type of research. I firmly believe there is serious research being done by other paranormal investigators who come from many disciplines. The task of these researchers is a difficult one: they are attempting to lay down the foundation of a new science. However, conducting research that results in verifiable documentation requires new methods of investigation. Most importantly, we must change our view of how science perceives reality; in other words, the scientific method needs to be revised so we can investigate the multi-dimensional universe in a "scientific" manner. Also, we must modify current cutting-edge technologies and invent new instrumentation to assist us in our understanding of paranormal events. Such technologies are now being developed by several researchers (including myself) and early prototypes of equipment have proven very promising, especially in the fields of electronic voice phenomenon (EVP) and digital photography sensitive to the electromagnetic wavelengths outside that of human visual perception.

My own initial study of the paranormal began with the investigation of UFO reports three decades ago, and over the course of those many years I have accumulated a considerable number of cases that involve channeling, hauntings, strange creatures, animal mutilations, poltergeist, and all forms of psychic phenomena. All of these cases came to my attention as a result of my research into the UFO experience. I found these paranormal cases so interesting that I spent quite a great deal of time looking into them and trying to understand their relationship to the UFO phenomena and the connection they have with the multi-dimensional universe. This book is the result of a small number of those cases that remained in my files for years. Although some of the cases presented in this book took place decades ago, some are much more recent and have never been published. The paranormal events presented in this work have undergone extensive scrutinizing by me and experts in various fields. I believe them to be authentic representations of an unseen world that exists beyond human perception. However, with modern computer technology an image of a ghost, strange creature, or even a UFO for that matter is only as credible as the word of the witness.

Over the past five years, many paranormal groups have formed and quite a number of television shows have aired all apparently with the intent of investigating and documenting paranormal activity. These groups, clubs, and television "investigators" do not objectively investigate—they go into a case with a predetermined belief of what is responsible for generating phenomena. For example, one "chief investigator" from a popular paranormal reality television show stated that they go into a case trying to disprove it. This attitude, in my opinion, is wrong: you must enter a case with a blank slate and let the evidence fall where it may, and then make a conclusion. Several of these reality paranormal television shows are scripted to make them more interesting with the purpose of increasing the ratings. I know this for a fact since I have taken part in a number of these programs over the years as a "consulting expert."

Coming to a definite conclusion after an investigation is very difficult since the resources of those trying to do serious research is limited. Because of this, there can only be three conclusions to any paranormal case: the first is that there is no evidence that anything out of the ordinary took place, the second is that the data is inconclusive and finally, that something out of the ordinary did take place, but unless you were able to positively identify it, then the case has to remain open and put in the category of "unknown."

Popular evidence suggests paranormal phenomenon is increasing substantially on a global level. Those who experience an event outside their normal reality come from all walks of life and are of every age. I firmly believe that what we call the paranormal or supernatural of today will be a new science of the late twenty-first century. Once the foundation is established for this new science, human beings will embark on an exploration into this realm of hidden reality and obtain a better understanding of the complex multi-dimensional universe in which we are an integral part. Over the many years and the hundreds of cases I have investigated, my exploration of the paranormal has changed from a scientific study to more of an adventure: I have witnessed some of the events presented in this book and to me, there is no doubting their realness.

It is also important I thank the following researchers whose previous work and tireless efforts aided my own and helped me stay on the correct path to get a clear view of what lies ahead. They include John Fuller, John Keel, Budd

Hopkins, Rosemary Ellen Guiley, and last but not least, my mentor, Dr. J. Allen Hynek. This is an exciting time, and like the voyagers of long ago who left their home shores to chart unknown oceans and explore new lands, we are about to set foot onto a strange, new, unexplored world full of wonder and danger.

Philip J. Imbrogno
January 2010

THE NEW SCIENCE

Human beings have always had a fascination with the supernatural. When the people of ancient cultures witnessed something they could not explain, they would attribute it to some god, spirit, or unknown elemental force of nature. Two thousand years ago, thunder and lightning frightened inhabitants of the Mediterranean and northern Europe; despite the attempts of the greatest minds of that time to find a rational explanation, not one had an answer for what caused this terrifying phenomenon. It was then said that the lightning and the thunder were beyond the understanding of mere mortals and the result of an angry god. The Greeks and the Romans called this entity Zeus and Jupiter, while the Norse, Anglo-Saxon and continental Germanic people called him Thor. Science later gave us answers and because of this knowledge, most people no longer fear the thunder and lightning of an electrical storm.

A study of the natural world is not an exact science. History has taught us that the theories and laws of the universe science has placed so high on a pedestal as being the absolute truth are shaky and changeable. Today's scientists continue to make the same mistakes as their predecessors by holding on to outdated ideas for reasons they only know. Perhaps keeping the old ways intact gives many of the older and established professors of the academic world feelings of certainty and security.

REPEATING THE SAME MISTAKES

In the seventeenth and eighteenth centuries, science was just starting to bloom as new discoveries were being made almost every day in all disciplines from astronomy to zoology. It was in this early scientific age that William Herschel discovered the planet Uranus using a relatively new device at the time called the telescope. The era also saw the beginning of great exploration as human beings began to understand the forces of nature. Using improved instruments and logical thinking, scientists realized a supernatural being was not necessary to explain wind, earthquakes, volcanic eruptions, thunder, and lightning. Yet, there were still many mysteries that science could not explain—one of them was our sun.

It was common knowledge in the 1700s that our sun was very far away from Earth and that every second it produced enormous amounts of energy. A heated debate among scientists and theologians emerged to explain the sun's energy source. No one had a definite answer as to what fuel source could produce that amount of energy for such a long period of time. In the eighteenth and nineteenth centuries, coal, wood, oil, and natural gas were the only fuel sources they understood. Since most of these were fossils fuels and all of them were formed on our planet, they didn't seem to apply to the sun.

Theories abounded, yet not one of the greatest scientific minds of the eighteenth century could offer a suitable theory to explain our sun's energy output. When asked what powered the sun, most scientists would reply that it was beyond man's understanding. Some even claimed that a supernatural being was responsible—an angel of fire (so to speak) who ensured the sun would continue to output heat and light uninterrupted for millions of years so humans could survive.

The scientists and philosophers of more than two hundred years ago had no knowledge of nuclear energy. They could not imagine—even in their wildest dreams and speculations—that when atoms are smashed together, a great amount of energy is released . . . great enough to power a star like our sun. Mankind would have to wait until the twentieth century before humans truly understood the power source of the sun. When nuclear fission and fusion were discovered, humans once again no longer needed a supernatural or divine being of great power to explain the energy output of our sun and other stars in the galaxy.

It's amazing to think that today in our modern world science still adheres to the rule that if your current ideas, knowledge, and theories can't explain something, it must not exist. Science is the pursuit of making what is unknown, *known* and *understood*. Yet, the scientists of today have forgotten their true mission and have once again turned their backs to reports of the unexplained. The human state of mind has

changed little over centuries past: many modern people attribute unexplainable events to a supernatural cause just like
their ancestors of a more unenlightened time. The confused
and often scared people begin looking for answers to help
them understand what has taken place and so look to the
scientist for answers. However, scientists do not have the instrumentation or knowledge to prove or disprove the reality of strange events; they give the unexplainable very little
attention and so these phenomena remain without explanation. UFOs and other forms of paranormal phenomena have
no easy explanation; because they are complex, the only way
we can begin to find answers is if we open our minds to ideas
considered impossible by the scientific community and society at large.

Speculation is the key to discovery; if people like Galileo,
Brahe, Priestly, Copernicus, and Kepler didn't speculate and
open their minds to accept new, radical ideas, modern science
would never have been born. We must give up our old ideas
of a finite expanding universe and consider that the cosmos is
more complex than any of us could have ever dreamed, possibly with multiple parallel universes each composed of several
dimensions. It is my belief that experiences mistakenly labeled as "supernatural" or "paranormal" originate from a parallel dimension or universe very close to our own. Recently,
the theory of not a single universe, but a mega-universe (or
"multiverse") has received considerable attention from not
only scientists, but the general public as well.

MY INTRODUCTION TO THE MULTIVERSE

During my early days as a student at MIT, sometime in the winter of 1977, I attended a lecture given by Dr. Philip Morrison called "How We Know What We Know in Science." I had read Dr. Morrison's work in theoretical physics and found his insights fascinating—I had to see and hear what he had to say in person. However, before I continue, let me give you some background information on Dr. Morrison and his contribution to our current knowledge of the state of the universe.

Philip Morrison's title was Institute Professor at the Massachusetts Institute of Technology, the highest academic honor bestowed on a university faculty member. In my opinion, he was one of the world's greatest physicists and an amazing teacher: Dr. Morrison could explain complex astronomy and physics theories so clearly that anyone, no matter the level of education, could understand it. He was a talented educator who spoke in complete sentences . . . and paragraphs. Dr. Morrison had a unique ability to verbally convey his thoughts and ideas to his students with crystal clarity.

If I had to describe him, I would say he was a friendly, down to earth, spirited, witty gentleman who loved science with all his heart. He once said "I teach because I was taught; my great love in life is to explain my craft." In 1959, Dr. Morrison suggested that a scientific project be initiated to search for extraterrestrial life by listening to the universe using radio waves. For his time, this was a radical suggestion. When asked about it, he would say "I just want to know if anyone is out there. Are we alone in the universe or are there countless numbers of civilizations in the galaxy also looking up to the night sky and wondering the same thing?" When members of the media asked him if this search would ever find "aliens," Dr. Morrison would reply: "The probability for success is hard to estimate but if we don't look, the chance of success is zero."

I was quite anxious to hear Dr. Morrison's presentation so I got there more than an hour before the lecture to ensure a front-row seat in the very large auditorium at the Mac-Laurin Building at MIT. I really didn't know what to expect, but as eight o'clock drew near, every seat in the house filled up. I looked around the auditorium and noticed some of the most esteemed scientists in the country were present, including the famous Dr. Carl Sagan. Dr. Morrison entered the room and began to talk, and I was very surprised that his presentation quickly turned to the topic of extraterrestrial life and suggested our current understanding of the cosmos could be very wrong. I wanted to mention this incident since it was the first time I heard a person of great standing in the scientific community talk not only about UFOs and alien civilizations, but also what was later called "string theory" and the concept of a multidimensional universe. Dr. Morrison's two-hour presentation was amazing—later that night in my small apartment in Cambridge, I considered changing my major at MIT from chemistry to physics.

Dr. Morrison's words rang true and still influence me to this day. He presented some amazing ideas that night—very radical for that time—but what I remember most were his closing words: "What was presented here tonight is a theory and we, as scientists, must look for further answers since what we now know about the universe is limited. However, extraordinary claims and ideas also require extraordinary evidence." This was a saying that Dr. Morrison used since the early sixties and was later copied by scientists in many fields including Carl Sagan. In case you were wondering, I did not change my major; I was informed that there were more opportunities in chemistry than physics in the worlds of industry, research, and education.

Dr. Morrison passed over in 2005 at age 89. When he died, this world lost a great man and, in my opinion, one of the most brilliant minds since Isaac Newton. Dr. Morrison's legacy continues to this day—he encouraged a group of young scientists (including myself) to look further for answers and not to be limited by what you have learned from your teachers.

A NEW THEORY REVEALS ANOTHER REALITY

In 1976, Daniel Z. Freedman, at SUNY Stony Brook proposed an idea that the universe was connected together by a four-dimensional force he called "super gravity."[1] Within five years of Dr. Freedman's published paper on the subject, our view of the cosmos grew larger, and it was found that super gravity could not explain the correct state of the universe; a forgotten idea called "string theory" was once again taken seriously.

---

1. Peter Breitenlohner and Daniel Z. Freedman, "Positive Energy in Anti-De Sitter Backgrounds and Gauged Extended Super Gravity," *Physics Letter B* (MIT) 115 (September 2, 1982): 197.

In the twentieth century, the popular view of the geometrical design of elementary particles that make up matter was that they are small spheres, so small that more than 100 trillion of them lined up could fit on the head of a pin and still have plenty of room. However, string theory states that the building material that makes up the elementary particles are much smaller and not spheres but two-dimensional strings with a length of one billion trillion trillionth of a centimeter (very small).

String theory was originally developed during the late 1960s and early 1970s as a never completely successful attempt to tie all the forces in the universe together and provide the physicists with a neat package of all and everything.[2] In the 1960s, Dr. Geoffrey Chew, then professor of physics at the University of California at Berkeley, discovered that mesons had unusual spins that could not be explained at the time.[3] This was later explained by Nobel laureate Dr. Yoichiro Nambu of the University of Chicago and Dr. Leonard Susskind of Stanford University to be the relationship that would be expected from rotating strings. Dr. Chew advocated making a theory for the interactions of these trajectories that did not presume they were formed by fundamental particles, but two-dimensional strings. At first, string theory was con-

---

2. Leonard Susskind, "The Anthropic Landscape of String Theory," Presented at MIT, February 2003.

3. A meson is a particle emitted from the nucleus of the atom with a negative charge. It is seen in beta decay of certain radioactive isotopes like carbon-14. When a meson leaves the nucleus, the atom receives one more proton and becomes more positive.

sidered (by the older, established scientific community) to be nothing more than a pipe dream invented by a group of wide-eyed scientists who allowed wild speculations to cloud their logical scientific judgment. Since the established scientific community at that time was so skeptical of the idea of strings holding the universe together, the theory was not seriously considered until the mid-1980s.

String theory is actually a theory of gravity and an extension of general relativity where vibrating strings are the glue that ties all the forces in the universe together. In string theory, all the properties of these elementary particles (which include charge, mass, and spin) come from the string's vibration. The more frequent the vibration, the more energy and mass the particle will possess. The sequence in which a number of strings vibrate will determine if they will become neutrons, protons, electrons, leptons, or other types of more exotic particles. As with a stringed musical instrument, the wire must be stretched under considerable tension in order to vibrate at a particular frequency, in this case the force would have to be close to 10^{40} tons. This is one of the flaws in the theory; scientists have yet to find this great celestial tension load required for a string to vibrate.

The Guitar and the Universe

To understand string theory a little better, consider the idea of a guitar being tuned. The tension and thickness of the string will determine what musical note is produced when played. Each note produced by the string can correspond to the creation of the elementary particles that make up all matter from the smallest atom to the largest galaxies. In string theory (as with a guitar string), the string has to be under tension in order for it to vibrate and produce a sound (energy). However, the guitar string is attached to a solid base, but the cosmological string is floating in time and space. The "base" holding the tension to the quantum string has not yet been found, but theoretical scientists are convinced of its existence!

To take this a speculative step further, imagine if intelligent super beings understood how strings work: they could tune them and then pluck them to play different notes that in turn would change one particle into another and simultaneously alter the properties of matter in the universe. Simply put, if you knew the secret of the vibrating strings and how to play the guitar of the universe, base metals like iron or lead could be changed into gold, the highest achievement of alchemists in antiquity. Throughout time, legends from many Middle Eastern cultures tell of "supernatural" beings called the *Djinn* (genies) who have the ability to shape-shift and change one type of substance into another. To mere mortals it appears as magic, but perhaps the Djinn and other beings like them know how to play the cosmological strings of the universe. The legend of the Djinn also states that they are invisible and live in a world (dimension) close to our own. Sound familiar? Let's explore these other dimensions in greater detail.

Dimensions Abound

String theory also predicts the existence of additional dimensions in the physical universe created when strings actually loop or fold around each other. These extra dimensions are actual physical areas of space existing all around us that we cannot see or enter. This is because human beings are limited to existing in three-dimensional space along one particular part of a string. Although one aspect of the theory predicts the existence of twenty-six dimensions, it has been proven mathematically that this model would be unstable since these extra dimensions would eventually collapse on each other. A stable model of string theory (called the M theory) places membrane-like structures that interact with the strings and provide support keeping them intact. The membranes also act like buffers between the dimensions, ensuring that one reality does not constantly clash with another. In this mathematical model, eleven stable dimensions can exist in any given physical part of the universe.

A good analogy would be to imagine a sheet of glass with many drops of water on both sides. The drops of water represent each dimension while the glass is the membrane, and the sheet itself represents our universe. If you have that pictured in your mind, now imagine an infinite number of glass sheets all with water bubbles on them. Each plane of glass represents another universe. So what would happen if two glass sheets hit each other? No one knows for sure, but the one thing physicists are certain of is that although two colliding universes might be annihilated, the information in the two realities would not disappear—they would still exist and most likely form into one large universe or many smaller ones.[4] Since scientists widely believe string theory is consistent with quantum gravity, many researchers, including myself, hope that it will explain the many mysteries of the cosmos, including paranormal phenomena.

ENTER THE MULTIVERSE

If string theory hasn't confused you yet with its prediction of eleven dimensions in our universe, hold onto your hat—a new idea states that all the stars, gas clouds, planets, and galaxies we can see from our viewpoint in time and space (called the Hubble Volume) is only one single universe, the one we happen to live in. The multiverse theory states that in all existence, there are countless numbers of parallel universes larger and smaller in size than our own, each with eleven physical dimensions! If this theory is correct, what we call our visible universe is one of many multiple bubble-like universes in the multiverse.

The multiverse (or "meta-universe" as it is sometimes called) is an infinite number of possible universes that interact together and make up what we call reality. In some of these other universes, the laws of physics are the same and in some quite different. Universes close by each other in the multiverse are called parallel universes; each could be inhabited by intelligent beings that rarely, if ever, get to meet their cousins who live in a nearby reality.

---

4. Stephen Hawking, *The Hawking Paradox*, Discovery Channel, 2005.

Imagine there is another copy of you reading this book in another galaxy billions of lights years away on another planet called Earth. The life of this person is almost identical to yours in every respect, until now. Let's say you decide to stop reading this book but your twin continues to read it until the book is finished: this would be the turning point from which the realities start to diverge. Most would find this idea very strange and unacceptable. We would like to think we are all unique, but according to the simplest theory in the multiverse, called the level I, this duplicate of you actually exists in a galaxy 40 billion light years from our planet. There are four levels of the multiverse theory, presented briefly in the following sections.

Level I: The Cosmic Horizon

In this version all matter in the universe is dimensional and expanding in all directions across space and time. The level I universe is so vast that eventually everything is duplicated with even a copy of you at a great distance somewhere in space beyond 40 billion light years. All intelligent beings in the level I universe experience the same laws of physics. This theory discounts the idea of you and your double(s) ever meeting; the distances required for the duplication to take place is too vast.

Level II: The Cosmic Bubble

This theory states that there is an infinite number of level I universes existing like bubbles throughout reality. Each universe would have a different space-time dimensionality and would most likely have different physical laws that govern them. Each bubble universe is predicted to be farther and farther from our own universe. Even if you traveled at the speed of light forever, you could never reach the closest one since the inflation of the bubbles continues to move them away from each other at greater and greater speed. Although in the level II multiverse we are unable to interact with these other realities, scientists can infer their presence indirectly by observing unexplained phenomenon in our universe and gravitational interactions with clusters of galaxies.

Level III: Infinite Diverging Realities

Level I and II deal with worlds that are too far for us to ever see. The level III theory says that they are all close by and extensions of our own reality. This idea originates from the concept that random quantum processes cause the universe to branch outward in time, space, and dimensionality into multiple copies, one for each possible outcome. Simply put, every action or decision being made or not made by every living being has multiple outcomes and each is branching out, creating their own separate reality. There may be a reality in which you got married, another in which you did not. In one reality you may have brought a green car, in another a red one and so on. Some of these parallel realities may be only slightly different from your own: if you switched places with your double, you may never know the difference.

Level IV: The Theory of the Parallel Multiverse

I like this theory best because it explains most paranormal phenomenon seen in our world. Level IV theory states that there are an infinite number of bubble-like universes attached to ours in a multidimensional state. At any time, two or more of these parallel realities may merge together and allow matter to stream from one universe to the next. Perhaps UFOs and other mythological beings and creatures reported throughout human history are all visitors from a neighboring universe. Some may have journeyed here with the intent of exploring our universe, but some could have arrived here by accident and can't find their way home!

THE MULTIVERSE IN SCIENCE AND RELIGION

The idea of a multiverse is not a new one—it has been hypothesized in physics, astronomy, philosophy, and science fiction for more than a hundred years. The concept of a multidimensional universe can be found in many religious beliefs that predate Judaism and Christianity. The earliest known records describing something similar to the multiverse are found in ancient Hindu cosmology. Ancient records expressed the idea of an infinite number of realities each with its own gods, worlds, and inhabitants all governed by different laws of nature. The legendary spirit worlds of the Druids and Native Americans also indicate belief in other realities that exist outside the physical realm. The Christian heaven, hell, and purgatory could also be thought of as existing in a parallel universe.

In modern physics, we have observed several theories of the multiverse and not one, but all of them may be the true state of reality. According to MIT physics professor Max Tegmark, each nearby parallel universe could be connected by wormholes allowing realities to merge for an indefinite amount of time. Wormholes are an interesting idea because many paranormal cases involving the appearance of strange beings and glowing lights also involve a portal-like structure that appears out of thin air, potentially allowing an entity or UFO-like phenomenon to emerge in our universe and neatly disappear when the transition is complete. It is my belief that all paranormal researchers, from ghost hunters to UFO investigators, should take into account that much of the phenomena they are trying to document does not come from our world, but another reality that occasionally merges with our own. It is not the purpose of this book to explore multiverse theory or the extra dimensions that exist in each; the reader should consider that paranormal cases presented in this book most likely have an origin in not one but multiple parallel realities.

INVESTIGATING THE UNKNOWN IN A MODERN UNIVERSE

Despite great technological advances and our growing awareness of the forces that power the universe, there are still many things human beings experience that they are incapable of categorizing; in turn, these experiences generate fear. Mysterious events have been called "paranormal" because they seem to emanate outside our normal reality. Over the past thirty years as a paranormal researcher, I have investigated and gathered information from hundreds of cases that span across the paranormal spectrum, including everything from ghost sightings to claims of alien contact and abductions.

One of the greatest problems a researcher faces is the collection of accurate information; are witnesses really reporting what they've seen and not what they *think* they might have seen? I don't think witnesses fabricate hoaxes all the time, but in some cases, people embellish their experiences by adding missing parts to satisfy the questions of the investigator. The investigator must learn to ask the important questions and pull back witnesses when they seem to get carried away. It helps to ground a witness by saying "Please, just give me the facts, just the facts." If you should ever experience a paranormal event, the most important thing to do is to find another person (another witness) because a greater number of witnesses make for a stronger case.

Although my growing database is filled with all types of paranormal events, I am still amazed by the similarities in many independent case studies. The bottom line is that credible people are reporting encounters with something incredible. After studying the data, no matter how skeptical a person may be, there are three things that cannot be denied: reports of paranormal events exist, they are a global phenomena, and they are increasing in frequency at an alarming rate.[5] Reports of various paranormal phenomena are similar worldwide; the only difference is witness interpretation of events. This similarity will be a key factor in how investigators document experiences. Differences in data collected from those who experience paranormal events are directly related to local culture, education, and religious beliefs. One of the greatest misconceptions the public has is that only "true believers" have paranormal experiences but this could not be further from the truth—my files are full of cases in which witnesses had no interest in ghosts, poltergeists, Bigfoot, or UFOs. The majority of these people never claim psychic powers and do not seek publicity of any kind. Many I've spoken with were afraid to tell even their closest friends or relatives for fear of being perceived as crazy or unstable.

After a paranormal event take place, a good number of once-stable people see their lives totally changed, some for the better, and some for the worse. The majority of witnesses I've interviewed have been reputable people with solid reputations whose testimonies would never be questioned in any court of law.

I must clarify that although I have investigated hundreds of cases, not all of them are unexplained; I have researched quite a few alleged encounters which, after lengthy investigation, turned up nothing outside the ordinary taking place. There are people who doctor photographs and falsify reports to get attention; an experienced, objective researcher will be

---

5. Based on information from data banks from a number of UFO-paranormal organizations, including MUFON, CUFOS, America Psychical Society, and the Paranormal Data Bank.

able to correctly identify hoaxes. Often, a hoaxer's story becomes more and more incredible with each subsequent telling, in order to keep everyone's attention.

Some charlatans use alien contact, channeling, exorcisms, and ghost hunting as ways to increase their income by preying upon the needs of an unsuspecting public. People want to believe there are mystical forces in the cosmos that will guide and protect through troubled times. Many "psychics" claim abilities of communication with the dead; these abilities fulfill emotional needs of those in grieving and fill the psychic's bank account in the process. While I'm convinced that a small number of people I've met and worked with over the years *do* have psychic abilities and the capability of doing extraordinary things, I feel these types of gifts are not as common as media hype and self-promoting "experts" would have us believe. There are people in our troubled world tired of their mundane lives who want to believe they have supernatural powers or have had some type of other-worldly contact, but their desire to believe exceeds their credibility.

There are real paranormal experiences taking place, and out of the 1,095 cases I have investigated over the years, in my opinion, 78 percent (about 854) of them have no conventional explanation. I do not personally investigate every case that comes to my attention since some are too far away and my profession as a science educator limits my time. However, every case that comes to me is given attention; sometimes I follow up or interview by telephone or email. To me, the numbers of legitimate cases indicate something very real is taking place—science should examine these cases more closely, but unfortunately, the majority of scientists have ignored the cries of the witness. By and large, science dismisses paranormal reports because they do not neatly fit into our current understanding of the universe.

Today, string and multiverse theories help explain the existence of parallel realities in a multidimensional universe. Accepting these theories allows us to achieve better understanding of how the elementary particles that make up the cosmos are produced. It's strange to think that it took the scientists of today's world so long to discover what the mystics, shamans, and Druid priests knew ages ago: these ancient people knew of the multiverse's existence and incorporated it into their teachings and religions long before modern science was born. The great thinkers of today are beginning to realize that to understand the true nature of our existence, new ideas have to be considered no matter *how* radical they may be. UFO sightings and paranormal events do not seem to be part of our physical universe, but if they are real occurrences, where do they come from? It's obvious to anyone who has done research in this area that most of it is very real; the majority of reports come from credible people who had encounters with other-worldly forces. If what we call "paranormal" does not originate in our reality, then where does it go when it can't be seen? If we take into account the theory that there are other dimensions in our physical space that we can't perceive in addition to other nearby parallel universes, then (and only then) can we begin to understand why paranormal events seem like nothing more than phantasms to humans trapped in a limited three-dimensional reality. We are indeed continually being confronted with experiences still mistakenly labeled as "supernatural," and these modern mysteries are greater than any human beings have ever faced. The scientific community must start taking the stories of those who've had a brush with another reality more seriously; the same mistakes must not be repeated. In the next chapter, I present a brief introduction to paranormal phenomenon showing that the Law of Uniformitarianism is its case. This law (some call it a philosophy of science) states that what has taken place in the past is now taking place in the present and will take place in the future, but perhaps at a different rate.

OUT OF NOWHERE

The first person who began a serious documentation of paranormal phenomenon was Charles Hoy Fort. Fort was born on August 6, 1874, in Albany, New York, and died in May 1932. Fort was a writer who spent most of his free time at libraries taking notes from newspapers, scientific journals, and various books looking for reports of strange occurrences. He felt strongly that science was suppressing anomalous data that didn't fit in with current theory. In his early days, Fort lived in poverty and, although he had a number of works published in small magazines, he had considerable financial trouble and often took on other, non-writing jobs to make ends meet. It was because of this that he had to put his work of collecting tales of unusual events on hold.

In 1916 Fort inherited his grandfather's estate and once finally free from financial burdens, was able to devote most of his time to what was a growing obsession: collecting reports of the unexplained. Fort meticulously looked through newspapers, magazines, and books for odd phenomena that science could not explain, and began to catalog them. Included in these detailed listings were frogs, fish, stones, blood, and ice falling from the sky. He also included mysterious fires, stigmata, fireballs, monsters, UFOs, and ancient artifacts discovered out of place. Out of all these strange anomalies, Fort seemed partial to reports of falls from the sky; they made up the bulk of his material. Until Fort began to write about these occurrences, no one realized how many bizarre events were taking place on our planet.

Charles Fort published his works in four books: *The Book of the Dammed* (1919), *New Lands* (1923), *Lo!* (1931), and *Wild Talents* (1932). Until the twenty-first century, the paranormal events mentioned above were known as "Fortean phenomena." Several organizations still exist today trying to continue his work. One of these organizations is the International Fortean Society Organization (INFO), and in 2000 and 2001 I was invited to speak at their annual convention in Maryland. At the convention, I presented two papers concerning my research on the stone chambers in the Hudson Valley of New York and the alien contact and channeling phenomenon. This work was published in two of my books: *Celtic Mysteries: Windows to Another Dimension in America's Northeast* (Cosimo Books, 2005) and *Contact of the 5th Kind* (Llewellyn, 2002).

A more recent attempt to record various anomalies was accomplished in 1979 by William R. Corliss, a freelance writer and author of twenty books on space technology. Corliss has published a number of volumes that document astronomical and atmospheric phenomena called *The Source Book Project: Mysterious Universe*. If you are doing research in this area, his books are a must for your library.

Like Charles Fort, my early days of paranormal research saw many Saturdays and Sundays at libraries in New York and Connecticut combing through old newspapers and journals looking for reports of unexplained events. I must admit that it was tedious, but thanks to Fort's early work, I already had a considerable amount of information to work with; I mainly concentrated on events he either missed or that took place after 1930. Although this chapter and book does not permit me the necessary room to list all the events collected during my research, I will present the most impressive ones from the earliest to the most recent. I want to remind my readers that I researched all the Fortean paranormal activity presented in this chapter, but I only personally investigated a handful of them. After collecting a considerable amount of data, I divided them into the type of event that took place such as falls from the sky, monsters, poltergeists, psychic phenomena, and finally, UFOs (what Fort called "strange meteors, lightning and clouds"). My detailed investigations appear starting in the chapter High Strangeness and although some of the very early case studies are now more than thirty years old, they have never been published in any form until now.

BALL LIGHTNING

The majority of the phenomena Fort cataloged still remains unexplained today; even modern science can only offer weak explanations for them, at best. For example, Fort collected reports of a strange ball of light that would glide around the sky before and after a thunderstorm. On occasion it would also strike the ground or enter a person's home through a closed window (not breaking the glass) and then crash into a wall with a loud boom and disappear. Fort thought that this was some type of bizarre electrical phenomenon that he eventually named "ball lightning." He noticed that reports of this ball lightning were one of the most frequent and widely witnessed phenomena he documented. Fort was sure it was some sort of rare variation of lightning created during an electrical storm.

The scientists of Fort's time didn't take these reports seriously at all because they insisted lightning could not take the shape of a sphere. Today, ball lightning has been documented and is now accepted by meteorologists as a form of atmospheric electrical discharge. A research paper published in 1960 by Harvard University scientists reported that 7 percent of the United States population reported having witnessed ball lightning during the twentieth century.[1] We now know that ball lightning is a real atmospheric electrical phenomenon, but how it is formed in nature is still controversial. Ball lightning can range in size from a pebble to up to nine feet in diameter. Unlike flashes of lightning that last a second or so, ball lightning has been reported to be seen for as long as several minutes. Scientists of Fort's time ignored the reports because they insisted that what people were seeing could not possibly exist. They refused to investigate and considered the occurrence impossible, so we had to wait decades for

---

1. Gregory, "Statistical Studies of Ball Lightning," *World Scientific Publishing* (1988): 80–94.

ball lightning to be accepted in the scientific community as a real phenomenon. As a scientist and paranormal investigator of more than thirty years, I am not surprised at the attitude science took at the time regarding ball lightning—that very train of thought is still prevalent today. The learned gentlemen of Fort's time refused to even consider the possibility of ball lightning's existence despite credible reports and repeated incidents. Following are several of these cases, two of which I have investigated personally.

Deaths by Ball Lightning

The first documented death by what was evidently ball lightning was recorded by the historian Flavius Josephus in 80 AD in Jerusalem.[2] Although what actually took place is not clear, the great historian mentions the sky darkening, turning to dark green, and then without warning, a ball of pale blue light emerged from a cloud and sped toward Earth.[3] The sphere of light went up the side of a building and moved across the roof, rolling like a ball. Roman soldiers present at the time watched the ball of light as it jumped off the roof and fatally struck one of soldiers with a loud boom. Witnesses considered this incident to be the judgment of God

2. Josephus Flavius (author), William Whiston (translator), *The Complete Works of Flavius Josephus: The Celebrated Jewish Historian* (London: Potter Publishing, 1880).

3. Karl Hoeber, "Flavius Josephus," *The Catholic Encyclopedia*, vol. 8. (New York: Robert Appleton Company, 1910).

since this particular Roman solider was known to be unjustly cruel.

On October 21, 1638, four people were killed by a ball of fire while attending church in Cherbourg, France, during a severe thunderstorm. The fireball was reported to have been more than six feet in diameter and entered the church through the ceiling window, destroying part of the roof. The ball smashed several of the pews and exploded, filling the church with a sulfurous odor. The minister of the church later explained the event as the work of the Devil who was upset with the good work they were doing saving souls.

In 1753, Professor Georg Richmann of Saint Petersburg, Russia, was attending a meeting at the Academy of Sciences when he heard thunder. He excused himself from the meeting and rushed home—he was performing electrical experiments and did not want to miss the chance of seeing a bolt of lightning striking a pole he had set up on his property. In a crude way, Richmann was trying to duplicate Benjamin Franklin's electricity experiment.[4] While watching for a strike near the back door of his home a ball of light flew down from the sky and struck him in the head, killing him. The ball left a red spot on Richmann's head, singed his clothes, and blew off his shoes. A nearby next-door neighbor was knocked unconscious, and the windows in the Richmann home were shattered.

---

4. Ronald W. Clarke, *Benjamin Franklin: A Biography* (New York: Random House, 1983).

Ball Lightning, Foo Fighters, or UFOs

During World War II, pilots described balls of light that were blue in color and ranging from the size of a baseball to that of a basketball following their aircraft as they flew over Europe. At first, Army Intelligence suspected they were some type of German secret weapon used to track Allied planes, but in 1944, they discovered German aircraft were also reporting the same objects. No one at the time had any idea what they were and since they didn't seem to interfere with the air missions or disrupt operations, they became of little concern.

Pilots called them "foo fighters" and all types of stories were created about their origin, including gremlin-like creatures and alien probes. One such encounter with foo fighters during World War II was actually mentioned in a non-fiction book about the October 14, 1943, bombing of ball-bearing factories in Schweinfurt, Germany.[5] I also found references to the account in a declassified file from the Air Material Command; unfortunately the document gives very little detail and most of the information containing the pilots' names was blacked out.[6] The story of this encounter is presented below.

As the Flying Fortress (bombers) approached their targets (the German ball-bearing factories), one of the most baffling incidents of World War II was to take place: an enigma that

---

5. Martin Caidin, *Black Thursday* (New York: Bantam, 1987).

6. Air Material Command document dated October 17, 1943: Declassified July 1987.

defies all explanation to this day. As the bombers of the 384th Group swung into their final bomb run, the German fighter attacks fell off. At this point, there were no enemy aircraft in the air and the pilots and gunners were puzzled and looked around the sky to see where they were, but they were gone. A moment later, the pilots and top turret gunners, as well as several crewmen in the Plexiglas noses of the bombers reported a cluster of discs in their flight path and approaching the 384th's formation. The startled airmen focused their attention on the phenomenon and the crew members talked back and forth, discussing and confirming the astonishing sight before them. The discs in the cluster were silver colored, about 1 inch thick and 3 inches in diameter. The B-17 crewmen could see them easily, gliding down slowly in a very uniform cluster. Then, something incredible took place: B-17 Number 026 closed rapidly with a number of discs; the pilot attempted to evade an imminent collision with the objects, but was unsuccessful in his maneuver. He reported at the intelligence debriefing that his right wing went directly through a cluster with absolutely no effect to engines or the aircraft surface. Number 026's pilot stated further that one of the discs was seen striking his B-17's tail assembly, but that neither he nor any member of the crew heard or witnessed an explosion and the plane was not damaged in any way. The pilot reported that about 20 feet from the discs, they also sighted a mass of black debris of varying sizes.

The foo fighters of World War II still remain unexplained, and although they have a similar description to ball lightning, most UFO enthusiasts claim they were alien probes following the development of our aircraft. In the twentieth and twenty-first centuries, these strange globes of light have been reported following aircraft, in addition to being seen near military bases involved with the space program and nuclear weapon development.

Over the years, I have personally investigated four cases of possible ball lightning, all reported around areas where UFOs had been seen. One of these incidents took place in 1978 just outside Newtown, Connecticut, near the sleepy little town of Sandy Hook. The encounter took place on a late summer evening and the weather was fair. In the past, electrical phenomenon like ball lightning seemed to be able to appear regardless of the weather, but it is reported more frequently in summer.

Encounter on a Bridge

After a hard day's work, the witness (whom we will refer to as "Jim") was driving home alone on August 30, 1978, at about 8:30 PM. He crossed the bridge near Newtown Road, about 60 feet in length and made of a steel alloy that shows a consdierable amount of oxidation in the form of rust (indicating high iron content). It was a clear night, and Jim was anxious to get back to his family in Newtown. He was listening to the radio as he crossed the bridge when suddenly the station faded and it was replaced by a great deal of static and other sounds he called "electrical interference." Without warning, the car engine died, but the headlights were still on. Jim grabbed a flashlight from the glove compartment and popped the hood to take a look. As the man got out of the car, his attention was drawn to a bright light just above the bridge. It was flickering yellow, green, and red and at first, Jim thought it was the planet Jupiter, which he had heard was bright in the sky at that time of year. Jim looked under the hood but couldn't see anything wrong. Looking up, Jim noticed the light was descending; now he could see that it wasn't a star or any other celestial object—it was a glowing globe. Jim climbed back into his car and the light from the object became so bright, it illuminated the bridge and the road ahead. As he watched, the globe of light appeared to be rotating faster and faster, shooting out "flares of fire" in all directions. The object then split up into three smaller balls: one went under the bridge, one circled outside the bridge, and the third circled his car.

Then, all three balls of light circled his car, moving slowly enough so he could see their shapes. "They were about the size of basketballs, and they had a deep amber color, almost like a dark yellow," he told me. After circling, the three lights went up in the air, merged together into one ball, and just disappeared. Still amazed at what had taken place, Jim began to look out of his windshield to see if the ball of light was still visible, but it was gone. About ten seconds later, the car radio came back on and he was able to start up his car.

Jim seemed to have no ill effects after the encounter; however, in the following days the local newspaper *The Newtown Bee* carried a number of stories about residents reporting unusual balls of lights in the night sky performing fantastic maneuvers.[7] A similar encounter had taken place two days earlier near the much-shorter metal bridge near Clearwater Road, also located in the Sandy Hook–Newtown area.[8] Here a witness described similar electrical interference with his radio and his car engine stalling. In this encounter, the object was said to be red and split into two balls of light. Did both witnesses have a close encounter with the same object? Was it ball lightning, an interdimensional energy source, or some type of alien probe? I guess we will never know for sure.

During the Hudson Valley UFO Flap of 1983–1985, a giant object the size of a football field was reported over this highly populated area of New York.[9] At times, the object hovered in one place while several balls of light the size of basketballs emerged from the bottom of the UFO and flew off in different directions. Several hours later, multiple witnesses at another location reported seeing the lights once again, this time entering the bottom of the object. During this time, there were also numerous reports of people being followed by a ball of red light while driving in their cars. There were also several reported encounters where some say these balls of light entered their living rooms, passing right through the window without breaking the glass. Supposedly, the ball of light would glide around the room and

---

7. *The Newtown Bee*, September 10, 1978.

8. This case is documented in my book, *Interdimensional Universe: The New Science of UFOs, Paranormal Phenomena and Otherdimensional Beings* (Woodbury, MN: Llewellyn, 2008).

9. A UFO flap is an outbreak of many UFO sightings over a relatively small geographical area..

then leave by going back out the window or right through the roof without doing any damage. In every case, witnesses reported some type of electrical interference with either television or radio signal reception. In some cases there were also confirmed widespread or isolated power outages. This all took place while a sphere of light was in sight, but after it vanished everything went back to normal.

More Electromagnetic Effects

On July 12, 1982, at ten o'clock in the evening, a resident of Stamford, Connecticut, was watching television when he noticed the power in his home slowly dying. The lights in the house faded to the point of visibility and his fan slowed down to almost a halt. The TV picture shrunk to the size of about 2 inches across, but the picture was still visible. The rest of the screen had a reddish glow, but there was no sound.

Sitting in his chair, the witness noticed the room and window glowing from a light apparently coming from outside. The man walked over to the window and looked out and saw a bright, round, orange-and-white object hovering above a tree about 50 feet from his home. He described the object as being the size of a large beach ball "floating" above one of the power company's transformers, seemingly attached to it by a glowing wire. He thought this object was draining power from the transformer, and it made him consider that it must be something living or under intelligent control. As he watched, the object shot away to the east at great speed leaving a luminous trail behind. After hearing

the man's story I called the power company, United Illuminating, and was told that there was a power drain in that
area of Stamford at that time that lasted several minutes,
the cause of which was unknown.

The balls of light seen at the time of the Hudson Valley
UFO flap all had similar characteristics to ball lightning, including the electromagnetic and physiologic effects on people and animals. Animals seem to get very uneasy, even before the light is seen, and people can feel a tingling sensation
on the back of their neck or a shiver up and down the spine.
A strange encounter with one of these balls of light came to
my attention in July 1984, when a middle-aged Connecticut
woman had an encounter that was too close and resulted in
injury.

Burned by a Glowing Sphere

On July 26, 1984, I received a call from a woman named Peggy
from Hamden, Connecticut, who said that she had a sighting
of a ball of fire outside her home at three in the morning—and
that it burned her face. In Ufology, we call this type of case a
"close encounter of the second kind" because the object left
some type of physical trace. In all my years of investigating,
this was one of very few trace cases that came to my attention
so I made arrangements to visit Peggy as soon as possible.
Any type of physical effect on a human after a paranormal encounter is a rare event—I wanted to make sure this one was
properly documented. I arrived at Peggy's home on July 27.
When she answered the door, I was a little taken aback—half
her face was a bright red, while the other half was normal (in

her case) pale white skin. Peggy told me that on July 25, just after a severe thunderstorm, she woke up at about 2:45 AM hearing strange loud cracking and buzzing noises that seemed to come from outside her home. Peggy's husband was away on a business trip that night, and her children are married and live in different parts of the state; whatever was making the noises she would have to face alone.

Peggy's greatest fear was that during the storm, lightning had struck the wires of her home and started an electrical fire. She walked toward the kitchen to the back of her home and looked out the sliding glass doors that led onto the deck. She noticed that the ground and trees were glowing red as if on fire. In a panic, Peggy opened the glass door and looked around the deck. Without warning, a glowing fireball the size of a basketball came up over the trees and started to move toward her. Fearful, she ran inside and closed the door. The ball of fire came to within 20 feet of the deck and Peggy stared at it, mesmerized: "It was almost hypnotic, I couldn't take my eyes off of it. It was scary but also beautiful."

Peggy noticed that the object started to get brighter and something like sparks began to shoot out from it in all directions. It changed in color from a crimson red to a bright yellow. It was so bright, she had to turn and shield her eyes. However, the right side of her head was still facing the object and it was then she felt a tingling sensation on her face. Peggy then ran to the phone, but it did not work—there was only static. Then, as if a light turned off, the fireball was gone. Bravely, Peggy once again opened the sliding doors, looked around, but the glowing ball had vanished. The entire incident lasted only ten minutes, but Peggy said it felt like a much longer time had passed. Her face felt very irritated so she grabbed a flashlight, ran to the bathroom, looked at her reflection in the mirror and noticed the side of her face that had faced the object was red. She tried putting ice on it and that made it feel better for a little while, but her skin was feeling like it was on fire; the burning sensation was getting worse.

Afraid that she had been exposed to some type of harmful radiation, the following morning, Peggy made an emergency appointment to see her doctor. After his examination, Peggy's doctor didn't have an explanation for the burn on the right side of her face, but said that it was only a first degree burn that should heal in a few days, with a little peeling. The doctor suggested that she may have fallen asleep on her deck and exposed one side of her face to the sun. Peggy told the doctor about the ball of fire, but he looked at her with disbelief so she said nothing more about it. The burn faded within a week (with no peeling) and she suffered no further ill effects. So the question is: did Peggy see an alien probe from a UFO or did she have a rare encounter with a form of ball lightning? The actual cause of the event remains unidentified in my case files.

A similar experience to Peggy's took place in the summer of 1986 at Fishkill, New York, when a limousine driver en route to pick up his customer was driven off the road by a "yellow ball of light the size of a basketball." The driver lost control of the vehicle and veered into a ditch on the side of the road. The time was nine in the evening and the road was quite desolate. He got out of the car and there was a strong smell of ozone in the air—so strong, it irritated his eyes and lungs. The man looked up and saw the ball of light hovering above a telephone pole across the street. He watched it for about five minutes, then the object started shooting sparks into the sky. After doing that for a minute or so, the sparks then focused to one point and created a tunnel in the sky into which the ball of light vanished. The next day, the driver had to visit his doctor because his skin was itching and his eyes were red and irritated. Although there were no other witnesses to this event, *something* caused him to lose control of his car and the irritation to his eyes and skin. I interviewed this witness to a great extent on the phone and was convinced he had an encounter with something that could not be conventionally explained.

IS THE SKY REALLY FALLING?

I have a number of cases in my files of sightings and close encounters with similar balls of lights sent to me from all over the United States and Canada. In the world of the paranormal, this type of occurrence seems common, but what is it? Are the glowing spheres some type of interdimensional intelligent life form, alien probes, or a rare form of natural electrostatic phenomena? Although sightings of unusual balls of light take place in many paranormal experiences, another type of frequently reported event is falls from the sky. These falls include; fish, frogs, stones, blood, and ice, just to name a few. I've also heard of an unidentified material simply referred to as "angel hair" because of its silk-like (ectoplasmic?) properties.

I have personally investigated thirteen cases in which different forms of matter apparently fell from the sky. Five of these cases involved stones that either floated silently in the air or came crashing down with a boom. Two of these falling stones turned out to be meteorites.[10] In the three other cases, however, the falling stones were indigenous to the area and involved as many as one hundred rocks ranging in size from a pebble to almost 5 pounds; these rock showers were reported to have periodically fallen over a several-day period.

Star Stones

Before the nineteenth century, observing a meteorite striking the ground would have been a paranormal event. The mentality of established science at that time was that since stones were not found in the sky, they could not fall from it, and the idea was therefore ridiculous. Even the great scientist and explorer Alexander von Humboldt (1769–1859), who Thomas Jefferson called "the most important scientist [he had] ever met," doubted the idea that rocks could fall from space despite the fact that he was one of the first scientists to accurately observe and plot meteor showers. Like many others in his day, Humboldt thought meteors originated in the upper atmosphere of our planet.

---

10. One of the meteorites is now on display at the Bruce Museum in Greenwich, Connecticut.

In the early afternoon of November 7, 1492, in the town of Ensisheim, in Alsace, France, a farmer looked out his window one morning and witnessed a fiery object fall from the sky into his wheat field.[11] The next morning he went out to the field and found a dark stone about 5 pounds in weight sitting in a small depression. He picked up the stone, took it to Paris, and presented it to the learned masters at the University of Paris. When asked by the scientists where he got the strange looking stone, the farmer replied it had fallen from the sky. The scientists all started to laugh and dismissed him as a nut; according to everything they had learned, it was impossible for rocks to fall from the sky. The rock was kept in the museum cellar for four hundred years after which it was re-examined in the mid-nineteenth century by scientists who by then had begun to accept the idea of rocks falling from the sky—they were even given a name: meteorites. The rock the farmer found on his land was in fact a stony-type meteor and one of the first of many that were recovered and identified as not having an earthly origin. When I think of the farmer's story, I wonder how many other falls from the sky are laughed at because they don't fit into currently accepted ideas of science. I'm sure the farmer felt quite silly and embarrassed when he left the museum. His negative experience most likely stopped many others from reporting similar phenomena to authorities.

---

11. Ursula B. Marvin, "Ernst Florenz Friedrich Chladni (1756–1827) and the Origins of Modern Meteorite Research," *Meteoritics & Planetary Science* 31 (1996): 572.

It wasn't until 1835 that some scientists began to take rock falls from the sky seriously, but the academic community was divided on this subject and spawned many heated debates. The famous Aristotle is credited with the idea of "falling stars" that could have landed on Earth more than two thousand years ago. The earliest record we have of falling meteorites is of one that fell at Aegos Potamos in 465 BC. It is so well described by great writer/historian Plutarch in his epic story *Lysander* that I quote the passage in full; it sheds light on ancient Greek opinions on such phenomena and possible causes.[12]

> There were those who said that the stars of Castor and Pollux appeared on each side the helm of Lysander's ship, when he first set out against the Athenians. Others thought that a stone, which according to the common opinion fell from heaven, was an omen of his overthrow. It fell on Aegos Potamos, and was of prodigious size. The people of the Chersonesus hold the heavenly stone in great veneration, and show it to this day. It is said that Anaxagoras had foretold that one of those bodies, which are fixed to the vault of heaven, would one day be loosened by some shock or convulsion of the whole machine, and fall to the earth, for he taught that the stars are not now in the places where they were originally formed; that being of a stony substance and heavy, the light they give is caused only by the reflection and refraction of the ether; and that they are carried along, and kept in their orbits, by the rapid motion of the heavens, which from the beginning, when the cold

12. Plutarch, *The Life of Lysander*, written in 75 AD. Loeb Classical Library (January 1, 1916). Copy available at the New York City Public Library.

ponderous bodies were separated from the rest, hindered them from falling.

In the 1820s, the U.S. government was trying to establish a more open line of communication with the Native American population. Scientists and doctors from a number of universities met with Native American medicine men and shamans. The meeting's purpose was to see if these Native Americans had any "natural cures" or medicine that nineteenth-century doctors could use. In one meeting, when asked if they used anything in particular to help fight infection, a medicine man emptied his medicine pouch on the table and out fell a number of strange stones. The doctors asked what they were and the medicine man replied that they had great power for healing. The doctors asked where he got them and the medicine man replied "they are star stones that fell from the sky." The doctors began to laugh and ensured the medicine man it was impossible—stones could not possibly fall from the sky. Well, the last laugh is on the doctors: one hundred years later, the so-called "star stones" that were part of many medicine pouches were analyzed and found out to be meteorites, some of them very rare ones.

Flying Rocks

The falling of rocks from the sky that seem to be thrown by an invisible force are frequent happenings in the paranormal world, especially in cases that involve poltergeist activity. In the late seventies I investigated an occurrence where rocks would fall down from the sky on a number of homes in an isolated neighborhood in Monroe, Connecticut.[13] Although the case history and investigation were both complex, I will present the basic facts here and focus on the falling of rocks, omitting the bizarre claims of alien contact that surfaced during the investigation. The rocks fell straight down from the sky several days a week and always after eight in the evening. Residents thought an angry spirit had invaded their property, but local police were sure that pranksters were involved. I personally investigated this event and on one occasion, while interviewing a witness in their home when a falling of rocks took place. The stones fell on the roof making extremely loud sounds; I ran outside but didn't see anything except the roof, now covered with a new layer of rocks. I went back inside and several minutes later, the rocks began falling again, but this time near the home's entrance. Once again I dashed outside where I saw several new stones ranging in size piled up against the side of the house. It's interesting to note that there was never any damage to the side of the home or the roof. I picked up one of the larger stones and it was very warm, as if just heated. The larger stones cooled down to a normal ambient temperature within several minutes.

The stones were all quite common granites and rhyolites found in the area, but the interesting thing about them was all of them were rounded and smooth as if they had been in a fast-moving stream for hundreds of years. I checked other

---

13. This incident is documented in my book *Interdimensional Universe: The New Science of UFOs, Paranormal Phenomena, and Otherdimensional Beings* (Woodbury, MN: Llewellyn, 2008).

homes in the neighborhood and, although they had experienced the rock falling phenomenon on previous dates, on this particular night the home that I was in was the only one affected. The rock falling took place two days a week for several weeks, stopped suddenly, and as of 2009 has never happened again. Despite a very involved investigation in cooperation with the Monroe and Newtown police, no conventional explanation was ever found.

The Litchfield, Connecticut, Poltergeist

On November 19, 2004, I received a call from a young couple who owned a home on a secluded dead-end street in Litchfield, Connecticut. After hearing me discussing the paranormal on a local radio talk show, they called to relate an experience they found both perplexing and terrifying. The couple told me that on numerous occasions, their house was "bombarded" by rocks of all sizes—the stones even entered their home by breaking windows. The frightened couple asked me to come and investigate since they were sure that it was an angry spirit that wanted them out of the house.

I arrived at their home on November 21 during the day and was greeted by the couple who at the time were recently married and in their late twenties. After some brief introductions, I asked to be taken outside to view the property. I walked around the perimeter of the house and noticed hundreds of rocks against the walls of the home and chips and cracks along the siding as if they had struck with considerable force. Just as in the poltergeist cases in Monroe, Connecticut, all the rocks were rounded and smooth as if they had been in running water for a very long time. I asked for a ladder and climbed up to look at the roof where I noticed only fifteen or so stones, several of them appeared to weigh at least 10 pounds. It seemed that most of the attention was focused on the south side of the home. We then went back inside and began the interview; it was two hours in length and the important facts are presented here.

It all started with a Ouija Board

The couple had just moved into the house in October 2004; neither of them had ever had a paranormal experience prior to that. The house is seventy years old, and the previous owners (whom I contacted) never saw or felt anything unusual in the twenty-five years they lived there. It was Halloween eve when the new couple finally moved in and they decided to "have some fun" and play with a Ouija board they found in the attic. As they began to ask questions, the couple was surprised when the planchette (pointing device) went "wildly" across the board and spelled the words "GET OUT." Both were quite scared and blamed the other for fooling around and moving the pointer around the board. The next night, at ten in the evening, they heard loud thumps on the south side of the house and, thinking some kids were throwing rocks, they both ran outside but no one was there. They went back into their home and the thumping started again, this time louder. The husband grabbed a flashlight to go outside, but before he even opened the door the noise stopped. He went outside anyway and walked along the side of the house and found dozens of rocks piled up in a row 2 feet in width and 8 feet in length. He went back inside and all was silent. That same night at two in the morning they heard the same sound, but this time it was coming from the roof. His wife became very frightened and called the police who found nothing and left.[14]

The house was quiet for about two weeks, then on November 15 at ten in the evening, the rock throwing started again and this time, they were not only smashing up against the wall, but also falling on the roof. Suddenly, a rock flew through the living room window, shattering the glass, and all was quiet. The couple called the police once again and after looking around, the responding officer suggested that someone they knew was having fun with them. The couple found this idea ridiculous and told me that although the officer seemed helpful, they got the feeling he did not believe them. He even asked the couple if they were drinking or smoking dope. They showed him the stone in the living room that came through the window; the officer picked it up and said it felt warm.

There were no more incidents until November 18 when at about ten in the evening, rocks began hitting the south side of their home once again, but every time they would run out to try and catch the culprit, the bombardment would stop. After my investigation and visit on November 21, the rock throwing stopped. I kept in touch with the couple for sev-

---

14. The Litchfield police report indicated that the investigating officers thought that squirrels were running on top of the roof; however, I checked the roof while I was there and found the same type of stones piled alongside the house.

eral weeks and all remained quiet. They were sure that an evil spirit or ghost was contacted when they used the Ouija board so they burned it in the fireplace. This case remains unexplained in my files. There was notable damage to the side of the house and roof so I think a hoax can be ruled out—why would these people damage their new home? This case is one of many in my files in which a paranormal event was triggered after the use of a Ouija board. Is there a connection between the two? Do they open a doorway to another reality?

A BERMUDA TRIANGLE IN THE SKY

Charles Fort thought that there was a "Super Sargasso Sea" in the upper atmosphere that would occasionally interact with our world and draw things up from the ground and the oceans.[15] Fort also felt that on the other side of this Super Sargasso Sea was another land composed of unknown forms of matter and home to strange creatures. This was incredible speculation for Fort's day; he was trying to express the idea of portals opening up from a parallel reality. During his life, Fort collected more than a thousand cases of identifiable and unidentifiable things that fell from the sky. After spending hours going through microfilm in the New York City Public Library, I actually found many of the original stories Fort used in his research and they seemed quite well documented. Believe or not, the *New York Times* ("All the news that's fit to print") was one of the only papers that carried

---

15. The Sargasso Sea is also known as the Bermuda Triangle.

these types of stories. Although some of the articles were short and used as fillers, others had a great deal of information indicating something strange did indeed take place.

Falling Out of the Super Sargasso Sea

We've all heard the saying "it's raining cats and dogs," but as far as we know, house pets never fell down to Earth from the sky. This saying seems to have originated in sixteenth-century England. Dogs and cats were not allowed in homes so when heavy rain fell, animals would jump on the roofs, lined with a considerable amount of straw for insulation. When the straw got wet, it became very slippery and animals would easily lose their footing, thus the saying was born. Fair enough, but when it rains fish, frogs, birds, and toads not normally found in the area, where do they come from? The cases are too frequent to be ignored, and although I have seventy-three cases in my files, only seventeen of them are presented below.

1666, September: Wrotham, Kent, England: Hundreds of fish of all sizes and species were found in a field. There was no rain for two days and no water around the area. The fish were all dead but there was no sign of decay, indicating they had fallen less than twenty-four hours before.

1683, October 24: Charles Fort's *Book of the Dammed* reports that frogs fell from the sky over Norfolk, England. Many of the frogs were still alive as they invaded the homes of people who lived in the village. It took ten days to get rid of all the frogs; the number of frogs was said to be in the hundreds (sounds like one of the biblical plagues).

1804, September 22: *The London Herald* reported that the town of Toulouse, France, experienced a fall of tiny frogs. The day was nice and sunny but without warning, massive grey clouds filled the sky and there was lightning with no thunder or rain but plenty of wind. After about ten minutes, the skies cleared and the sun once again was seen—it was as if the storm never took place. Then, tiny little frogs fell from the sky, totaling more than one hundred; they were all cold and appeared frozen.

1859, October: The magazine *Nature* reported a dense shower of fish 5 inches in length that covered the roofs of many homes in South Wales. The report was investigated by a Dr. Gray of the British Museum who was puzzled by the event.

1860, June 2: The *New York Times* reported that on May 28, 1860, the Port Jervis area of New York experienced a rain of toads. The author of the article, a Dr. Isaiah Deck, said "these experiences are not rare" because he also saw a rain of toads and fish in 1846 in Norfolk, England. The Port Jervis toads were all dead but they were fresh—the mouths were all open and there was no sign of decay.

1877, January 15: *Scientific American* reported small snakes falling from the sky after a violent freak thunderstorm over the town of Sandhaven, Scotland. An investigation team from the British Museum said the small garter snakes were most likely transported by a water spout from France; all the snakes were dead.

1878, July 16: The *New York Times* reported an exceedingly large number of small toads fell from the sky covering the ground during a heavy afternoon shower in La Crosse, Wisconsin. The toads were most numerous in the Vine Street Depot area where they excited and caused wonder among residents there. A Captain Moulton testified that he saw them fall from the sky; the reporter considered his statement "good testimony" and included it in his story.

1881, May 30: From the *Worcester Daily Times*: During a severe thunderstorm at three in the afternoon, there were heavy rains and hail that "tore through the trees." In the town of St. John's, thousands of periwinkles fell from the sky; residents picked them up. In the days to follow, locals were still picking them up.

1885, July 26: The *New York Times*: "Where did all the toads come from?" After a heavy shower passed over Troy, Pennsylvania, in Pike County, the town found itself covered with toads. There were so many toads, it was impossible to walk along the streets without crushing them. They were reported to be at least 1 inch in length and they swarmed into the streets, yards, and gardens. People in the area said roads and fields for miles around were swarmed with toads in the same way. By noon, the toads had all disappeared as mysteriously as they had come; no one was able to explain how they came and went.

1896, October 15: The *Philadelphia Times* reported that dozens of dead birds fell from the sky on a clear day over Baton Rouge, Louisiana.

1897, July 16: The *New York Times* reported a shower of toads that appeared during a heavy evening rainfall in the village of Leeds, New York. The toads fell in a limited area only about 100 square feet. This area was covered with perfectly formed, still-alive toads. The toads were all of the same size, about an inch or so in length and of a very strange translucent white color.

1922, September 5: The *New York Daily News* reported that the French village of Brignoles experienced a freak tornado and thunderstorm. After the weather cleared, small live toads fell from the sky over a two-day period. The total number of toads was said to be more than three dozen.

1929, July 8: The *New York Times* reported a tiny toad shower on a hill just outside New Brunswick, Canada.[16] One witness said "The toads fell like rain from a clear blue sky and many of them were still alive and jumped away when they hit the ground." Scientists from the New Brunswick Museum investigated, but could find no answer concerning how the toads got there.

1933, July 22: The *New York Times* writes that a couple living on a farm in Enfield, Connecticut, reported toads falling from the sky during a "frightening" thunderstorm.

1954, June 12: The *New York Times* reported a fall of little frogs after a thunderstorm in Sutton Park, Yorkshire, England.

1973, January 2: The *Camden News* of Arkansas reported showers of tiny frogs the size of quarters during a violent thunderstorm that seemed to form out of nowhere.

1973, September 22: A small article in the *New York Times* said that thousands of tiny toads were seen falling from the

---

16. Most stories of falling toads and fish, especially from the period of 1830 to 1899, can now be found in the online *New York Times* archives at newyorktimes.com.

sky during a freak thunderstorm near Kent, England.[17] A local meteorologist theorized that a water spout must have lifted the toads from another location and transported them to Kent. The toads were found to be not common to the area; the article does not go into detail from whence they came.

Fishing in the Sky

A case of small fish falling from the sky came to my attention in 1986 from a neighborhood in Rhinebeck, New York. On September 23rd, at two in the morning, there was a violent thunderstorm with winds that actually blew over several trees. The next day, many residents in the northern section of this very rural suburb found their property covered with little minnow-like fish. Several days before this occurrence, I did a series of cable television shows in the area on UFOs and the paranormal. One of the families that found fallen fish on their property had seen the show and decided to give me a call in hopes of shedding light on this mystery. I arrived on the 23rd, sometime in the early afternoon where property owners were still raking up fish and placing them in baskets. There were hundreds of them scattered over the yards of four homes, but not one on any of the roofs—the strangest thing was many of these fish were still alive.

One of the dead fish was sent to the Connecticut Department of Wildlife Management where the species of minnow

---

17. I found this one in 1973; the actual day it took place seems to have been lost while taking notes from the microfilm. I could not find it again in the archives.

was identified as the bluntnose minnow, found across the Midwest from Louisiana to New York. The bluntnose is the most common type of minnow. One resident, an avid local fisherman, joked that he'd wasted years fishing in area lakes—perhaps he should have started casting his line up in the sky!

Fallings of toads, frogs and fish from the sky are the most common, but there also exists many reports of blocks of ice, blood, meat, unidentifiable organic substances, jelly-like material, blocks of limestone, and the most perplexing of all due to its white, silky appearance: angel hair.

DO ANGELS SHED THEIR HAIR?

Angel hair, so named for its similarity to fine silver threads, is a substance allegedly dispersed from UFOs as they fly overhead; some think it similar to spider webs. Paranormal researchers most often compare it to ectoplasm due to its tendency to disintegrate shortly after being found.

Reports of "angel hair" falling are worldwide; the greatest numbers comes from North America, Western Europe, Australia, and New Zealand. In the Portuguese city of Évora, angel hair was collected and analyzed by a local school director in November 2, 1959. Later, armed forces technicians and scientists of the University of Lisbon took interest in it as well. Their conclusions were that angel hair was formed by a small insect of an unknown species or perhaps some kind of single-celled organism. An unconfirmed report also states that angel hair was seen falling from the sky on November 3 of that year as a UFO passed over the Air Force Base of Sintra; soldiers were seen collecting the material in containers.

Other Noteworthy Angel Hair Fallings

Milwaukee, Wisconsin, 1881: *Scientific American,* volume 45, p. 337: People of Milwaukee were astonished by the fall of a web-like material that appeared to come from over Lake Michigan. The strands seemed to fall from a great height and were 2 or 3 feet in length. They covered the ground and trees over many miles. In all instances, the material was said to be strong in texture, very white and vanished five minutes after reaching the ground.

Port Hope, Ontario, September 26, 1948: A story entitled "Cobwebs or Flying Saucers?" appeared in the December 1949 issue of *Weather.* At 2 PM eastern time, a number of objects that looked like stars were seen streaking across the clear sky. Shortly after the objects passed over the town, residents witnessed a silk-like material in the shape of long threads falling from the sky. The threads quickly dissolved after touching the ground.

Montreal, Canada, October 10, 1963: *The Marine Observer* reports that a Captain R. H. Pape noticed very fine white threads falling from the sky while his ship, the *Roxburgh Castle* was moored in her berth. Calling the attention of the chief officer, the captain picked up one of the threads from the ships deck and said that it was "quite tough and resilient and after keeping it in [his] hand for three to four minutes, it disappeared completely." Looking up, they noticed "small cocoons" floating down from the sky. They tried to pick up the material and preserve some of the filaments, but they disappeared very quickly.

A Recent Fall of Angel Hair

On July 24, 27, and 30 of 2008, a considerable number of UFO close encounters took place in the small New York town of Hopewell Junction.[18] I received calls and emails from a total of fourteen people reporting that a very bright object, triangular in shape and the size of a large aircraft flew silently over their homes at about ten-thirty at night.[19] The UFO circled one particular neighborhood for ten minutes and projected down a beam of red light that moved across residents' properties. After "scanning" the ground, the object moved northwest and vanished.

On October 10 of that same year, I received a telephone call at six in the morning from one of the witnesses from the aforementioned sighting stating that he once again saw the object that very morning, this time at 4 AM. When he went outside at sunrise, his lawn and trees were covered with a silky, white material that looked like "cobwebs." When he picked up the material in his hand, he said excitedly, "it just

---

18. At the present time, I am still investigating these sightings since they involve possible encounters with an alien intelligence. I hope to publish my finding in my next book.

19. Most of the people who called or emailed had read my book, *Night Siege: The Hudson Valley UFO Sightings,* and knew how to contact me. A local newspaper, *The Journal News,* also ran a story on my research in the summer of 2008.

dissolved like it wasn't even there!" I made arrangements to drive to his home from my place in Connecticut—I wanted to get there as soon as possible because it sounded like a rare case of angel hair. With my research in mind, I knew this phenomenon would likely completely dissolve a short time after its fall from the sky. I arrived about two hours later at the witness's property; he told me most of the material was gone, that it just "vaporized," but some of it was still left on the front lawn.

I picked up a small amount and it felt like fine threaded silk. It wasn't sticky like a spider web and the strands were so thin that the slightest breeze blew them up into the air. I collected as many of the threads as I could and placed them in a specimen jar, took some photos and left. I was hoping to take the material to a laboratory in the area that I often used to perform quantitative and qualitative analyses. Unfortunately, half an hour into my trip, the material in the jar was gone and nothing at all remained. I called the property owner and was told all the "cobwebs" were gone; just "evaporated away." I was able to get my laboratory associates to take rubs from the inside of the glass jar, but nothing was found. The next day I discussed the incident with an entomologist who guessed I had found spider silk. She explained that spiders often use a finer thread-like material spun into sheets or balls for transportation. Air currents take them up in the air and they're used to migrate from one place to another. I then asked if they could dissolve. The entomologist replied that yes they could over time, if exposed to moisture, but she could not explain why this mystery material vanished on touch and inside the jar so quickly. As of 2009, the angel hair (or spider silk) never reappeared, so the question remains whether those wispy silk threads were from a UFO or nothing more than a migrating spider web.

HIGH STRANGENESS

"High strangeness" is a term used to describe an event that is more unusual than a typical paranormal experience. Although Fortean phenomena are strange to begin with, there are reports and claims that are so bizarre they must be placed in a special category. The term "high strangeness" was originally used in UFO research to describe encounters that involved more than just a sighting of an unknown object; today it is used in all areas of paranormal to denote a very bizarre case.[1] UFO investigators have always been in the forefront of paranormal research and because of this, many of them (including myself) have had the opportunity to investigate a number of very bizarre cases.

The majority of these high strangeness reports seem to involve some type of extra- or ultra-terrestrial contact, but in most of the claims, no UFO was seen and some experiencers never had a sighting in their lives. The stories present, in

---

1. "High Strangeness" was coined by the late Dr. J. Allen Hynek in his attempt to classify UFO encounters.

my opinion, some type of contact with a being from another physical dimension, or perhaps another universe. Although the claims may be very hard to believe, witnesses (or experiencers) are relating what they believe is the truth. Because the intelligence behind the contact never fully represents itself in its true form, the experiencer is left trying to interpret the encounter and make sense of it by drawing from their education and cultural beliefs.

HIGH STRANGENESS CASE NUMBER ONE: MOVING THROUGH TIME

In September 1982 I received a call from a man then in his early forties. His real name is Frank, but to protect his identity, I will not publish his last name. Frank had an outrageous story to tell and his claims seemed to be so fantastic that I felt no one—not even the most imaginative science fiction writer—could invent what he was to tell me. I agreed to meet Frank the next day in the afternoon at a restaurant in Darien, Connecticut. I arrived at the restaurant early and when Frank arrived, I invited him to sit at my table. The first question he asked me was "What day and year is this?" Frank claimed that since his interaction with an "alien" intelligence, he had been moving backward and forward through time. Frank said, "I was thirty years in the future and the towns from Norwalk to Greenwich were destroyed by an atomic explosion set by a terrorist who will soon become known only as

"Carlos."[2] I asked him to slow down and start his story from the beginning and tell me how this all started happening to him. Frank's claim was so fantastic that I will present what he told me word for word. I was interested in what he had to say; according to my background check, he had until this point led a pretty normal life as a successful corporate executive and property owner in Connecticut.

Frank's Story

"I guess you can say my life was normal until I had my first contact with what I thought at the time was an alien emissary from another planet. I owned my own home in Darien, had been happily married for ten years, and although we had no children it was still something considered for the near future. In December 1981, at about eight in the evening, I was watching television alone at home when suddenly the power went out. My wife was away visiting her mother who lived in New York City; the thought of spending the night alone without power did not sit well with me. I tried calling the electric company, but when I picked up the telephone there was no dial tone. I went and got a flashlight, looked out the window, and noticed that the power was still on in the neighborhood. I then started to go down to the basement to check the circuit breakers when the phone started ringing in short, loud bursts. It didn't even sound like my phone, but as I picked up the receiver there were two voices:

---

2. This would make it the year 2012—strange coincidence?

one of a man and the other of a woman, but they didn't sound human. I think they were computer generated.

"The voices took turns speaking and said: 'Greetings. We are from another galaxy and have chosen you to communicate with. Do not be alarmed—we mean you no harm but we have neutralized the power to your home so that we could speak with you.' I tried talking back and asked them what they wanted with me, but it was as if they used some type of pre-recorded message; they didn't respond to my questions. The voices also said that in ten seconds after the communication ended, electrical power in my home would be restored and at that time I was to go back into the living room and sit by the television. This seemed like a strange request, but the voices did not sound threatening and were very polite; they often apologized for the inconvenience and they often said the word 'please' when they wanted me to do something.

"The power came back on just after the voices stopped and the dial tone on the phone returned. I walked into the living room and sat near the television. As I sat there the set turned on all by itself and although the picture was fuzzy there was an image of a person. He had very large eyes that wrapped around his head, which looked almost like the shape of a pear. I could not see a mouth moving, but the being spoke and said, 'Greetings to you from the light of the radiant ones. My name is Lomunk and I am projecting my image to you from a ship located behind your moon. I come from a race of beings called the Ashtar which has been observing your planet for over ten thousand of your years. We are now making contact with individuals who have been genetically programmed to assist us in saving your planet.'

"I told this Lomunk guy that I wasn't interested and they should find someone else. He said, 'You have no choice in the matter and we shall have your assistance even if we have to use force.' I then went over and pulled the plug on the television, but it was still on and this Lomunk said, 'You can't get rid of me that easily. I am very real and control all that you see and hear on this primitive device.' I was really getting scared! I picked up a glass ash tray and threw it at the TV screen which made the tube explode, causing glass to fly everywhere. I was so scared, my hands were shaking so I went into my private supply of alcohol and drank several shots of whisky. I convinced myself that the whole incident was just a bad dream or hallucination of some kind. I cleaned up the glass in the living room and wondered how I was going to explain all this to my wife when she returned home. I was very upset, but the alcohol made me sleepy so I decided to go to bed and try and forget what had taken place. My wife would be back the next day, and my life would hopefully return to normal."

A Shadowy Night Visitor

Frank went to bed, and for some reason he was very tired and "drained." He slept until the wee hours of the morning and woke up in a cold sweat with a feeling of terror. Here, his story continues: "When I woke up, it was about two in the morning and the room had a heavy-like atmosphere to it. I felt incredible fear as if something awful was in the room with me. I can only describe it as a presence of pure evil somewhere in the dark, waiting to pounce on me. I sat up and the bed began to vibrate. A shadowy mist came out from under the bed and hovered at the foot. Although the room was dark, it was partly illuminated by a night-light, but this cloud was jet black. The mist formed into a human-like shape; it was very tall and seemed to have a hood. It looked like the angel of death and the first thing that came to my mind was that it was there for me because I was dead or about to die. I could not see any facial features, but this image had long arms with no hands. It stood at the foot of the bed and pointed its arm to me and as it did, I yelled at it asking why it was here. Then it formed back into a black cloud and went through the ceiling. I turned on the light and noticed a slight smell of cigar smoke in the room. The feeling of fear was still with me; I stayed up all night with the lights on until sunrise. My wife returned about noon the next day and asked what happened to the television set. I told her everything that had taken place, and she didn't say a word but just looked at me with a concerned stare of disbelief."

I didn't know it at the time, but what Frank described was an encounter with a shadow person. Shadow people seem to be some type of dimensional entities that exist in a reality very close to our own. They also seem connected to UFO-contact-abductions and cases of demonic possession. Paranormal researcher Rosemary Ellen Guiley has done extensive research on the shadow people and has complied hundreds of case studies.[3] Her initial findings indicate that encounters with this type of entity are increasing and are

---

3. Ms. Guiley has compiled an online database of encounters with shadow people (http://www.visionaryliving.com/2008/10/06/

global in nature. Shadow people sightings are discussed in the chapter "Entities from an Unseen World."

Encounter With the Silver Ball

Frank was so upset about his nighttime visitor that he stayed home from work the next day. At one in the afternoon he decided to go for a ride in his car to clear his head. Frank drove down to Greenwich, Connecticut, into the backcountry, and as he was driving, he heard a buzzing sound. He looked back and noticed a silver ball about 2 feet in diameter behind his car just above the hood, following him. No matter how fast he went, the object kept up with the car and the buzzing sound was getting louder. He looked around for another person, but no other cars were on the road. Suddenly, the object shot down three red laser-like beams on the trunk of the car, causing the vehicle to vibrate wildly. Frank began losing control of the car and finally had to pull over to the side of the road; as he did, the engine died. Frank looked around and to his relief the object vanished. He opened the door, got out, and walked around his vehicle looking for damage. Looking at the trunk, he noticed three silver spots where the silver ball shot its "lasers."[4] Shortly later, a Greenwich police officer stopped and helped him with his car. Frank didn't tell the officer about the object because he didn't want to look

---

category/shadow-people), and has been collecting reports for nearly twenty years.

4. The silver spots were very similar to what Betty and Barney Hill found on their car after their close encounter and contact experience in New Hampshire in 1961. Betty also described the spots' "magnetic properties" in an interview I conducted with her in 1986.

"crazy." The officer gave him a ride home to Darien and about an hour later, the tow truck delivered the car.

The spots on the trunk were still there, and when he placed a compass near them the needle spun around in circles. Later that evening, Frank's wife came home from work and asked about the car. When Frank told her his story, she once again gave him a strange look and said she did not believe him. Frank then took her out to the car to show her the circles but they were gone. Frank's wife started to yell at him, "What's wrong with you? First the TV, now the car!" She suggested he see a doctor and get some tests done since what he was saying happened to him was "just plain crazy." To make a long story short, Frank did see a doctor and had a CAT scan of his brain and it showed nothing abnormal. His doctor suggested that Frank should see a psychiatrist, but he was reluctant to do so despite his wife's insistence.

Several days later after the encounter with the silver ball, Frank began hearing voices that spoke in some language he didn't understand. He also claimed that at night, he would close his eyes and have visions of people and alien-looking beings in some type of operating room. Two days later, Frank would disappear for forty-eight hours, returning home with an even more incredible story for his disbelieving but concerned wife. Below is his account.

A Trip Through Time

"Things were not going well for me: my wife thought I was losing my mind and I could not function at work so I decided to spend the day walking through Bruce Park in Greenwich,

Connecticut. I parked, got out of the car, and began to walk down the path when all of a sudden everything around me got blurry and I felt as if I was spinning around in a circle. After a minute or so, things settled down and the dizziness stopped. My vision was clear but something had changed. The path ahead of me looked different, with plants and flowers that were not there before. I continued to walk and saw three people, two men and a woman, walking toward me on the path. They were dressed strange, like what people wore in the mid-1800s. As they approached I said, 'Nice getup, are you going to a costume party?' One of the men replied, 'Excuse me, what do you mean, sir?' They looked at me like I was some kind of nut and walked past me. I looked back to apologize and they were gone. Then, without warning, the dizzy feeling and blurry vision returned; I fell to the ground and looked up and saw an alien being. It was that Lomunk person from my TV. I got up to my feet and he told me that I moved from one hundred years in the past to thirty years in the future. He then said he had something to show me, but first we had to go up to a ship cloaked and five hundred feet above us.

"Lomunk waved his hand and a device attached to his wrist glowed. I saw a bright light and the next thing I knew, I was in a room that had all kinds of equipment with people strapped to five tables. The people were human; two of them (a man and a woman) looked at me, smiled, and said hello. I asked this Lomunk guy what they were doing and he said that these people like me 'were volunteers who are being conditioned to help us save your planet from disasters that will take place at different points in time.' I yelled at him and said I never volunteered for anything. Lomunk told me that I did and pointed to a wall where a screen appeared. The screen played some type of video of me when I was a teenager, talking with him and agreeing to help. It's strange—I remember that experience, but always thought it was a dream. Lomunk pointed to another screen and told me to look, and what I saw shocked me. Several cities along coastal Connecticut were in burning ruins, thousands of people were dead. Lomunk said that a terrorist set off a nuclear device, and it was my task to stop the disaster by disarming the bomb. He then said that they were going to take me back in time twenty-four hours and place me at the location of the bomb. I told him that I didn't know how to do this and he replied, 'We will teach you.'

"He took me into a room and instructed me to sit in a chair. Another alien-looking guy came into the room and attached a small circular disk to the right side of my head. He pressed a button on a device that looked like a remote control and I felt a vibration that shook my skull. It felt as if electricity was being shot into my brain. It only lasted about ten seconds and when the procedure was finished, I had all the knowledge to do what they wanted. I was then taken into a room that Lomunk called the 'travel chamber' and was told that they had the ability to travel 175 years back or forward in time. Lomunk said that I would be transported to the correct time and place to disarm the bomb, and when the mission was complete, they would transport me back to the park in the year 1982, close to the time that I left. I asked him why they didn't do it themselves and he replied, 'We would, but we can only stay in your dimensional reality for a short period of time.'

"I was transported to the site by a beam of light and saw the bomb—it was in the basement of a large building, and I did what they trained me to do; I disarmed it. I then found myself sitting on a bench back in the park. I walked to my car and found myself drifting through time—every five minutes or so I seemed to be in a different time period.

"After what seemed like forever, I felt steady enough to drive home. As I pulled in my driveway my wife yelled, 'Where were you?!' She told me that I had been missing for two days and that she filed a missing persons report with the police. It's strange, because I was not hungry or thirsty; my beard hadn't grown and I didn't have to go to the bathroom, so how could I have been gone for two days? I told my wife what happened and she said, 'That's it, *now* I am calling the doctor!' To make a long story short, I was forced to see a psychiatrist or my wife was going to divorce me. The doctor said I was having delusions to escape reality and was afraid to face life. I tried to explain that my life was fine until this Lomunk person appeared. The doctor and my wife forced me to take medication and although I no longer heard voices during the day, just before drifting off to sleep at night I would find myself traveling through time to different periods of human history. On several occasions, my consciousness was beamed aboard Lomunk's ship where I was introduced to others from his race and was introduced to other humans from around the world who were also helping them."

Beings of Plasma

If we limit our thinking to what we were taught in school,
Frank's story would be impossible to believe. Eventually, Lomunk identified himself as not an alien from another galaxy,
but a being that represented a race that exists in a very nearby
dimension. After multiple meetings, Lomunk told Frank that
his race really didn't care about humanity and if we wanted
to destroy ourselves, it was our own business. According to
a conversation with Frank in the spring of 1983, he discovered that Lomunk's civilization was so near us, the atomic
explosion would also have damaged his world. It seems that
Lomunk's race is susceptible to magnetic fields and EMPs
(electromagnetic pulses). When taking a look at some of the
entities reported in paranormal cases, the sensitivity would
make sense—many otherworldy beings seem to have shape-
shifting abilities and don't appear to be composed of matter
as we know it.

According to Islamic legend, an ancient race of beings that
predates humanity called the Djinn exist in a very nearby
parallel dimension. It is said they are composed of smokeless
fire, which sounds a lot like plasma to me. Plasma is often
called the fourth state of matter, and although many schools
still teach that there are only three states, there are actually four. To put it very simply, plasma is an ionized gas into
which sufficient energy is provided to free electrons from atoms or molecules. The gas allows charged atoms and electrons to coexist. It might sound strange, but this fourth state
is actually the most common one in the universe.

A charged particle soup has powerful electrical properties and creates a magnetic field—the excited, charged particles radiate light and other forms of electromagnetic radiation. The biggest chunk of plasma in our solar system is the sun. The sun's enormous heat rips electrons off the hydrogen and helium atoms that make up our star. Plasma can be found on earth in glowing neon lights and in severe electrical storms. Plasma can be manipulated or disrupted by an intense magnetic field or an EMP. A being composed of plasma would not have a definite solid form and might be able to change its shape by rearranging the magnetic field that contains it. Any type of EMP might be very dangerous to a creature of this nature, perhaps that's why Lomunk's race needed a human to disarm the bomb—a powerful EMP is emitted during an atomic blast.

Endgame

In the long run, Frank's contacts with Lomunk were not beneficial to his existence in our world. As time went on, Frank lost his job and filed for divorce. I wonder how many people are out there who have been judged as mentally ill after having a paranormal experience. Our mental hospitals may hold quite a number of people who are now heavily medicated and permanent residents because they claimed to have had some type of alien contact. Society has locked these people away because they don't behave in a normal manner, but they may be the first ambassadors of a new world. It's a travesty of justice, the result of a society that restrictively judges reality by what the five senses and instruments of our making

can record. Science and the governing bodies of this world
find it difficult to accept the fact that some individuals may
have touched an unseen reality; clearly their experiences are
beyond what is "normal," but these experiences may be very
real, in fact. Recently (2009), I was able to track Frank down
and had a lengthy conversation with him. Although his contacts with Lomunk are no longer taking place, he has dedicated his life to helping others who have had similar experiences. Frank is single now and seems to have gotten his life
back together. He is employed as a sales executive in a major
corporation and lives happily in New York.

Although many of the contact cases in my files are referred to as "aliens," this does not mean that they originate
from another star system. Concerning experiences like the
one mentioned above, it is my opinion that we are dealing
with intelligence that hails from that part of the unseen
physical universe that eludes human perception. These cases
are best suited for the paranormal researcher and not the
UFO investigator. Most people who investigate UFO sightings have narrowed their objectivity by looking for nuts-and-
bolts spaceships and evidence of alien explorers. As a result,
these people ignore case studies presented in this chapter.
However, in order to fully understand the complexities of the
paranormal world, all claims must be considered.

The next story is another case of a contact experience that
seemingly involves a race of dimensional beings. Why they
chose people like Frank and the person mentioned below to
make contact is still beyond my complete understanding,
but I do know that many of these people have one connect-

ing thread and that is they all seem to have psychic abilities.[5] Perhaps there is also something in their emotional, spiritual, or biochemical makeup that may also allow them to cross the bridge of one reality to another.

HIGH STRANGENESS CASE NUMBER TWO: THE UGLY ALIEN

I received a letter from the Center for UFO Studies in April 1982 describing a Milford, Connecticut, resident's "alien" contact experiences. I had a working relationship with this organization at the time; the information was sent to me mainly because I lived in that part of the country. The letter was from a young man in his twenties who claimed to have met people from another dimension.

This person's name is Robert. The first time Robert had a "visitation" was when he was five years old. He woke up very early in the morning to find his room glowing with a pale blue light. Then, a "monster" appeared at the foot of the bed and looked like it was about to say something when Robert covered his eyes and began screaming. His parents came running into the room, concerned he had fallen out of bed and hurt himself. Turning on the overhead light, Robert's parents expected to find him on the floor, but he was still in bed. Robert began telling them of the monster that appeared out of the blue light. Robert told his parents that the

---

5. Tests were done by me during the interviews. Details on this procedure can be obtained by emailing me at the address in the appendix of this book.

creature was so ugly, he had to hide under the covers; he said that it was tall and had dark skin like leather with a pointed nose and ears; he was sure it was the devil. Robert's parents assured him that it was just a dream and that he should go back to sleep, but Robert insisted that the light stay on. Over the next several years, the ugly being would appear before Robert's bed several times a year at the same hour during the night and each time the creature would attempt to communicate with him.[6] However, Robert was too frightened and would always cover his head with the bed covers and start screaming. When Robert was fourteen, he finally mustered enough courage to ask the entity what it wanted and it only replied "you" and vanished. The entity did not make another appearance until Robert was in his early twenties; the rest of his childhood was quite normal.

Underground Bases

At twenty years old, Robert enrolled in the University of Arizona and concentrated on his studies; he felt a passion for engineering—in many of his dreams involving the ugly alien, he was shown devices he was sure he could build providing he was taught the skills. Robert's early college years were not easy: "I could not concentrate on the lectures or do any of the homework because as soon as I went to my dorm and rested, I would hear voices and then drift off to sleep. In the

---

6. The time of these nighttime visitations was always about three in the morning. This is interesting since most paranormal events of this type also have been reported at this hour.

sleep state, I was often taken out of my body and brought to some type of laboratory with aliens and humans working on some type of instrumentation. Once, I was taken to what seemed like an underground base, and there I saw government people and aliens working together."

Robert told me that one of the underground bases was located near Brewster, New York. He knows this for sure because just before he was led through a tunnel, he saw a sign that read "Southeast." Since he never heard of a town called Southeast, Robert looked it up on a map and found there is one such town in southern New York—Southeast is actually a part of Brewster. At the time, I didn't think too much of what Robert said, but later I was to find myself in Southeast on many occasions, exploring underground tunnels that were the remains of a nineteenth-century mining operation. The location where Robert saw the "Southeast" sign in his dream has been the scene of many paranormal events and close encounters with aliens, strange creatures, and UFOs. Nearby are Reservoir and Upper and Lower Magnetic Mine Roads, which lead to underground tunnels connected to the old mines. It is at these locations that strange hooded beings and mysterious lights have been reported. According to local folklore, they are the ghosts of miners killed in an 1895 mining accident. Today, I still find it amazing Robert knew about these underground tunnels ten years before I began exploring them.

Materialization in a Car

One morning, Robert woke in his Arizona dorm with a strong feeling that he should get into his car and drive to Colorado— he seemed to do it without thinking and says it was like some outside force was controlling him. While driving through a pass in the Rocky Mountains, he heard a voice say "Hello, Robert." Robert turned his head and saw the ugly alien creature from his childhood dreams in the passenger seat! He said the creature was so ugly and the smell of burning sulfur was so strong that it made him vomit. The creature laughed and said, "At last we meet in person. Now I am really with you, and not a projection."

Robert described the creature as being long and slim with greenish, wrinkled skin. It had a long pointed nose, and pointed face and ears with no hair. He also described horns or tubes coming out of its head. He asked the being who it was and it replied, "Some say I am the devil," and it laughed. The creature would not give Robert its name or where he was from. It only replied, "I and others like me are from another dimension and we like to play games with you pathetic humans." Robert asked why it tormented him all these years and the being replied, "I could have killed you a long time ago, but you are just too much fun." Robert said to the being, "You can't control me!" The entity replied, "Well! I made you drive all the way here, did I not?" At this point, Robert stopped the car and got out. The being followed. The entity then pointed to the sky and a swirling black portal opened up and the creature flew in it and as it entered, yelled back, "You will see me again!"

Robert got back into his car and returned to Arizona. Things didn't go well for him. He flunked out of school and moved back to Connecticut to live with his parents. The night-time visitations increased in frequency. Robert saw shadow-like beings walking into his bedroom almost every night— they would stop at his bed, look at him, and disappear. It got so bad that Robert stayed awake for an entire week because he was too afraid to close his eyes. At night, he would keep all the lights in the house on and turned on all the television sets and radios: he discovered that when there was a great deal of noise and light in the house, the shadow beings would stay away. Finally, Robert's parents could not take it any more and forced him to see a psychiatrist. The doctor diagnosed Robert as a paranoid schizophrenic and placed him on a number of medications.

I tried to follow up with Robert, but it was very difficult. In 1993, he moved out of his parents' home into a small apart-ment in Bridgeport, Connecticut. Today, he is a member of a local born-again Christian group and although his contacts with the ugly entity still continue, he claims he is no longer afraid because "the Lord" is protecting him. To me, what Robert encountered sounds very much like the Native Ameri-can legends of the Trickster or the Middle Eastern Djinn. The contacts were not extraterrestrial in nature; Robert had no in-terest in UFOs and has never had a sighting. There seems to have been no purpose to the contact except to torment Robert and manipulate his life. It is also interesting to note that when Robert kept all the lights, radio, and TV on, the ugly alien and shadow people stayed away. Perhaps if these entities are composed of plasma, the magnetic field produced by the electrical devices acted like a repellent to keep them at bay.

HIGH STRANGENESS CASE NUMBER THREE: THE THREE VISITORS

On July 2, 1987, I received a call from a thirty-six-year-old woman named Gail who at the time was living in Toms River, New Jersey. She found my number after hearing me on a radio talk show. When she called, Gail sounded very troubled and wanted to tell me about a number of paranormal visitation experiences she'd had. Sometime in late June 1987, while lying down on her bed, Gail began to feel uneasy, as if someone was watching her. The time was around 10 o'clock and she was alone. Her seventeen-year-old daughter was away visiting her father in New York; Gail is divorced. As she lay on the bed, she heard a voice say, "We have come for you . . . you will not be hurt." Gail realized her entire body was paralyzed and she could only move her eyes. Lying on her back, she saw three strange-looking beings standing in the doorway to her bedroom.

Gail said the three beings were dressed in something that looked like tightly fitting black jumpsuits and they stood single file, one behind the other. As Gail watched them in great fear, she noticed the leader seemed to have a problem entering the room—it was as if some type of invisible shield was blocking his way. The leader lifted his hands and pressed them against the invisible shield, as if taking measurements. The light in the hall was dim, and Gail could not see their facial features clearly, but noticed they were about five feet tall with very long arms. The leader took some type of rod from a side pocket and unscrewed the bottom of it. The rod glowed with a green light and then the leader passed it over the doorway. The entities then walked into the room without any effort, still in a single file. Gail noticed that they had large heads and eyes that looked like a cat's eyes that extended around to the sides of their heads. She never heard them speak out loud using vocalizations, but realized that the leader was communicating with the other two, because she perceived a variety of buzzing and clicking sounds in her head. When she heard these sounds, the other two moved; one pressed down on some type of black pad attached to its arm.

Gail tried to scream but couldn't—she was only able to move her eyes. The leader moved to her right side, the other beings each went to the foot and the left side of the bed. The beings on each side of her then placed their hands under her head and raised it up. Gail said their hands were ice cold like the dead and all she wanted was for them to stop touching her skin. Gail then noticed that the being on the left had a tube in its hand that looked like a narrow roll of white cotton it started pushing up her left nostril. At that moment, she felt extreme pain in her head and started to lose consciousness. Gail remembers feeling as if she was falling from a great height, then everything went black. The next thing she recalled was waking up at eight in the morning with a very bad headache. As she walked to the bathroom, both nostrils started to bleed. She felt as if something was stuck up her nose but nothing seemed to be there. She looked in the bathroom mirror and noticed her nose was puffy and swollen; there was a vivid red rash on her neck and legs as well as a mild rash on her arms. Gail had hoped that the experience from the previous night was nothing more than a bad dream. She did not want to believe it and tried to block the entire episode from her mind.

When her daughter arrived home that evening, Gail began to tell her what happened, but before she even finished her story, her daughter started shaking. She revealed that on the same night, about the same time, she and her father were followed by a UFO on Route 116 near Croton Falls, New York. She described the object to her mother as a large, dark craft, triangular in shape that paced the car for five minutes just above the treetops. I found this report very interesting since Croton Falls is near the border of Westchester and Putnam Counties and lonely Route 116 was the site of more than one close encounter in the mid- eighties. I also found it quite interesting that both mother and daughter, even though widely separated by physical distance, had an experience with the paranormal at about the same time.

Gail's rash and headaches lasted for the next few days and then disappeared, but Gail's story does not end here. Several weeks later, I received a call from her telling me the entire experience repeated itself. She said, "Those creatures returned at the same time of the night and they did the same exact things they did before. It was as if I was watching a replay of the first time they came into my bedroom. They even had the same trouble getting into the room and the leader once again took out the glowing rod and had to wave it in front of the doorway so they could enter." Her daughter was visiting her father, but did not have any UFO sightings this time. One night in October 1987, while walking into her kitchen at ten in the evening, the "alien" beings appeared out of nowhere. Gail fell to the floor and started screaming. She passed out and woke up the next morning with bruises on her legs and arms. To my knowledge, Gail continued to have visitations well into 2007. I am still working with Gail, attempting to document a complex series of continuing abduction experiences with beings that are not a part of this world. Her daughter married and no longer lives at home, so every night as the sun sets, Gail keeps all the lights in the house on, afraid her "visitors" will return.

HIGH STRANGENESS CASE NUMBER FOUR: THE SILVER SHAPESHIFTER

This next case involves a professional nurse; I will refer to her as "Kate." Kate had a number of visitations as a child of a tall, silver, "robot-looking" creature that had the ability to change shape. The being would enter her bedroom by walking through the wall after a flash of blue light. Every time the being appeared, she would not be able to move or call her parents for help. In many cases like this one, sleep paralysis is a common occurrence and although the experiencers are not harmed, they lose the ability to move or speak while the entity is in the room. The only body part in which the person seems to be able to move is the eyes. The being said his name was Leenal and that he came from another land (dimension?) very close to her room. In one visit, he actually picked Kate up in his arms and walked through an opening in the wall to show her his world. She doesn't remember much except that it was foggy and had all kinds of colored lights in

the air that illuminated the mist. Could it be that another reality intercepted or crossed near her bedroom? When I heard
of this case in 1993, it reminded me of a *Twilight Zone* episode
("Little Girl Lost") in which a young child accidentally falls
into another dimension after a portal opens up in the wall
behind her bed.[7] Although her parents could hear her, they
couldn't find her. Finally, just before the portal closes, her
father and a scientist friend who figured out what is going
on are able to rescue her. This episode was filmed in 1961;
most people don't know that Richard Matheson wrote the
short story based on a real-life incident involving his young
daughter, who rolled off her bed while asleep against a wall.[8]
Despite hearing her daughter's cries for help, Matheson's
wife was at first unable to locate the young girl.

Leenal started appearing to Kate when she was five years
old; her contacts with the being would continue on a regular basis until she was ten. Leenal would always enter the
room the same way: walking through the wall on the east
side of the house and at about the same time, between two
and three in the morning. The contact took place once or
twice a month, and during the visit she would be unable to
move. Kate said that Leenal looked like a tall silver "robot"
with a gentle and kind voice. The entity would often change
shape into a dog or storybook character as if to entertain

---

7. *The Twilight Zone*: 1961, season 3, episode 31.
8. Richard Matheson, born February 26, 1926, is an American writer
   whose work often appeared on Rod Serling's *Twilight Zone* television series. Now in his eighties, Richard continues to write science
   fiction and fantasy.

her or allay her fears. Leenal's efforts were successful, because eventually, Kate no longer feared the alien's appearance and began looking forward to seeing it. Kate tried to tell her parents about Leenal's visits, but they told her it was just dreams. When Kate was eight, her parents took her to a child psychologist who found her "an intelligent child with a vivid imagination." The doctor told her parents it was common for children her age to have imaginary friends.

The night after the visit to the doctor, Leenal paid Kate another visit and was very upset she had told the psychologist about him. Kate was puzzled—how did the entity knew about the visit? It couldn't—unless it was watching her. Leenal told her that if she continued to tell people about their conversations he would become *very* angry and go away forever. Kate kept silent about subsequent contacts with the silver robot and didn't mention them anymore to her parents or anyone else. When Kate's mother asked her once about Leenal, she "admitted" to making him and his visits up—they were "imaginary," like the psychologist said. Two days after her tenth birthday; Leenal appeared for the last time to Kate as a child and said goodbye. The "silver robot" told her that he would contact her once again in the future. It would be twenty years before Leenal would once again appear to Kate. By that time, she was thirty, working as a nurse in Arizona. Below is her story of her final contact (to date) with the shapeshifting entity.

Kate's Story

"I got a job at a hospital in Scottsdale, Arizona, just after I graduated from nursing school. I lived in a small apartment about a mile from my job so I walked back and forth to work when the weather was nice. I lived quite a simple life and had no strange things happen to me until several days after my thirtieth birthday. It was June 1992 and I had just finished the evening shift at the hospital where I worked as a nurse in the cardiac intensive care unit. It was almost 11:30 PM when I left my job; I was very tired and could not wait to get home to rest. Normally, I would take the streets to walk to my apartment, but that evening I had a strong impulse to cross a field (a shortcut), but it was pretty dark and isolated. The moon was almost full that night so I figured it would be safe since it was quite bright out. I slid under the fence and started walking through the field. It was about half a mile long and I'm not sure who owned it, but I thought if someone objected, I would never do it again; besides, there were no signs telling me not to trespass. I carried a small flashlight in my purse and took it out to see where I was going because there were many holes and I didn't want to sprain or break an ankle.

"I was halfway through the field when three deer came out of the brush to my right; they were walking as if they were drugged and they just collapsed on the ground. Then several birds dropped from the sky and fell to my left and right—they seemed dead. At that moment, several rabbits ran by me and one of them rolled over on the ground and looked like it was having a convulsion. I then heard this loud humming sound and a yellow ball of light appeared in the air several feet above the ground. I was quite startled and stopped in my tracks, since whatever this was it affected the animals and could possibly hurt me. I felt strange, like when I was a child and would have those nighttime visits with the silver robot Leenal. The only difference this time was that I was still able to move, but couldn't because I was so scared. I just stood there transfixed looking at the light.

"After several seconds, a mist shot out of the light with a loud 'swoosh.' The mist then formed into a shape that turned into Leenal! He looked just like I remembered him, tall (maybe 8 feet) and all silver with a helmet and visor like thing where his eyes should have been. He then spoke, 'Hello Kate. I told you I would be back.' It was quite upsetting to see this being again because I had convinced myself that those childhood experiences were not real and just dreams. I yelled, 'Why are you bothering me now? It's been twenty years!' Leenal said that time had no meaning to his people and that he had to show me his world. He waved his hand and I felt myself go numb and fall to the ground.

"I opened my eyes and was in a different place that didn't seem like planet Earth. The sky was red and a fog was all around me. Leenal was standing in front of me and started to change shape, first into a horrible creature that looked like the devil. When I turned away and screamed, he turned into a tall, handsome young man with long blonde hair, very pale white skin and the greenest eyes I have ever seen. He said he could take any form and be anything or anybody I wanted him to be. He told me we were in his world and he had to bring me there to establish a 'permanent connection' with my mind.

"Leenal explained that he was part of a very ancient race that existed before mankind, and that many of his people were trying to establish mental links with selected humans so his race could come into our world. He then turned back into the tall silver robot-like form and put his hand on my head. Once again, my body went numb, but this time I didn't feel myself falling to the ground, I kind of floated. When I opened my eyes I was in the field and it was daylight. I looked at my watch—it was 6:23 AM. The passage of time felt weird because it only seemed like I was in Leenal's world for under an hour, yet at least five hours had passed.

I went home, opened my door and found my apartment a mess. Furniture was overturned and all my dresser and kitchen drawers were pulled out and emptied. I thought at first that I had been robbed, but my jewelry, money, television, stereo, and other valuables were still there. I asked my neighbors and the people who lived above me if anyone had heard or seen anything, but no one did."

Although Leenal never appeared again to Kate since that summer night of 1992, she continued to have paranormal experiences in the form of poltergeists and saw shadow-like beings in her home and at the hospital when she worked the night shift. Kate felt as if the shadow figures were spying on her. In 2005, Kate would experience being abducted, not by aliens or dimensional beings, but by flesh and blood humans she said were government agents. This is one of two accounts that have come to my attention in which, after a paranormal or UFO experience, the individual involved was taken by a group of men to some type of secret laboratory. I will relate the story below as told to me by Kate just twenty-four hours after the kidnapping took place.

Abducted by Government Agents

On August 23, 2005, at about seven in the evening, Kate received a phone call by someone who identified herself as "Brenda," a close friend of hers. There was a great deal of static on the phone and the voice was very low and hard to make out. Kate said that it didn't sound like her friend and there was so much static on the line that she really could not tell for sure. "Brenda" said that her car had broken down in a town near the Chandler Fashion Center in Chandler, Arizona, in an underground parking lot, and she needed help because she had no money to pay for a tow truck. Kate quickly jumped in her car and got there in about twenty minutes since the mall was only about 14 miles from her home. As she drove around the underground parking lot, Kate was surprised that there were so few cars for that time of the evening. She did not see her friend's car, so Kate decided to park, get out, and look around. As she stepped out the door, a white van and a black car came screeching towards her and stopped. Out of the van, four men dressed in black with ski masks on their heads grabbed Kate, and one put something over her nose that made her almost pass out. Kate was still awake but was unable to move her arms and legs and when she tried to look around and call for help, everything began swirling.

She was terrified, but there was nothing she could do. Kate was placed in the back of the van in a sitting position with two of the men on each side and one almost face to face with her. At no time did any of them talk. As she went in and out of consciousness, Kate thought she heard a female voice on a radio transmission say "approaching home base with target 8V2." Then the van stopped and the back door opened quickly. A man in a white coat came in and gave her some type of an injection. She was then taken out of the van by the men and felt herself slipping away. She noticed that the men brought her into a building and one of them took out a card and swiped it through a magnetic lock and then entered a code on a key pad. The door opened, but she was so drugged that she could not make out any faces or what the place looked like—the lights in the room were very bright. The last thing Kate remembers is being strapped on a table where someone moved a device that could have been an ultrasound over her chest and face. She then heard the person who was doing the procedure say, "There. We found it." Kate then blacked out and when she regained consciousness, she was in her bed at home—it was one in the morning. She got up and besides a slight headache, she felt all right. The next day she called Brenda and asked about her car. Brenda said her car was fine, but she had been trying to call Kate since nine yesterday evening and only got her machine. Kate didn't tell Brenda about the experience, but after she said goodbye she checked her machine and found two messages from her, one at 9:10 and the other at 9:55 PM.

Kate tried to convince herself it was just a dream, but could not. She thought that the abduction was somehow connected to her contact with Leenal. There is no doubt in her mind that both were very real, and she thinks Leenal put something in her the government wanted so badly that they sent agents to kidnap her. When I asked Kate if she went to the police to report the incident she laughed saying, "Yeah, then I would have to tell them the whole story and most likely lose my job. I am responsible for the lives of people in the cardiac intensive care; how would my patients react if they knew the person giving them medication through their IV had contact with a being from another dimension?" I kept in contact with Kate well into late 2008, and although Leenal and the "government agents" never paid her another visit, she continued to see the shadow people in her home almost every night moving quickly through the house.[9] She told me that on a number of occasions at night, she would wake up and see one standing by the bed and it would quickly disappear as if it didn't want to be seen. As of the writing of this book, Kate came into a very large inheritance and quit her job and moved out of Scottsdale. Kate informed me that despite relocating halfway across the country, she is still seeing the shadow people in her home.

---

9. I was going to use Kate's story in my book, *Interdimensional Universe* (2008) but decided against it because the case involves a considerable amount of high strangeness and is more applicable here.

HIGH STRANGENESS CASE NUMBER FIVE: THE CREATURES FROM THE SWAMP

There are sixty-two cases in my files involving some type of contact with terrifying animal-like creatures. The case I now present involved a grandmother, mother, and her young daughter taken out of their normal reality, brushing against a world they thought existed only in nightmares.

On April 22, 2002, I received a call from a woman named Margaret, a single mother who lives with her daughter and mother in a small Connecticut town. Margaret told me she saw a strange light and a number of unusual creatures in a swamp very close to her home. She said her mother and thirteen- year-old daughter, Jessica, had also seen the "things" and found them terrifying. Margaret also mentioned the creatures took their dog, a six-year-old dog named Thunder. Margaret had heard me on a radio show talking about the paranormal and decided to call me. She had called the police but could tell that despite their politeness when taking her story, they did not believe her. When we spoke, she sounded sincere and like she had a solid case so I made plans to see her.

Margaret's home was located in an isolated section of Connecticut backcountry, down a long driveway impossible to see from the street. This was before I had GPS, so it took me quite a long time to find the house. It was a good thing I left home very early in the morning since I arrived at Margaret's home almost two hours late. After ringing the doorbell and going through introductions, I was asked to come into the living room, the side of the house that faced the swamp. I looked around the room and was surprised to see the windows were boarded up. I asked Margaret about it and she replied, "I boarded up the windows to make sure that if the creatures ever came back, they could not get into the house." In the room was her mother and daughter, Jessica. All three ladies were still quite excited about the experience and tried to tell their story at the same time. The interview ended up being more than two hours long; the important parts of their story are presented below.

An Evening of Terror

On the evening of April 19, 2002, just after a late dinner, Margaret and her daughter decided to have a quiet evening listening to music in the living room. Margaret's mother was upstairs in her room listening to the radio and things seemed quite normal. Their dog, Thunder, was lying on the floor next to the television, fast asleep after a large meal. At about eight, Thunder jumped to his feet and began growling and barking as if someone was on or approaching the property. At the same time, the CD player began to make strange sounds as the music started skipping and an electrical-like noise played through the speakers. The noise was so bizarre that both Margaret and Jessica indicated that at times it sounded like the howling or growling of some type of animal. In other words, it wasn't your normal sound coming from a player having trouble. At that point, the grandmother (Margaret's mother) came downstairs and said that the radio upstairs had all static on it and she couldn't hear the music. Margaret then turned on the television set and it seemed to be working fine. Jessica tried the CD player again and the noise was still there so she changed CDs—the strange noise seemed to get worse. Margaret then said that it no longer sounded like static; it actually sounded like the groaning and howling of a monster. The dog began barking louder and then started crying as if very frightened of something that could not be seen. Margaret's mother indicated that she heard almost the same sounds coming out of the radio upstairs after the music faded away.

At a quarter past eight, there was a total loss of power in the house; the lights went out. The women brought out the flashlights and lit candles when Jessica noticed a light in the swamp. All three of them looked out the large living room window and wondered what it could be. At first they thought it was a car that ran off the road and got ditched in the mud, maybe after hitting a telephone pole, causing the power outage. Margaret picked up the phone to call the police, but it was dead—no dial tone, not even static. She told her mother and daughter to wait inside as she went out the back door to the deck to get a better look at the light. As Margaret left the house, Thunder ran past her and into the swamp barking and growling. She tried to call him back, but he disappeared into the darkness.

As Thunder got farther away, his barking started to fade and eventually just stopped. Once again, Margaret tried to call him, but there was no response . . . the dog seemed to have vanished. From the deck, the light seemed to be about a hundred feet away. Now walking closer, Margaret realized it wasn't the headlights of a car but a large sphere that was yellow in color with some type of swirling in the middle.

When I asked her to estimate the size of the light, she indicated that it was at least 6 feet in diameter.

As she continued to watch, the light started to change color from yellow to red and appeared to be pulsating. Then, a dark human-sized figure jumped out of the light. Two others followed. Since the light was so bright, she could not see them clearly and they appeared only as silhouettes. Margaret noticed they seemed to walk on two legs, but they swayed back and forth and were crouching. As she stood and watched, her daughter yelled from the window that they saw them also. The creatures seemed to hear Jessica's voice and started moving toward the house at a much quicker rate. Margaret said as they got closer she heard growling, as if these creatures were animals of some sort. When I asked if she could compare the noise to some common animal, she said it was very much like a dog's growl.

Jessica and her grandmother yelled for Margaret to come back to the house because the creatures were coming closer. Margaret told me with a shaking voice, "As they got closer I could make out their form: they seemed to have hair all over their bodies with long arms that almost reached to the ground. I was so scared that I couldn't move; the feeling was of pure terror. I stood transfixed—the hair on the back of my neck stood up. Finally, I heard my daughter scream. [I] turned around, ran into the house, locked the door, and yelled to my mother to close the shades."

All three women stood close together in the living room, trembling in fear when suddenly, they heard a loud pounding on the back door, outer walls, and living room window that faced the swamp. The pounding on the window was so hard, they were afraid the glass would shatter. The noise stopped, then after a minute or two, Margaret slowly lifted the shade. One of the creatures *was standing by the window!* The apparition was so scary that the women all screamed. Margaret quickly pulled down the shade and moved backward from the window. The three women described the creature as being as tall as a man but with hair all over its body. It had long, skinny arms with claws on its hands, circular eyes, and long ears that went to a point. The most terrifying part, they said, was its mouth—full of long, sharp fangs.

Terrified, the three women didn't know what to do. Young Jessica was screaming so loud her mother tried to calm her by saying, "If we are quiet, perhaps they will go away." After ten minutes of standing in the middle of the room in the dark, Margaret cautiously went to the window and pulled back the shade. She told me, "I saw three of them standing together in the middle of the yard, they were pulling something apart and placing it in their mouths like they were eating. I had a horrible thought that they may have killed Thunder and ate him. Then the creatures ran back into the woods toward the light and I lost sight of them. A short time afterward, the lights in the house blinked several times and then the power came back on."

Margaret picked up the phone; to her relief she heard a dial tone and called the police. When the officers arrived, they could find nothing on the property and there was no sign of the dog. Interestingly, they refused to go into the swamp and said that a patrol car and a detective would come by in the morning to do a more complete investigation. Despite the next day's extensive police efforts, the dog was not found. The police report said there were no footprints or any other signs that someone or something had been on the property.

My Investigation

I looked around the grounds and walked into the swamp where the light was seen and found nothing. The marsh was still thawing from the winter and smelled slightly of methane. The local electric company reported no outages in the area that could account for Margaret's home losing power. As of the writing of this book, Thunder was never found and it was the opinion of the police and the animal control officer that the dog must have just run away. This explanation didn't make any sense to Margaret; the dog was treated very well and was quite loyal.

Margaret knows a local nature expert who offered the possibility that the light she had seen was nothing more than swamp gas, also called a will-o'-the-wisp or *ignis fatuus*. Swamp gas has been reported as a ghostly light appearing over a bog at night or twilight. Science has explained the phenomenon as methane gas being released from rotting vegetation after a spring thaw. The methane rises into the air and ignites when coming into contact with oxygen. Much folklore surrounds the lights and many still believe they represent fairies or the souls of the dammed trying to escape from hell.

When I heard these tales, I almost laughed out loud— back in the sixties, Dr. J. Allen Hynek suggested that a rash of UFO sightings in Michigan was the result of swamp gas igniting and glowing. Dr. Hynek never lived down his swamp gas statement—many UFO skeptics later used "swamp gas" to jokingly explain away sightings they did not want to address. Throughout his eighteen-year position as a scientific consultant with Project Blue Book, Dr. Hynek was told to explain away all sightings at any cost.[10] I have seen swamp gas on two occasions: it appeared to be a bluish glowing flame, rising up from the ground and then exploding with a "pop!" Although there have been reports of the phenomenon lasting several minutes, the two I witnessed were no more than three seconds in duration.

Margaret and her family never saw the light or the creatures again. I find it hard to believe that "swamp gas" was responsible for the glowing light, and that the creature sighting was nothing more than three panicked women's overactive imaginations. The swirling, glowing yellow sphere in the swamp may have been a portal that opened a doorway to our world from another reality. The creatures that came through acted more like animals than intelligent beings—could they have been gathering information for their masters or were they simply hunting?

---

10. Project Blue Book was one of a series of systematic studies of Unidentified flying objects (UFOs) conducted by the United States Air Force (U.S.A.F.). Started in 1952, it was the third revival of such a study. A termination order was given for the study in December 1969, and all activity under its auspices ceased in January 1970.

THE GHOSTS OF
THE LOST MINES

The story of Robert's experience from the previous chapter describing a network of underground bases and tunnels in the town of Brewster, New York, intrigued me enough to do more research on the subject. Despite my efforts at the time, however, I couldn't find any data pertaining to any type of underground paranormal activity or locations of old mines. It wasn't until March 1983 after the UFO sightings in the Hudson Valley that all types of paranormal reports started to be brought to my attention; many were from that particular area. At the time I was already occupied with investigating the hundreds of UFO sightings that had recently taken place so I didn't think too much more about underground tunnels and mines until the summer of 1983 when two letters appeared in the editorial section of the *New York Daily News*.

MYSTERY TUNNELS

The letters were from concerned residents in the towns of Brewster and Southeast who claimed the U.S. government was doing little or nothing about the recent rash of UFO sightings. One letter, from a Southeast resident, claimed that he lived near the old abandoned mines and on numerous occasions he saw military vehicles heading down the narrow dirt paths that lead to the entrances. One letter writer claimed he also observed large cargo helicopters of the Chinook class landing somewhere in the hills behind the mines. Needless to say, this caught my interest but the name of the person who wrote the story was not published and the editor at the paper told me it was signed "Anonymous." Several days later I had a water leak in my study; the files that contained most of my recent work on the mysterious tunnels were severely damaged, but I was able to save one of the editorial letters dated July 1983.

An Interesting Letter

Why are people seeing all these UFOs, all of a sudden in the Hudson River Valley area? The answer is simple: there seems to be some kind of underground activity in the Brewster area, in the old abandoned iron ore mines. Some years ago the Government went out of its way to purchase the land that the mines are located on and people who live in the area including myself have seen military vehicles entering the dirt roads and they never come out. Also, we have seen helicopters landing in the hills close to the mine entrances. These areas have quite a few sightings of UFOs and people who live close to the mines have

*reported strange sounds and unusual lights as well. I feel that
the Government has established an underground base in which
some type of experimental aircraft is being kept. There is also
a possibility that the mines are being used by our government
and an alien intelligence to hide some type of operation in the
area.*

Signed,
Anonymous

If this letter printed in the *Daily News* was not enough
to get my interest, three years later (1987), just after *Night
Siege*'s first publication, I received a call from a friend who
is a CIA operative living in the southwestern United States
who read my book. Part of my past military background was
dealing with the Intelligence community, and I still had limited contact with individuals who are working not only for
the CIA but also military intelligence. This person told me he
came across a number of documents that were actually supply requests for an underground operation in the Brewster
area. The documents said that the operation was located in
an old iron ore mine near that town, but it failed to mention
which mine and its exact location. My informant also told
me that according to what he found out, the underground
base was a lab that was being jointly used by a special operations unit. The underground lab's purpose was unknown,
but he told me he saw equipment lists that might be used in
biological experiments. I told him that I was going to investigate the matter and go out there to see what I could find out.
His last words to me were to "stay away from this, just let it
go. The people involved are too powerful and are protected

by the National Security Act." Shortly after the phone call, I couldn't reach the contact. It seems he no longer had an active phone number and all mail sent to him was returned "address unknown."

My next course of action was to get detailed maps of the area and mark locations I thought should be explored. Doing so would save a considerable amount of time—the area in question has very steep hills with thick brush and few apparent roads and paths. I also purchased a topographic map for the area that included elevation, and locations of pits, swamps, caves, tunnels, and mines. As I studied the maps, I wondered where the entrance to these mysterious mines and underground tunnels might be found. I was pleasantly surprised when I saw that several isolated dirt roads around the Croton reservoir had the names "Lower Magnetic and Upper Magnetic Mine Road." This was promising: many hiking trails and secondary roads are named after something in the immediate area. There was also a path marked "Reservoir," which seemed to be more of a road rather than a trail. Reservoir Road connected to Stoneleigh Avenue, which in turn ended in Route 6, a major traffic artery for the towns of Carmel, Southeast, and Brewster. To my dismay, the topographic map showed no symbols indicating where the mines might be found. My next step was to drive there and survey the area. I picked a clear, warm day in April of 1988 and drove to the destinations eager to explore the locations marked on my maps. As I drove around the secondary roads, nothing really stood out so I decided to pay a visit to the nearby Brewster Museum, the Putnam County Records and Archives, and the Putnam County Historical Society.

THE OLD MINES OF PUTNAM COUNTY

My first visit was to the Brewster Museum, located on Main Street right in the center of town. Although the museum was small, it did have a good number of artifacts left over from the mining days in addition to a number of photographs. I entered, thinking I had found the right place but despite the wealth of available information, I could not find the location of the mine entrances. I spoke with the curator who wasn't sure exactly where they were, but she heard that one entrance to the Brewster Mine was located on Marvin's Mountain behind the train station. She suggested I visit the Putnam County Records and Archives located just one mile away. I took her advice and found a great deal of historical information about the towns in Putnam County and the old mining days that seemed to have been almost forgotten by current residents. To my disappointment, the people working at Records also had no idea where the mine entrances were located but the clerk was sure they had all been sealed off sometime in the early part of the twentieth century and are now inaccessible.

Although I could not get a clear answer as to why all the mine entrances were sealed, one person, a volunteer, told me quietly that it had something to do with the local legend of "ghosts and devil worship." This statement furthered my interest enough to spend the rest of the day carefully reading documents dated back to 1790. The hours seemed to pass quickly and before my research was completed, one of the volunteers asked me to leave—it was closing time. I returned every day for four days early in the morning to continue my research. I spent hours going through piles of materials that included old news clippings, several of which were so incredible, they would result in months of research and numerous field explorations. However, before I go into further detail, let me give you a clear understanding about the history of the mines and how they were formed; it will act as a cohesive to bind this chapter's materials together.

AN ANCIENT BEGINNING TO THE MYSTERY

A *very* long time ago, our planet Earth was much different than it is today. The continents were in different positions and part of the northeast section of the United States was at the bottom of an ancient sea. Six hundred million years ago, the body of water we call the Atlantic Ocean did not exist; another smaller ocean lay in its place. A geologist would know this ancient ocean as Iapetus, named after the Greek mythological figure, father of the titan Atlas (for whom the Atlantic Ocean of today was named).

During this time period, much of the eastern coast of New York lay at the fringe of proto-America; what was to be the state of Connecticut was divided into a number of sections mostly located on the floor of the ancient Iapetus ocean. After about two hundred million years, North America and Africa came together and closed the Iapetus Ocean and combined with other land masses to later form the supercontinent of Pangea.[1]

---

1. The Greek word *pangea* roughly translates to "entire earth."

The African and North American plate collision pushed the Iapetus Ocean floor upward, creating Connecticut in addition to the Appalachian mountains. As the two continents continued to collide, a great metamorphic process took place on the border where the Iapetus Ocean and the North American plate met: granite was changed into gneiss and quartz was fused into quartzite. If you drive along the highways of southeastern New York and Connecticut, you can still see the effects on the rock today as they are twisted and bent into bands. As the plates collided, many rocks, minerals and ores were also melted and forced to the upper crustal layers. These included serpentine, talc, chrysotile, and a highly desirable iron ore in a very high-grade form called magnetite. As the iron ore was melted from the friction of the two plates moving into and over each other, it was forced upward in a dramatic uplift that formed veins of ore between the layers of gneiss in the hills that were to become the towns of Carmel, Brewster, and Southeast. This geological history allowed settlers to find some of the purest iron ore in North America; it was mined for much of the late eighteenth and all of the nineteenth centuries. The mining days in New York are long past and the mines themselves have been closed for about a hundred years. Many residents who moved into the Brewster area within the last fifty years have no idea the mines even exist and that underneath their homes is a complex network of tunnels.

MINE HISTORY

There are five major mines in the Brewster area, and they all produced a high-grade iron ore, but Tilly Foster in Southeast was the largest. The mine was first owned by James Townsend from 1810 to 1830 and during this time, high-grade iron ore was taken out of the earth and shipped to Danbury, Connecticut, where it was then transported by railway to several cities in New England for further processing. The iron ore was almost pure magnetite with low levels of impurities (such as sulfur and phosphorus); this high-grade ore was in great demand by steel manufacturers, so the mining industry in Brewster began to flourish. In 1830, Tillingham ("Tilly") Foster purchased the mine and surrounding farms. Although the Foster family never used the land for its mineral and ore rights, it still bears his name. I found this very strange since according to the records Mr. Foster paid a considerable amount of money for the mine and the land surrounding it. There is no historical record to indicate why the family never exploited the riches of the area, but there is a local legend that may explain it all.

The story goes that shortly after purchasing the mine in 1830, Mr. Foster couldn't sleep one summer night and decided to go for a walk. The night was clear and warm and he decided to walk to the mine entrance. As he approached the path that led to the mine, Mr. Foster felt a very cold wind that seemed to be coming out of the opening. He stopped dead in his tracks and saw a glowing mist emerge from the adit (mine entrance). As Mr. Foster stared at the mist, he noticed the center of the cloud was glowing much brighter than the rest of it. The mist took the shape of a human and started floating toward him—when this took place, a violent wind kicked up and he thought he heard a voice speak in an unknown language. He watched in terror as the figure slowly drifted by him and returned to the mine entrance where it vanished. He later talked about his apparition sighting at the local tavern in town where a very old local Native American medicine man told him that what he saw was the ghost of a Native American princess who was buried in or near the mine and was upset that her tomb had been violated. Legend says that because of this ghostly encounter Mr. Foster never took the iron ore out of the earth; he was concerned the ghost would come back or put a curse on his family.

Mr. Foster died in 1842 and his widow sold the mine in 1844, but it wasn't until 1853 after General Thomas Harvey brought the land that the ore was once again extracted. In 1848 with the arrival of the Harlem railroad, transporting the ore became economically feasible. Shortly after his acquisition of the Tilly Foster mine, General Harvey also purchased the nearby Brewster and Theall-McCollum mines. The Brewster Mine produced three hundred tons of iron ore in two years and in 1849 part of the land was sold to a Mr. Aaron Marvin who built a home on top of the highest point of the mountain; today this area is called "Marvin's Hill."

Sometime in 1850, Walter Brewster opened a number of shafts around town that connected to the main mine tunnels.[2] This was an easy way for workers who were staying

---

2. Walter Brewster founded the village in 1848, motivated by nearby mines (which he partially owned), an abundant water supply, and the railroad's plans to pass through the area. The railroad helped

at local homes to go to work. All they had to do was go into the basement of the house and climb down a shaft that led to the main part of the mine. These shafts still exist today in the basements of the older homes. I wonder if the current owners are aware that somewhere in their cellar is a doorway that leads to a forgotten underground world. The last big mining boom was in 1870; by 1880, the Brewster mine had not been in operation for a while and was sealed off.

Satan's Cave

General Harvey purchased the Theall and McCollum mines in 1848, located two miles southwest of Brewster, on the west bank of the Croton River and mined them until his death in 1880. A year later, a John Cheever bought the mines and connected the two together with a 1,400-foot adit (horizontal tunnel), thus the Theall and McCollum mines were now known collectively as the Croton Magnetic Mine. The Croton Magnetic Mine was in operation from 1882 until 1899. During this time it produced more than one hundred thousand tons of high-grade magnetite before closing down. The reason the mine closed was unclear to me at the time, but it seemed to be the location of a considerable number of paranormal events, including sightings of unexplainable lights on the ground and in the sky.

---

to foster two local industries: iron mining and dairy. By the 1870s, Brewster was a thriving community, due in large part to these industries' successes.

After the mine was closed, the entrance was sealed some-time in 1904; shortly after, local residents called it "Satan's Cave"—in the early part of the twentieth century, a local cult of "devil worshippers" known as the Fallen Ones went into the mine to perform rituals. According to police documents dated from that time period, local residents accused the group of being responsible for a number of missing children. Although no evidence ever connected any cult members with the alleged crimes, information I uncovered indicated local authorities dealt with and forced the cultists to stop. How they were dealt with seems unclear. To this day, the "old tim-ers" whose families still live in the area will not discuss it. The actual number of people that belonged to this "devil worshipping group" is unknown, but the description from state police documents indicates they wore dark red robes with hoods. When I read this, chills went down my spine: at the time, a number of reports had come my way describing sightings of ghostly hooded beings near Reservoir and Lower Magnetic Mine Roads, very close to the entrance of the Cro-ton Magnetic Mine. It became clear to me why the mine was now known as "Satan's Cave."

THE HOODED BEINGS

Between 1910 and 1990, there were twenty-seven reports of people seeing one or more hooded beings along the Res-ervoir and Upper and Lower Magnetic Mine Roads. In most cases, the figures would appear out of thin air, sometimes right in front of a moving car, causing the driver to suddenly swerve off the road. In every case when the driver got out of the car to check if someone or something was hit, nothing was found. Fourteen of these reports indicate that the creatures had glowing red eyes, and all the ghostly encounters took place in the summer or fall after 9 PM. Some people in that area believe the hooded beings seen alongside the dark roads close to the mines are the ghosts of the devil worshipping cult known as the Fallen Ones, while others think they are alien visitors from another dimension. Whatever their origin, there is no doubt people are seeing *something*—sightings of these entities date back a hundred years. Although I could find several actual short news stories in the *Danbury News Times* dated between 1911 through 1950, a number of more recent accounts came to my attention during my investigation of UFO sightings in Putnam County.

The first was a 2003 phone call after I did a radio show on a New York station. Although the person who had the experience would not give me a name and phone number, he described an encounter I found quite interesting. The case involved a family of four, driving on Lower Magnetic Mine Road at about 10:30 PM on a hot summer's night in July 1999. The children, ages eight and ten, were complaining that they were tired and were getting a little cranky. The parents, therefore, wanted to get home sooner rather than later. The father decided to take a shortcut to Route 6, and he bravely turned down the dark secondary road, driving very slowly and cautiously with the bright lights on. The area is known for deer that jump out of the woods and sprint across the road, so he wanted to be careful. About halfway through Lower Magnetic Mine Road, the kids complained that they felt "sick" and nauseous. Suddenly, a "man dressed in a hood and a long robe" seemed to appear out of nowhere from the left side of the shoulder and started waving his hands as if trying to get their attention. Their first impression was that someone was in trouble, so the driver slowed down the vehicle and as he did, a number of other hooded "men" came out of the woods from both sides of the road and approached the car, all of them waving their hands wildly in the air. The father yelled for his wife and kids to lock their doors and roll up the windows. He floored the gas pedal and sped off, never looking back. The family drove to the sheriff's office to make a report with the Putnam County police. The impression the deputy gave them was that they had heard of this type of occurrence before but when the family asked who and what the hooded men were, the question was shrugged off. The police promised to investigate, but nothing was ever found and for some reason a police report was never filed.

During my investigation, the local police claimed they had "no such reports from that time." This lack of cooperation with local authorities was not unusual; my reputation as a paranormal investigator seemed to precede me. In the early and mid 1980s, after the first publication of *Night Siege*, hundreds of people began UFO watching along the roads in Carmel, Brewster, and Kent Cliffs. On many clear nights, residents called police several times because the UFO watchers were blocking traffic and disturbing them. Perhaps the police didn't want people driving up and down the dark roads looking for anything strange. A contact of mine who worked in the Putnam County courthouse told me paranormal and UFO reports that came to the attention of the police were filed as "closed reports" and were not available for viewing as public records. I can understand the want for security—after the excitement of the Hudson Valley UFO flap, local authorities were reluctant to release information concerning reports of the unexplained.

The hooded beings seem to be able to disappear and reappear and solid objects like cars passed right through them. Knowing this, one would assume they are not physical creatures but more like ghosts. The next account I will present also took place in July, but in 2002. This encounter indicates these creatures have the ability to become physical as you or me and can interact with the material world if they so choose.

The Beings With the Red Eyes

In the summer of 2002, a young woman left her friends house at 11 PM in North Salem, New York, and began her drive home to Brewster. She decided to take the back roads and drive around the reservoir; it was very beautiful that time of the year. As her car turned down Lower Magnetic Mine Road, she saw a figure standing in the road up ahead. At first she thought it was a deer, but when she flashed her bright lights, she could clearly make out an outline of a person. The figure started walking toward the car and it was apparent this mysterious apparition wanted to get her attention. She stopped the car, rolled down the window, and yelled, "Are you OK?" Without warning, her car was swarmed by "at least fifteen men and women" in long red robes who pounded on her car hood and started shaking the vehicle. The woman screamed when one of them opened the driver's door and *tried to pull her out of the car!* She reported that when it grabbed her arm, its hands looked like leather and felt very cold, "like something dead." Although the terrified woman could not see any facial features, she noticed clearly that when these figures turned their heads directly toward her, their eyes looked like glowing red coals. The woman fought back, kicking the creature away with one foot and used the other to step on the gas. As she sped off, she looked in the rearview mirror and saw the figures running after her until they just faded away in the dark. She arrived home, locked the door, and pulled down the window shades. She was afraid that the creatures would find her and try to abduct her in the night. To feel safer, she called two of her friends to come and spend the night. The next day, she debated whether or not to call the police and report the incident, but, decided against it.

There are many incidents like the two mentioned above that took place on this dark, isolated stretch of road. One very interesting encounter was made by a Mr. Harold Eglin Jr. who actually witnessed the hooded beings emerge out of solid bedrock. Harold's story is fully documented in my book *Interdimensional Universe: The New Science of UFOs, Paranormal Phenomena, and Otherdimensional Beings* (Llewellyn, 2008). Apparently, sightings of the hooded beings near the old mines have increased—there have been more reports in the last two decades than in the past eighty years.

SPOOK LIGHT

The area around the old mines is very strange indeed, with reports of UFOs, claims of alien abductions, ghostly apparitions, and strange creatures, but the greatest mystery was yet to come. In my final days of research at the Putnam County Records building, I found a number of old newspaper clippings so yellowed they were hard to read. The news stories covered a mining disaster at the Tilly Foster mine in 1895. According to local folklore, the ghosts of the men killed in a mine cave-in still haunt the area and have often been seen from Brewster to Southeast. At the time, I had more than ten unique reports in my files telling of a mysterious ball of light observed in the backcountry of Brewster; I was very intrigued. This ball of light was somewhat famous; it has been photographed and observed numerous times over the past hundred years.

The older residents of Brewster say the mysterious light(s) are ghosts of miners killed in the accident, while others say a UFO is to blame. To me, the reports seemed more like a phenomenon known in the paranormal world as "spook light." Spook light is an unexplained light source that appears in the distance at a particular location with a regularity that seldom disappoints those who come to view it. Glowing in the night with an eerie, soft color, the light sometimes will pulse, change color, and dance about near the ground or at treetop level. When the curious try to approach the light, it will vanish as if purposely keeping its true nature a secret. Spook light is sometimes known as ghost light and has baffled the human race for centuries. Many theories have been offered to explain their presence, including hallucinations, UFOs, automobile headlights, ball lightning, electrical discharges caused by tectonic forces, and even ghosts, as the name implies. They are seen in every inhabited continent on earth, but for some reason, North America has the most well-documented reports. The curator at Putnam County Records advised me to visit the Library in Danbury, Connecticut, since all the old newspapers for the past hundred and fifty years on microfilm are kept there. My research would be easy: the exact date of the Tilly Foster disaster was November 29, 1895.

THE TILLY FOSTER MINE DISASTER

After spending a considerable amount of time looking around in the dusty cellar archives of the Danbury Library, I found the *News Times* article on the Tilly Foster mining disaster. It seemed to be big news at the time; the paper published stories on the tragedy over a period of almost a month. As I mentioned before, it is important to cover the mines' history to get a full understanding of the folklore that developed over the years. The stories that began to be told after the mines closed down influenced the way paranormal events would be perceived by future generations.

The Tilly Foster mine saw a decline in production in the 1880s; the ore was now deeper underground and very difficult to safely remove with the technology at that time. In 1884, Andrew Cosgriff developed a system to remove the ore and replace it with artificial pillars because the greatest fear was that tunnels would cave in.[3] Cosgriff's method proved unfeasible; man-made pillars crushed easily under the weight of the rock above them. The lower levels were becoming dangerous and expensive to mine; water seepage was another developing problem. It was first thought that the water was coming from the Middle Branch Reservoir, but even after emptying it, water continued to seep into the lower levels. The next idea was to convert the Tilly Foster mine into an open pit by removing the cap rock and overhanging walls. For two years, workers chipped and hauled away rock. By 1889, the mine was a funnel-shaped pit 450 feet wide and 300 feet deep. Over the top of the pit, a steam derrick controlled cable cars that allowed workers to descend into the pit and remove ore.

Work continued to go deeper and by 1895, the mine reached a depth of 600 feet. The mine had a major problem: at this depth, the ore was at a steep angle and very difficult to extract. To make matters worse, there were a great number of faults (large cracks in the bedrock) and because of this, cave-ins were commonplace. On November 29, 1895, thirty-four men working in the pit removing ore from the northwest wall were trapped as tons of rock gave way along one of the faults. Thirteen men were killed and twenty-one were rescued after considerable time and difficulty. Ten bodies were pulled from the mine over the next forty-eight hours and three were never found. To this day, no one knows the

---

3. Andrew Cosgriff was born in New York City in 1821. In 1865, he was mining in Pennsylvania. In 1868, he came to Putnam County and became the superintendent of Tilly Foster Mine.

THE GHOSTS OF THE LOST MINES 115

names of the men who died in this accident; workers were mostly transient immigrants identified only by number, a method of making payroll and bookkeeping much simpler. The tragedy had a solemn effect on the mining community and although accidents were common, the number of deaths was so shocking it made national news.

UNDERWATER SPIRITS

Tilly Foster was closed permanently in 1897; today the pit is filled with water that has an eerie greenish tinge to it. From 1941 to 1945, the U.S. Navy used the pit to train soldiers in deep-sea diving. After World War II, the military no longer used the pit—according to retired Chief Petty Officer Charles Burdent, a great deal of "weird stuff" took place underwater. Divers reported seeing apparitions of human-like figures working on the walls and floor that would disappear and reappear. They also claimed to hear clanging sounds (both faint and sometimes loud) like someone was using a heavy hammer to pound metal. At first, Navy doctors considered it some type of hallucination caused by the great depth, but not one of the divers exhibited any kind of abnormal physiological effect and the ghostly occurrences never took place at any other test site. The divers knew the site's history, so perhaps stories of the ghosts influenced them and let their imaginations run wild. Divers also say they actually saw the old miners who died in the disaster, still working, trying to bring up the ore, unaware of their being dead. The mystery continues today: people who walk by the flooded pit at night claim to hear the faint cries of the men who died there, but if you try to discuss it at the local pub in downtown Brewster, the old timers will tell you, "It's just the wind, but you shouldn't go back there."

THE "GHOST" OF THE RESERVOIR ROAD

According to local newspapers dated 1899, the phantom lights were not seen until after the cave-in of 1895.[4] The number of cases of the "spook light" in my files as of 2009 is thirty-six, all from the locations of Tilly Foster, Reservoir, and Upper Magnetic Mine Roads in Brewster. It's interesting to note that sightings of the light made before 1950 were called "ghost sightings," while reports from witnesses after 1960 refer to the phantom lights as UFOs. In December 1995, I received a report from two young people who were out for a Halloween Eve drive, but had a terrifying close encounter with the ghost of Reservoir Road. The two witnesses I identify as Jane and Carl are residents of a nearby town.

The two drove down Reservoir Road at 11 PM. Everything was quiet until Carl mentioned he had just heard a noise that sounded like a voice whispering in his left ear. The voice startled him, and was very deep and sounded like a man trying to talk with a very sore throat. Carl had trouble understanding the voice, but it seemed to be getting clearer. He was sure that the voice told him to "back away and leave this place." When he told Jane, she laughed and expressed

---

4. This information is from a microfilm at the Danbury Library.

disbelief; she thought he was making up this "voice" because it was Halloween.

Carl insisted that he *did* hear a voice. He abruptly stopped
the car and got out to see if anyone was on the road, but
neither of them saw anything. Carl walked down the road,
away from the car. For some reason, Jane suddenly felt very
concerned—a wave of fear rushed through her. At first, Jane
attributed the fear to being in a dark, lonely place, but just
then she heard a sound in the empty driver's seat: right before her eyes, a depression formed in the seat as if someone
invisible had just sat next to her! Carl returned to the car
and when he opened the door, he immediately asked, "Do
you smell that?" Jane didn't smell anything unusual, but felt
very uneasy.

Although scared, Jane was still convinced that Carl was
trying to play some type of trick on her. Again, Carl pressed
in a very shaky voice: "Jane, do you smell that?" At that moment a strong smell both people described later as burning
sulfur permeated the car. Now nearly choking, Carl and Jane
jumped out into the cool night gasping for fresh air. Jane
yelled, "What was that smell?! It must be the Devil!" Then,
both of them heard what sounded like chanting in the woods
alongside of the road. Carl reported it sounded like Latin
and guessed that someone was doing some type of ritual.
Carl and Jane were very scared, and they started to pray for
help from angels, good spirits, and other positive beings.

The chanting and sulfur smell stopped almost instantly
and was replaced by a strong and pleasant fragrance of lilacs.
They got back into the car—the smell of lilacs was almost

overpowering. They began to drive slowly to the southeast end of the road when suddenly they heard an explosion that vibrated the car. They stopped the car fearing an engine fire, got out, looked around, but saw nothing. Without any sound or warning, a bright globe of blue light the size of a basketball appeared on the north end of the road and with incredible speed, whisked past them, turned, and vanished into the woods. Carl and Jane both reported that as the sphere of light passed by them, it was so close it pushed them both against the car. They also noticed that when the light was at its closest, they felt a prickly feeling like ants were crawling up and down their backs. The feeling faded as soon as the light passed, but now they were pretty spooked—they definitely got more than they bargained for that night. Carl and Jane really wanted to get out of there, but the experience was not over!

As they entered the vehicle, another loud explosion shook everything once again. It seemed to be coming from the woods on top of a hill to the left of the road. They looked toward that direction, and Jane reported that she saw something large (she thought it was a truck) coming down the path. Carl frantically started the car, put it into gear and sped down the road. Jane remembers looking out the back window and seeing a lit object come out of the woods to the road and shoot straight up into the sky. They drove home and never returned to Reservoir Road and the old mine again—at least not after dark.

The entrance of the Croton Magnetic Mine was less than a quarter of a mile from where Carl and Jane had their encounter. From 1992 to 2005, the Putnam County Sheriff's

Office investigated reports of strange lights and "weird" little men in that area. Several nights during the summer of 1998, local police chased a small hooded being into the mine entrance. Thinking it was a child, they called in a rescue team but nothing was ever found.

THE "GHOST" LIGHT CAPTURED ON FILM

In the past, many so-called "ghost hunters" have used infrared film to try and capture the image of a ghost. The idea is that infrared (IR) film will pick up an apparition's energy interacting with the air molecules around it. Attempts to capture such phenomena have met with very limited success; the film detects heat, however, a physical object will lose its infrared trace signatures quickly, especially on cold winter nights. In June 1994, a close friend of mine (at that time adjunct professor of physics at Princeton University) suggested that scientific emulsions should be tried instead of standard films to image paranormal phenomenon. My colleague was very interested in my research and on one July evening, he drove up to Reservoir Road and stayed most of the night with the hope of seeing something. He called me excitedly the next day and said that at approximately 10 PM, he saw a faint sphere of white light approach from the west end of the road. Using his 7×35 wide-angle binoculars, he was able to determine the object was about 35 meters away and about 30 or so centimeters in diameter.

He tried to approach the light but it seemed to keep its distance. He stopped in his tracks and felt compelled to say, "Please, come closer. I am a scientist who is interested in what you are." After he said this, the light began to approach him. His camera contained only standard film, but he raised it anyway and took five frames before the light vanished. He stayed on Reservoir Road for another hour, then drove along Lower Magnetic Mine Road, and back to Reservoir, but didn't see anything. Over the next five years, he returned to Reservoir Road with an array of scientific equipment, but never had another sighting. My friend mailed me copies of the prints he took that night proving that the phenomenon, whatever it was, could indeed be captured on film. The images he sent me were very faint and somewhat underwhelming, but there was definitely something with him that night beyond all conventional explanation.

After reading more than two dozen reports and looking at several blurred photographs of the Reservoir Road spook light phenomenon, it was obvious to me that something new had to be tried. Commercial cameras are set to focus on visible light; any attempt to image electromagnetic energy beyond this range would result in a faint, blurry photo or no image at all. I conjectured that the phenomenon may be giving off another form of energy absorbed by the air, resulting in a slight increase in IR radiation when remitted. This could be the reason, I concluded, why images of the spook light look faint even when commercial infrared film is used. I felt this IR signature was only a secondary effect. If I wanted to capture the spook light of Reservoir Road on film, it was clear to me the source of its energy would have to be positively identified. After much consideration, I came to the conclusion that an initial ultraviolet source might be responsible for creating the faint heat signature on infrared film. A UV source would also explain the strange feeling of "ants" crawling on the skin that some people reported.[5] So, in the summer of 1994, I began an experiment with the hope of obtaining an image of the spook light using a special type of film once used in astronomy called 103ao-8.[6] This film is very hard to acquire and must be kept in cold storage before and after use. It is developed in Kodak D-19 (a special developing chemical) and one must have access to a dark room to process it. Being involved in astronomy, I was lucky to have one 24-exposure roll in the freezer at the observatory. Manufactured by Kodak, the film is blue sensitive. When used with the proper filter, the film has a sensitivity peak around 200 nanometers, well into the ultraviolet range. Using this film would ensure that any other light would be blocked out and the resulting image would be of UV only. I was now prepared to visit the "ghost's" haunting grounds and attempt to document its existence and perhaps even prove my theory.

---

5. Electromagnetic radiation in the wavelength range 4-400 nanometers (known as ultraviolet light). This range begins at the short-wavelength limit of visible light and overlaps the wavelengths of long X-rays.

6. I called Kodak Labs in the winter of 2009 and was informed that the film had been discontinued.

My Investigation and Sighting

I arrived at Reservoir Road at about midnight, parked my car alongside the road and got out to take a look. Everything seemed very quiet and I thought that this just might be a waste of time—I would rather be home watching television. The night was clear and since it was late July, it was rather hot and humid. After fifteen minutes or so, my eyes adapted to the dark and I looked toward the northwest section of the road. There, I noticed a blotch of faint light that appeared like a fog illuminated by an external source. I started walking down the road and the closer I got, the less diffuse it appeared. It was still about 75 feet from me and was quite faint, but as I slowly moved closer, the object took shape into something round and about the size of a beach ball. The sphere hovered about 5 feet above the road and as I continued to approach the light, it slowly moved backward trying to keep its distance. I decided to walk back to the car and get the camera and tripod—if this was the famous spook light of Reservoir Road, I didn't want to miss the opportunity to photograph it. Knowing how fleeting the phenomena was; I thought this might be my only chance.

As I walked back to the car, the light (which was still barely visible) seemed to be coming closer . . . it was moving very slowly and reminded me of a curious but cautious animal. I set up the camera to use a shutter release and a timed exposure of five to thirty seconds. I took a number of photos but really didn't know what to expect; the light appeared to be a faint nebulous sphere to the eye. Readers who have seen the Ring Nebula through a telescope know what I am describing. After taking ten frames, the object could no longer be seen visually. I continued to take photos, knowing my film would pick up an invisible UV source. As I exposed the last frame, I gently rewound the film and placed it in a cold storage container. Since the night was quite warm and the film was sensitive to heat, I drove home quickly to develop it.

I arrived home and developed the film in my own darkroom. To my surprise, eight frames showed an incredibly bright light source. This was amazing—what I was trying to image on the road appeared like nothing more than a faint blob but on the UV film it was blazing! There was no doubt now that whatever the object was, it emitted energy in the UV spectrum. Since human eyes are not sensitive to this wavelength, it would appear very faint to us if visible at all. The combination of the film and the filter blocked out all other wavelengths of stray light in the area; only a very strong UV source was recorded. When I printed the photographs, I noticed the light appeared to be changing shape and frequency. This proved two things to me: the spook light of Reservoir Road in Brewster really exists and my theory that this phenomenon emits light in the blue end of the visible spectrum was correct. This information is important: I had proven that 103ao-7, 8, or 9 film is perfect for photographing this type of paranormal event. Unfortunately, the film is very hard to find today because most astronomers now use digital imaging; demand has dropped so low that Kodak no longer offers it. However, UV-sensitive films are still out there and it may be possible to create a digital card that can record the blue end of the spectrum.

A COVERT OPERATION

After imaging the spook light, I was determined to find the entrance to the underground tunnels; my first objective was to locate the Croton Magnetic Mine because a great deal of paranormal phenomenon seemed to be associated with it. Local residents also suspected the military was using the old mines for some type of covert operation. I wanted to investigate any possible military involvement and find any evidence that could support these suspicions. So, in late summer of 1994, I began taking a closer look at locations that had a great number of reports of not only government activity but also paranormal phenomena. I decided to take a hike through the woods near the Croton Falls Reservoir in the town of Southeast. This particular location has had more than its fair share of otherworldly events over the past ten years so I thought it would be a good place to start. The land around the reservoir is sparsely populated; if you were going to hide some type of covert operation in an otherwise densely populated area of the United States, this would be the place to do it!

As I walked through the woods and down some of the more established back trails, I noticed tire marks made by small trucks that appeared to have four-wheel drives. The tread marks were wide and deep—typical of military-type vehicles—but I was cautious in my conclusions: they could have been made by hunters driving up to the paths looking for deer. I proceeded down Reservoir Road and came to another blocked-off road. On the map, the road was labeled "Upper Magnetic Mine Road." I continued to walk and saw quite a few "No Trespassing" signs on the trees posted every 30 feet. I began to walk up the narrow road and noticed fresh tire marks made by a jeep. As I proceeded farther up the road, I noticed large stones containing iron ore scattered around—evidence that the mine entrance was near.

Suddenly, I heard someone behind me. I turned and saw a police office running up the trail yelling, "Stop and go no farther!" I was a little surprised, but stopped. The officer introduced himself as a member of the Putnam County Sheriff's Department and informed me that I was trespassing on federally owned land and that no one was allowed up the road. When I tried to get more details from the officer, he refused to answer and told me that he only had orders to keep people out of the area. I was then escorted back to my car and was told to follow him. The officer led me to Route 22, a major road in Brewster that led all the way to lower Westchester County, about 20 miles away. I stopped my car as the officer pulled over to the shoulder of the road and got out of his cruiser. He approached me and said in a very serious tone, "Mr. Imbrogno, if you are caught trespassing in that area again the Sheriff's Department will have to arrest you." I left, but knew I had to come back and find out what was at the top of that hill.

I returned to check out the area two weeks later. In order to avoid the "No Trespassing" signs, I decided to try and find my way through the opposite side of Route 22 in Brewster. I parked my car near the side of the road and walked into the woods. It was difficult to approximate where the location of the top of Upper Magnetic Mine Road was from my position in the woods. After walking for thirty or forty minutes and periodically checking a map, I came to a ridge that overlooked a driveway with a small house and a number of smaller buildings surrounding it. My position was about a hundred meters away and located high enough above the house, allowing me to see all of the roof and most of the structure.

As I pulled out my binoculars, a jeep drove up the dirt path and parked outside the house. Two professionally dressed men got out. They had short hair and looked like police or federal agents. I was able to get a good view of them using the binoculars; my impression was that they were military or government types. The men entered the house, which from my view point showed no signs of drapes or other things that would indicate a home. There were no plants or flowers in the yard and the entire property appeared quite bland, even sterile. My first thought was that it was a well-hidden "safe house" being used by federal agents. It was strange to find a house so deep in the woods on an isolated dirt road with only one way in and out. I discovered later that this dirt path connected to Upper Magnetic Mine Road. The jeep did not have a New York or Connecticut plate; it was blue and white in color with just a number I could not make out: this type of marker is typical on vehicles a government agency uses. The jeep itself was white and appeared more civilian than military but then again, intelligence organizations like the CIA and NSA use modified vehicles of a similar nature.

I also noticed a number of power lines and telephone cables on poles running to the house and the small buildings that surround it; someone had gone through a great deal of trouble and expense to maintain this installation. As I continued to watch, two large dogs came out of the house and started patrolling the area. They came to the bottom of the ridge where I was lying down and started looking in my direction. Although the dogs were too far away to definitely identify, they appeared to be two large Rottweilers. I was a little nervous since the dogs seemed to know I was there and started barking. At that point, one of the men came out of the house with binoculars and started scanning the hill where I was hiding. As he scanned across the ridge, he stopped and locked in on my position.

For a brief moment, it looked like were were staring at each other—remember, I was using binoculars too. I felt very uneasy since there was no way he could have gotten a visual on my position because I was camouflaged by the brush. The man must have been using some type of high-tech thermal detector because my feeling was that this person definitely saw me. The man quickly ran back inside, and the dogs continued to bark although they did not advance. I knew I had to leave the area, so I carefully and quietly made my way back through the woods to my car. I guess my military combat training paid off that day—I was able to obtain information and slip away without getting caught. I wondered just *who* these men were and why the local police went out of their way to make sure no one traveled up that road. Most importantly, what was it they wanted to keep secret? I decided to let some time pass before trying to check out the location again, but a number of personal family matters prevented me from returning to my research for some time.

A Hidden Underground World

On a hot summer day one year later, I decided to walk up Upper Magnetic Mine Road again. It had been some time since the warning from the police officer, so there was a good chance that if caught I would not be arrested. Besides, the fine for trespassing in Putnam County is only fifty dollars—a fair price to pay to see what was on top of the trail. This time I was not alone; with me was Marianne Horrigan, a fellow author who has worked with me on a number of paranormal investigations. We made it all the way to the top of the dirt road without harassment and there was no indication that anyone was around—even the "No Trespassing" signs were taken down. As we continued, the dirt road turned into a trail and we began to feel a cool breeze. I knew the breeze was caused by an opening inside the earth; during my spelunking days I learned cave openings hidden by brush were often found this way.

I began to notice signs of occult activity everywhere: symbols such as inverted pentagrams and the names of fallen angels were painted on the larger boulders and exposed bedrock. We then turned a slight corner, saw the opening of the Croton Magnetic Mine, and stopped dead in our tracks. The mine adit was an amazing sight and looked like something from a science-fiction movie. Alongside the mine entrance were the names of Satan and his fallen angels in red paint. It was now very apparent to me why locals called this old mine "Satan's Cave." Here was the exact location where the cult known as the Fallen Ones performed their demonic ceremonies at the turn of the twentieth century.

The mine entrance was partially sealed with rocks and dirt, but this didn't stop us from digging it out. As I opened up the adit, we noticed the main tunnel went underground about 10 feet and was flooded. There was no way that we could explore this mine today—the water was so deep that we'd need a raft. I turned my attention to the house where I had seen the dogs and the two men. According to my notes, it was just above the trail to our left, less than 200 meters away. We walked up the trail and saw the house; it looked abandoned and the smaller buildings around it turned out to be storage areas. We went inside the house and found it trashed. It was as if someone wanted to get out of there fast and destroyed any evidence that would connect the structure to any agency or operation.

We left the house and explored the grounds. I found an electrical power junction box with circuit breakers rated at several hundred kilowatts. I wondered who could use that kind of electrical power and for what purpose? It was possible that the house was used as a base of operations for some recent activity in the mine. The next step in my investigation was to purchase the proper equipment and, I hoped, return a week later to explore the mine.

The Gateway to Hell

The next few days were spent looking through old mining journals; Marianne and I even made a trip to the New York City Public Library where we found articles in scientific journals about the mines and a layout of tunnels dated 1901. I wanted to get as much information as possible before venturing back where no one had gone in almost a century. This was an investigation in which I needed some help, and

Marianne was more than happy to journey with me inside the mine. After purchasing rope, proper clothing as well as an inflatable raft, we were ready to start our adventure. We arrived at the adit of the Croton Magnetic Mine early in the morning and noticed a mist coming out of the entrance; I learned later the phenomenon was known as "the devil's breath." It actually has nothing to do with the devil and has a scientific explanation: the mist is formed when the cold air coming out of the mine hits the warmer and humid air outside, causing condensation.

We inflated the raft and dropped it into the water. After we were properly seated, I took the front with the light and Marianne used the paddle to propel us into the darkness. The water in the tunnel was red due to the iron ore being turned into rust and reminded me of blood. As we approached the main chamber, I shined the light on the wall ahead and noticed writing: "ABANDON HOPE YE THAT ENTER—THIS IS THE GATEWAY TO HELL". The words were painted in white and judging from their position on the wall in relation to the water level, were written before the mine flooded. Marianne and I spent five or six hours exploring this mine; I could fill several chapters describing geologic wonders we saw, but perhaps most interestingly, we found tunnels that were *not* in the 1901 mining journals. These tunnels seemed recently made using modern equipment. We also noticed that many of these new tunnels only extended 20 or 30 feet and were sealed off by rock and dirt. The sealing also seemed recent, and it appeared as if someone went through a great deal of trouble to cover their tracks.

The tunnels were so dark that when the flashlights were turned off nothing could be seen. It was quite an unsettling thought that someone could be standing right next to you and unless you shined the light on them you wouldn't have a clue! As we explored the tunnels, we often stopped just to listen to the echoes. The entire time we were in the mine, there was a sound coming from the water behind us as if we were being followed the entire way. Also, when we stopped and listened, we could hear a moaning sound from the darkness ahead. Was it the ghost of a miner, or just the wind? We never found out for sure. Although we did not see any hooded beings, spook lights, or aliens that day, I did confirm much of my research concerning the occult connection with the mine and that the house was used for some type of covert operation. Over the next year, we explored the other mines and found new tunnels and other evidence to indicate that someone was using them long after the mining days of Brewster ended.

THE ELLENVILLE TUNNELS

Although the strange occurrences mentioned so far took place on the east side of the Hudson River, equally mysterious things were being seen or discovered on the western side as well. In Pine Bush, New York, a great number of UFO sightings and paranormal phenomenon took place beginning in 1983 and continue to the present. However, it is not the scope of this book to cover these events in great detail. If the reader is interested, I recommend reading *Silent Invasion* by the late UFO researcher Ellen Crystal. In *Silent Invasion,*

Crystal mentions underground tunnels and caves in the area where she claims a secret agency in the U.S. government has a joint operation with an alien intelligence. These tunnels are located outside the town of Ellenville, New York, and, unlike the tunnels in Brewster, there is no historical record of who made them so they remain a mystery to local historians. One theory suggests that Dutch miners looking for pockets of minerals carved the tunnels into the mountain, but no evidence has ever been found to support this conclusion. The two things the Ellenville tunnels and Brewster tunnels have in common are how they were made and the number of paranormal events that have taken place in and around them. The most-reported phenomenon seen near the tunnels is spook light. As in Brewster, the lights are referred to as the ghosts or UFOs of Ellenville and have been seen since the early part of the nineteenth century.

Tunnels To Nowhere

I visited the Ellenville Tunnels on September 10, 2001, to get a better understanding of what they looked like and how they were similar (or dissimilar) to the underground tunnels on the eastern side of the Hudson. Although I found only three of them, they were very hard to explore; the water was at least knee-deep. The only tunnel that seemed to have a modern look to it was the one located near High Point Mountain.

The High Point Mountain tunnel was first discovered in 1905. In 1907, a water company bought the land and used the natural springs to sell bottled water. The water company went out of business several years later, but activity there did not stop. In the mid-1980s, local residents claim to have seen military vehicles traveling up the road leading to the tunnel opening. Some of these people speculate that the government may have had some type of underground operation there sometime in the past; this may have been the basis of Ellen Crystal's claim in *Silent Invasion*.

Although I explored all three tunnels, my investigation was short compared to the research done in Brewster. I found evidence of chisel and drill marks on the walls that appeared to be made by tools used in the eighteenth and early nineteenth centuries. At the end of each tunnel, I noticed a great deal of rock and dirt as if someone collapsed the walls to seal off what lay beyond. It is my opinion that the tunnels of Ellenville were originally made in the eighteenth century by colonial settlers looking for iron ore. However, who or what took them over in modern times is unknown. Pine Bush and Ellenville have many mysterious secrets and in the years to come, my pursuit of High Strangeness would take me to these two towns repeatedly.

MY CONTINUING INVESTIGATION OF THE SPOOK LIGHT PHENOMENON

It's interesting that spook lights are a worldwide phenomena. Many locations around the United States have their own variation of the phenomena. As a science educator for the past twenty-seven years, I have a considerable amount of free time to pursue my passion in the summer, so I made it a point to visit states in which spook light has been well documented. Spook light seems to be associated with areas that have had a great number of UFO sightings and underground tunnels or caves. The connection is still unclear and speculation differs: some feel the phantom lights are probes from extraterrestrial spacecraft, some say they are disembodied spirits, and others think they come from the lower levels of the earth's crust and are released into our world during mining operations.

The Hornet Spook Light: Joplin, Missouri

Just southwest of Joplin, Missouri, near the old town of Hornet is an isolated countryside road where a ball of light has been seen for the last hundred and fifty years. It has been called many things, including the "Devils Promenade," "Hot Devil," and finally, "The Hornet Spook Light." It has been reported to spin down the center of the road at great speed then rise into the air and disappear. Local legend says that the light is the collective spirit of the Quapaw who died in the area many years ago. Others believe the light are the ghosts of a miner's murdered children. Whatever the explanation, the Hornet Spook Light is very similar to the Reservoir Road Spook Light in Brewster, not only in appearance, but also that it is reported near an old mine entrance. In August 2001, I made a trip to Joplin to track down this phantom light. Over several nights, I parked alongside several dark secondary roads off Route 43 near Hornet, Missouri. During my time in the area, I did not see the light(s) despite spending several days there, but I did talk to a number of people who witnessed the phenomenon—one person even claimed he took a shot at it but the bullet had no effect.

The Crossett Spook Lights:
Crossett, Arkansas

Information about the Crossett Spook Lights came to my attention in 2003. Over spring vacation of that year, I decided to take a trip to Arkansas with the goal of tracking down another mystery. When I arrived in Crossett, I was surprised that almost everyone (who was willing to talk) knew about the lights. The lights have been described as being various colors: red, blue, green, and sometimes a yellowish white. These lights always keep their distance from the curious who try to approach. During my three-day visit, I drove one night along Backwater Road and witnessed a ball of green light off the side of the road in the woods. I stopped the car and got out to try and get a better look at it. The light bobbed up and down in the trees, causing me to periodically lose sight of it. I watched it for three or four minutes before it quickly rose into the air and fell into a heavily wooded area. I could find no rational explanation for the phenomena, and although I took about ten photographs not one came out clearly enough. This may be because the light was never stationary—it continuously moved quickly above and below the tree line. Local legend says that the spook light is the ghost of a switchman at the nearby railroad who was killed by a train sometime around 1850. I wasn't surprised when I discovered a mineral mine less than one-eighth of a mile from the location where the light has been reported.

The Dover, Arkansas, Ghost Lights

The local Dover, Arkansas, newspaper reports that the "Dover Ghost Lights" can be seen almost every night, just 15 miles outside the city. After leaving Joplin, I paid a visit to Dover to try and catch a glimpse of another local legend. Just off highway 7 is a lonely stretch of dirt road considered a scenic route for the area—and the ghost lights' main drag. It is reported that the light behaves like a curious animal that responds to other lights and sounds. I spent the entire night switching positions using Route 7 as a center point so I would not get lost. At three in the morning, I noticed a faint ball of light ahead of me on the dirt road. At first I thought it was a motorcycle headlight, but quickly ruled this out because I heard no sound and at times the light went at least 10 feet in the air. I flashed the bright lights in my car and was amazed that a second later, the light flashed back! I did this five times and was able to obtain the same clear response. I started the car and slowly drove down the road with the headlights off; the light then seemed to shift in color from a yellow to a blue and quickly moved to the right into the woods. The next day, I went into Dover and asked about the ghost lights. To my surprise, I was given the names of eight people who had encounters with it. Since my time was limited, I was only able to interview one of them. I did not find a mine in that area, but noticed a very large pit filled with water about 15 feet wide and very deep. A volunteer at the local museum told me there were as many as eight such pits and no one knows who dug them.

The Surrency, Georgia, Spook Light

In 2004, I was visiting a friend in Georgia and decided to look into another report of a spook light that has been seen in Surrency, a small town of about four hundred people in the southeast corner of the state. According to the locals, the light can be occasionally seen along the railroads tracks that belong to the Macon/Brunswick line. In the local library, I found eighteen news stories about the lights indicating sightings began shortly after the railroad was constructed in 1911. According to the news stories, the light is the size of a large beach ball and bright yellow in color. During a regional seismic survey in 1985, geologists from the University of Georgia found a bizarre anomaly deep under the town of Surrency. The anomaly is unlike anything they have seen before: a dome-shaped pocket of unknown liquid at a depth of 7 miles. Some believe this strange underground anomaly is responsible for the light while others say it is the ghost of a resident killed in 1870. From 1925 to present, a number of town residents reported poltergeist phenomenon accompanied by mysterious noises, things being thrown around, and disembodied voices.[7] I spent two days in the town and although I didn't see any strange lights or other strange occurrences, I did leave with a great deal of information that proved Surrency is one haunted little southern town.

---

7. *The Savannah Morning News*, August 1875.

The Marfa Lights of Texas

The most famous of the American spook lights can be found in Texas in a small town called Marfa, located about 190 miles southeast of El Paso. Although the lights do not appear every night, they are said to be quite regular such that even visitors to the area have claimed to have seen them. The first recorded incident took place in 1883, when cattlemen first thought they were Apache campfires, but soon realized that they were something else, something strange. The lights have been reported to be yellow in color, and float up and down (or sometimes back and forth) in the sky. Several of them have been seen frolicking around as if in play, chasing each other like baby animals.

In 1973, a team of geologists from the University of Texas went to Marfa to make observations between the months of March and June. On one outing on March 19, they were able to see the lights, but as they tried to get closer, the lights moved away and kept their distance. On March 20, the scientists observed the spook light uninterrupted for twenty minutes. They reported the phantom lights swinging in the air, rocking back and forth then started looping around each other. One of the geologists remarked that the lights appeared to be playing. The lights have been photographed many times since 1986. In my analysis of these images, my impression is the photos are inconclusive. The Apache of the region were familiar with the Marfa Lights; they perceived them to be spirits. According to historical records, nineteenth-century settlers of Marfa believed the lights were ghosts of massacred natives. Later in the early twentieth century, Texans believed the lights were spirits that guarded hidden treasures. Finally, in the twenty-first century, many think the lights are probes sent by an extraterrestrial intelligence!

There are a great many locations in the United States and around the world that have their own spook or ghost lights; the cases are so numerous, a book could be written on this phenomenon alone. Whatever they really are, science lacks a definite explanation. Spook light sightings are very well documented and deserve serious study, in my opinion.

CREATURES FROM
A HIDDEN REALITY

The vast diversity of paranormal phenomena provides many avenues of research—enough to fill a very thick book. One important part of paranormal research is cryptozoology, the study of unusual creatures.[1] Under this branch are creatures such as Bigfoot, lake monsters, the Chupacabra, mothmen, and other creatures we once thought could only be found in our worst nightmares. In our modern age, people still report encounters with monsters; it makes you wonder if all mythological creatures like the minotaur, griffin, cyclops, dragon, gargoyle, and a host of others really *did* exist and were not the product of medieval over-active imaginations. Throughout history, these strange creatures of time and space appear in certain areas of the world but then vanish without a trace—only to reappear once again at some point in the future. Perhaps they are not

---

1. Cryptozoology (from Greek, "hidden" + zoology; literally, "study of hidden animals") is the study of and search for animals that fall outside contemporary zoological categories.

part of our world, but from a nearby parallel reality. If we accept the fact that over the centuries even a small percentage of these reports have substance, we have to consider their origin may be interdimensional. However, the frequency of reports seems to indicate the nature of their appearance in our world may be cyclic.

HALF HUMAN

Way back in 1960, when I was very young, I saw a movie on television called *Half Human*. The movie was supposedly based on a true story of the Yeti (also known as the Abominable Snowman of the Himalayas). The story centered on a peaceful creature somewhere between an ape and a human that lived high in the mountains with his family. One day, greedy hunters who had heard of the creature found and shot his mate and child. The bodies were taken to a village for storage until the hunters could arrange transportation back to England where they planned to display the creatures and sell them to the highest bidder. Well, the surviving male went berserk; he attacked the village and got his revenge but the story had a sad ending. The Yeti was finally hunted down at the edge of a cliff where he fell off after being shot several times. The Yeti portrayed in the movie was a terrifying creature, but it made me wonder who the bad guys really were in the story: this creature was peaceful and minding its own business until greedy profit-seeking humans found him and his family.

I was quite surprised when they played a short documentary at the end of the movie informing the audience that the creatures in the film were real and have been seen in the isolated Himalayas, and in many other parts of the world, including the northwest part of the United States. I felt safe in my apartment in New York, but I was greatly interested in the topic and began going to the library to see what books I could find on the Yeti and his American counterpart, the Sasquatch or "Bigfoot." You have to keep in mind, this was 1960; the public libraries did not carry many books on the paranormal—especially for kids. With the help of a librarian I was able to find two books, one about the Yeti in Asia and the other called *Tracking Big Foot*, which centered on one individual's search for the elusive beast in northern California. For some reason, the two were not shelved with the few books on the paranormal, but in the zoology section. I looked at some of the other nearby books, and they were science books about known animals, so my first impression was that the Yeti or Bigfoot was a real creature. Today, I no longer consider the shelving strange; at that time, books about what were called "flying saucers" were located under astronomy!

THEY ARE EVERYWHERE

As time went on, I began to do more research and found that sightings of similar creatures are not restricted to Nepal, Tibet, or the backwoods of the United States. There have been reports of Sasquatch-Yeti-like creatures in almost every state in the United States, including New York and my present home, Connecticut. According to the Bigfoot Field Researchers Organization (BFRO), these creatures have been seen in almost every country on every continent. The following report of a

Bigfoot-like creature was published in *The Republican*, a Connecticut newspaper still in print today. I am very familiar with this paper—for the past ten years it has been carrying my column on astronomy. The sighting that appeared in *The Republican* was made in Winsted, Connecticut; today this creature is part of local folklore and is called the "Winsted Wildman."

The initial sighting was made on August 21, 1895, and was made by Selectman Riley Smith, a local town official, according to newspaper clippings from the time. Other Winsteders supposedly saw the creature later as well, but it was Smith's sighting that was given the most credibility. According to the report in the paper, Smith had gone up to pick berries near the Colebrook town line on Lowsaw Road in an area then known as Indian Meadow. He had his dog with him, a six-year-old bulldog named Ned. When Smith bent over and began picking berries, his dog began barking as if someone was approaching. A short time afterward, a "large man, stark naked and covered with hair all over his body," ran out of a clump of bushes and, with fearful yells and cries, made for the forest at great speed where he disappeared.

According to *The Republican*, "Selectman Smith is a powerful man who has a reputation for having lots of guts, and his bulldog Ned is also noted for his pluck, but Riley admits that he was badly scared and his dog was fairly paralyzed with fear." Word of Smith's tale spread through the little town quickly and eventually caught the interest of newspapers from New York to Boston. Soon after the sighting, newsmen converged on Winsted not only to write about the incident, but also to try and capture the Wildman and bring him back to the city on the train! According to the story, the gang of reporters was unsuccessful and all they went home with were "sunburns and hangovers from the local beer." Townsfolk were scared, however, and a local posse was formed to find the mysterious creature; but like the reporters, the posse was also unsuccessful. Winsted residents speculated on who—or what—the Wildman was. Some newspaper reports from the time even said the Wildman may have been an insane artist named Arthur Beckwith. Beckwith reportedly escaped from a New York insane asylum in 1894 and was thought to be hiding somewhere in the Litchfield, Connecticut, hills. He was found six months later in Cuba, living naked in the tropics and eating raw fruits and vegetables from the jungle. Today the Winsted Wildman is a local legend and people who live in the backcountry still claim to hear his cries in the night; some say they have even seen the creature running through the woods.

In the summer of 2007, I took a trip to Winsted to see if I could get more information about the legendary Wildman. Many of the newer residents had never heard the story, but a trip to the local historical society proved worthwhile. Although many believe that something was seen during that time, no one will say exactly what. You have to remember that in 1895, the Sasquatch, Bigfoot, Yeti or whatever you want to call this creature was unknown. However, people in many different parts of the United States encountered human-like ape creatures in the woods and, as in the case of the Winsted sighting, were simply referred to as "Wildmen." During my visit, I found the original news story and talked to several people who knew about the infamous creature. I was also told of another sighting that took place in the late sixties in Kent, Connecticut, only about 10 miles north of my home. Concerning the report below, I was not able to track down the original witness, but I did get the story from the *Danbury News Times,* which carried an account of the sighting in 1969.

The Bulls Bridge Bigfoot

This sighting happened in 1968 when the witness was a young boy, about seven or eight years old. It was a cloudy day in late September and the boy was playing near a window in a two-story farmhouse when something outside caught his attention. He watched as a hairy nine-foot-tall creature came over a hill and crossed the front yard. It had a huge stride, as if in a hurry. It kept looking back as it walked, swinging its long arms. When it turned its head, the creature had to turn its shoulders to be able to look toward his direction. The young boy stood motionless, watching as the hairy ape-like figure moved up a hill. The creature slowed down and made eye contact with the boy for only a second. Its eyes glowed like an animal at night when light is shined in its face. The boy later said that he could see the creature clearly because it was still daylight, and he didn't get scared until it disappeared around the side of the house. That's when he ran in to the kitchen where his parents were playing cards with another couple. The boy tried to get their attention, but they took it as whining for a treat; a nuisance. It wasn't until the parents escorted the boy out the front door and slammed the door in his face that they figured out something was wrong: he started yelling, screaming, and kicking the door. Terrified, the boy continued screaming, beating and kicking the door, crying to be let in. His parents let the boy inside and with fearful tears, he told them about the "hairy man."

His father and a friend went outside to look around, probably thinking they would find a loose cow. The witness then recalls what happened next: "I'll never forget the look on their faces when they saw the footprints that dwarfed their own." The father's friend was a tall man of around six-foot two or three, and when he stretched his legs to step from one footprint to another, it was nearly impossible for him to match the creature's stride. Their disbelief had turned to fear. Wanting to follow the tracks that went across a recently plowed field, they agreed going in a car would be quicker and safer. They drove down a dirt road and followed the tracks as they crossed the road and up a small hill. The tracks then went into another plowed field and just disappeared as if the creature vanished into thin air.

Since this report also came from Litchfield County, Connecticut, I wondered if this was another sighting of the infamous Wildman. I had learned through local residents that there were eight more sightings of the creature from 1969 to 2008, mostly by hunters in the deep wooded areas of Shelton, Kent, Sharon, and New Milford, well away from populated areas. I explored one of these locations with three other people in 2008. As we walked into the woods, we heard a loud whooping sound that turned into a scream and then a growl. Whatever was making the noise, it sounded like we were getting too close and the creature wanted us to stay away. I later listened to a number of alleged Bigfoot sounds taped from all parts of North America and I must say, several of them sounded exactly like what my research team and I heard that day. If this creature is an ancient ancestor of man, it's remarkable that it could hide out in one of the most populated areas of the United States for so many years without being shot by hunters or captured on camera. However, if we take into account that this may be a creature that is able to merge in and out of our dimensional reality, its appearance, disappearance, and elusiveness would make sense.

Bigfoot On Video

The following case is a classic in Bigfoot history because it involves the first home movie of the creature ever taken. If the film is not a hoax, it represents undisputable evidence that Bigfoot does exist and the creature can be photographed. Over the years, a number of skeptics have claimed the movie shows nothing more than a man in an ape costume walking in front of the camera. They also claim that when still images are blown up, you can actually see a zipper in the back of the costume. I have looked closely at the video and never saw a zipper or any other evidence to indicate that it is a large man in an ape suit. I have to remind my readers that when a photograph of any type of paranormal event is very clear and sharp, people question it and say it must be fake. On the other hand, when a blurry photograph is presented in which you cannot make out what is on the video or still image, for some reason, there are more skeptics and true believers who will give it validity.

THE PATTERSON FILM

On October 20, 1967, Roger Patterson and Bob Gimlin were out looking for Bigfoot in the Bluff Creek Riverbed area of northern California on horseback. Their intent that day was to gather footage of the Sasquatch habitat—they really did not expect to actually see one. While riding their horses, suddenly one reared, bucking Patterson off, but he was able to grab the 16mm camera from the saddle bag just in time. Gimlin held his horse firm, and watched in awe as the sequence unfolded. Patterson thought his horse reared because of a cougar or bear, and wanted to film it. Instead, they were confronted with a large, dark, hair-covered body crouching down in the riverbed. With only a little more than one minute left of film, Patterson began filming. As he did, the creature stood up and began to walk away quickly. With his camera in hand, Patterson began chasing the animal, while Gimlin spoke a major concern for Patterson's safety. Patterson tried to catch up to the creature and filmed what has become the most compelling film evidence ever gathered of a live Sasquatch. The film is shaky in the beginning, but becomes more stable toward the end when the animal can be clearly seen and identified. Twenty years after the video was shot, several men who lived in the same town as Patterson came forward and said they were in an ape suit and that Patterson paid them to help perpetrate the hoax. When I heard this, it made me laugh; it reminded me of a similar claim after UFO sightings in the Hudson Valley. Several groups of pilots came forward and claimed that they were responsible for the sightings by flying in close formation and attaching unconventional lights to the wings of their planes. Actually very few people believed their claims, and those who actually saw the UFO didn't buy it at all. As in the case of the Patterson film, someone is always going to claim responsibility for a dramatic event to achieve their "fifteen minutes of fame" and perhaps make some money on the side.

Today, this Bigfoot footage is called "The Patterson Film" and in the late sixties, the film appeared on all major television networks in the United States and then on TV stations around the world. Just like a controversial UFO sighting with great photographs, there are those who believe it is real, while others insist that it's a hoax. In my opinion, it is the best image of Bigfoot I have ever seen.

Searching For the Hairy Bogeyman of Thailand

The only thing I found beneficial about my enlistment with the U.S. military was the travel. I was stationed in countries I most likely would never have seen, especially those in the eastern part of the world. From 1969 to 1971, I was stationed at a number of different military bases in southeast Asia, but the country I found the most interesting and beautiful was Thailand. Thailand is called the "land of the smiling faces" and for good reason: when people come up to you and say hello, they have big smiles on their faces and really mean it. During my stay, I was able to travel through the backcountry of the north, explore many of the old ruins, and track down some local legends. I found the scenery extraordinary and the people a refreshing change from Westerners. My Italian heritage and the hot Asian summer sun made my skin very dark so I didn't look like a typical American. Thai people occasionally mistook me as a visitor from India and although my Thai was choppy, I could get by in most conversations. Also, because of the American military presence at the time, many of the more educated Thai people spoke perfect English, so communicating my needs and getting information was not a problem.

While exploring old temple ruins near the village of Phimai, I was invited to join the local residents at a community lunch and dinner. People there are mostly Buddhist and are taught to always welcome you into their home, even if you are a stranger. At the time, the village had a population of perhaps two hundred people and was located down a dirt path about a mile or so from the Phimai ruins. Over dinner one night, the elders of the town told me of a "hairy wild man" that lived in the jungle and would occasionally come into the old temple to sleep at night and collect food the villagers would leave for him. The creature was described as being 8 feet tall with long red and black hair all over his body. I was told that it stood straight up like a man but could not talk and had the face and eyes of a human. Although the beast stayed out of the village, the people would bring food to the center of the old ruins hoping that this would satisfy it and it would leave them alone. I asked if the creature ever harmed anyone. One of the elders replied that as long as they left it food, the beast (which they thought was some type of nature spirit) would not harm them. One of the villagers who spoke English told me that fifty years ago (1920) the creature came into the village at night. He took food, broke into a hut, and stole two young sisters aged fourteen and sixteen. The beast picked up both of the girls with one arm and with the other arm, threw a sack of rice over its shoulder and ran back into the woods.

The girls were never seen again, and local legend says that the "Wildman" took them for mates. The villagers believed that the ridge above the temple is where the creature lives with his family. According to the story, several children were born that are a hybrid between a human and the Wildman. The stories of this beast are very similar to the Western tales of the bogeyman. Children in this village were told that unless they behaved, the Wildman from the hills would come down at night, take them away, and they would disappear forever, never to see friends and family again.

My Day in the Temple

After my conversation with the village elders, I asked permission to look through the ruins just to see what I could find. Although the legend of the Wildman was on my mind, my main purpose for visiting this location was to study and photograph the old temple. I still had at least six hours of daylight and decided to make the most of it. I was alone at this time and, as I was young, I often took foolish risks and traveled into the backcountry alone with only a concealed 45-caliber hand gun for protection (which, by the way, I never had to use).

I walked through the halls of the eight-hundred-year-old temple and marveled at the sculptures and carvings. Some of the inner sanctums and chambers were quite dark and—I must admit—a little scary. I walked down a dark corridor and shined my light ahead, almost expecting to see the creature's face. I spent the next four hours taking notes and photographs; but as the sun started setting, I remembered what the elder said about the beast coming down from the hills to gather food the townspeople left for it in the temple. As I began walking toward the main entrance, I heard a very loud sound in the jungle as if something very large was coming down the hill. It was twilight and at least a half hour's walk to the village so yes, I admit it, I chickened out because it was getting closer and sounded very big!

I quickly exited the temple and was greeted by a number of the villagers carrying prepared food and flowers to place in the ruins. I told them about the sounds I heard and they seemed quite frightened, but one brave lad took the food and ran into the main part of the temple, dropped it on the stone floor, and ran back out yelling that he had seen the creature walking down the corridor that joined with the main hall. I shined my light in the hall and saw nothing, but the young man then grabbed my light and said, "You will make it angry!" I grabbed the flashlight back from him and told them that I was going to walk inside to see if I could see this thing. One of the older boys said I was *ba ba bow*, Thai slang translating to "very, very crazy." He held on to my arm and said "Don't go! You will make the beast angry, it will come and steal our animals and take the children!" At that point I acquiesced; I needed a place to spend the night and if the elders thought I was breaking their laws or putting them in danger, they probably wouldn't have let me stay in the village for the night—I would have been on my own. The thought of traveling back through the jungle at night was not a pleasing one; the nearest town with transportation was a 10-mile hike away!

After returning from the temple, I had dinner with a family that was kind enough to let me sleep in one of their rooms. At about two in the morning, I woke and heard the cries of some type of animal in the direction of the ruins. The best description I can offer was a yelping, growling, and screaming noise unlike any animal's I had ever heard. Whatever it was sounded almost human, but then its vocalization would shift and become more animal-like. It seemed to be coming from at least three creatures, and I heard it most of the night. As I listened, my thoughts went back to my younger days in New York watching *Half Human*. Not in my wildest dreams would I have thought that someday I would be in an Asian jungle possibly encountering a Sasquatch-like creature.

The next morning I went back to the temple to see if there was any trace of what was there the night before, but I found nothing. The creature had left no evidence of its existence, like it was some type of phantom not from our world. I thoroughly searched the ruins and afterward, returned to the village to say goodbye. I asked the elders for permission to return with two or three of my friends to spend the night in the ruins. At first they were reluctant, but agreed if we left behind our weapons and anything that could be used to harm the beast. I agreed, thanked them, and journeyed back to the city I was staying in which at that time was called Korat. Korat was the location of an American military base and was 70 kilometers southeast of Phimai village.

STAKEOUT

Due to military obligations (and the fact that the Vietnam War was in full swing), I didn't get back to the village and the ruins for another two months. Meanwhile, I had another problem: trying to talk a couple of my buddies into coming along with me. At that time I was something of a platoon leader and had to promise them several days R & R (rest and relaxation) in Bangkok after the trip. Finally, two guys agreed, Charlie and Bill whose home states were West Virginia and Tennessee, respectively. I want to remind my readers that this adventure took place forty years ago and we were all at the time a part of Special Forces and attached to the 173rd Airborne; despite our young age, all three of us had seen a considerable amount of combat action. As it turned out, however, not even that would prepare us for what was about to take place.

We arrived at the village in the late morning and were greeted by the locals. By then, the villagers had come to know me and welcomed my companions with open arms. I had brought a number of gifts for the children, the elders, and of course the family that was kind enough to let me stay in their home during my last visit. We were due back at the base in four days so I had only planned to spend one night in the ruins and leave the following morning. Now, I must make it perfectly clear that we were not part of a research team and had a very limited budget; we were soldiers so the extent of our equipment was two flashlights with extra batteries and one camera. If we did find anything, documenting it was of little concern. I didn't really care who believed me;

all I wanted to do was to get a glimpse of this creature, most likely due to my fascination with *Half Human*.

As the afternoon drew to an end, we dropped off our weapons with the elders and proceeded to the temple ruins. I wanted to camp in the courtyard next to the side entrance that led to the main hall—this doorway was in close proximity to the jungle and the hill where I heard the noise during my last visit. The area was quite overgrown but we were able to make ourselves comfortable. As evening approached, I told my companions we would take two-hour shifts during the night. Darkness fell and the sounds of various animals could be heard in the distance, mostly birds and monkeys, but every now and then there would be a cry or shriek from something unidentifiable that brought all three of us to our feet looking out to the dark jungle.

At midnight all was quiet, and if it weren't for the bats buzzing around our heads, it would have been peaceful. The temperature was 85 degrees or so with high humidity; the sky was partly cloudy with no moon. We began our watch as two lay down on the stone floor using our sleeping bags as beds while one person stayed awake with a flashlight. I took the first shift and for those two hours all was quiet. I then woke up Bill for his shift. I went to lie down and drifted into a very light sleep. About an hour later, I saw flashes of light and heard thunder in the distance—a storm was approaching. I lay back down and thought to myself that once it started raining, I would move everyone into the main chamber and stay close to the entrance.

Fifteen minutes passed when Bill got my attention and gave me hand signals that something was in the woods coming our way. I sat up and looked where he was pointing but saw nothing. Charlie had woken up by then, so the three of us stood motionless with our eyes transfixed on the dark jungle as we heard the sound of something big slowly approaching. The foliage was so thick that nothing could be seen, but the creature sounded like it was walking on two legs. We had spent quite a bit of time in the bush on ambush at night, and after awhile we learned to tell the difference between the movements of an animal and a human. Whatever this was, it was bipedal, very large, and headed in our direction. Charlie ran over to Bill and said, "Give me the light." As he shined the beam into the heavy foliage, the noise stopped. When he turned the light off, the creature resumed moving toward us.

The storm was intensifying and rain started to come down heavily. Bill was still the closest to the jungle barrier while Charlie and I started pulling sleeping bags and supplies into the temple. While my back was turned, I heard Bill scream, "What the hell?! What are you?!" I looked around and saw a tall dark humanoid figure about 10 feet from where Bill was standing. As I watched, it turned its head toward me and its eyes flashed a deep yellow. It was very dark and all I could make out was a shape, but it dwarfed Bill who was 6'2"; this creature had to be at least 8 feet tall! As I raised up the camera to take a photo, the creature turned and jumped into the jungle as if it bounced off a trampoline. Strangely, we didn't hear any plants or branches rustling or snapping, it seemed to have floated right through the thick brush. All this action happened so fast I didn't even get a chance to take a snapshot. Our flashlights were fading quickly; the only real light we had was the occasional flash of lightning. This was also strange since we just changed batteries before the creature was spotted. In those days, there were no long-lasting lithium or alkaline batteries—just plain old dry cells—but the ones we were using should have lasted much longer. After countless investigations many years later, I would discover (like many others) that portable DC power sources seem to drain very quickly in areas active with paranormal events.

Although we could no longer see the creature, Bill stayed outside in the pouring rain. He was jumping around excitedly yelling "Whoop—whoop!" I called out to him asking what the hell he was doing. When he yelled back at me his voice was barely audible through the rain that was coming down so hard and the nearly deafening thunder. Bill said that he was trying to "entice the thing" to come back out so we could all get a better look. From my location inside the temple, I shined the beam of the flashlight into the jungle and was quite startled when my light illuminated three pairs of glowing yellow eyes—no bodies could be seen—only eyes. All six eyes seemed to be staring at Bill imitating an ape; they must have been amused because they didn't move. Charlie started to panic, saying "Why did we leave our guns at the village?!" I replied, "Because the villagers knew you would shoot the creature if it showed up." Charlie then picked up a good-sized rock and threw it in the direction of the center pair of eyes. There was a loud thumping sound as if the rock hit a very dense animal body. Then all the eyes blinked out at once and nothing more was seen or heard. We all stood by the entrance to the temple looking out into the torrential storm for the rest of the night.

At sunrise, I went to the location where we saw the dark figure jump into the brush but found nothing—no footprints or broken branches. Bill got the best look at the creature in the encounter and described it as being more than 8 feet tall with long, reddish brown hair. He didn't remember what its face looked like, but said it had eyes that glowed yellow. Bill wanted to stay another night armed with his gun; his intention was to lure the creature out and kill it. When we returned to the town, the elders got very angry and said they had a "peaceful" relationship with the creatures for more than fifty years and if one was killed, family members would no doubt seek revenge and destroy the village. The village's shaman-priest was worried for Bill; he was the only one who had looked into its face and stared down the creature. The shaman said that anyone who looked at the creature directly would die within six months. The three of us all left the village late that afternoon still talking about what took place the previous night. Both men really wanted to return to the ruins with firearms, shoot this creature, and bring it back to base. About three months later, Bill was killed by enemy fire on a helicopter rescue mission in Cambodia. Charlie died from gunshot wounds in a firefight soon thereafter. As for me, I was injured several times but of course am still alive today. Why? The shaman and the elders of Phimai would say it was because I didn't make full eye contact with the creature, unlike Bill and Charlie.

FOLLOW-UP

Approximately four months after our encounter, I made an appointment to see Dr. Kamiah Sutadsanajina, a zoologist/anthropologist at Bangkok University. I told him of our encounter at the Phimai ruins and he seemed interested. He said that it was possible we saw a family of orangutans. I replied by saying that it was my understanding orangutans weren't found in Thailand. He said that no one knows for sure; although then (1970), the orangutan was only found in Borneo and Sumatra, fossils have been found indicating they once lived in many parts of southeast Asia including Thailand and Vietnam. He said it was possible a small family still existed in the forest of that area. When I told him that the creature we saw was more than 8 feet tall, he laughed and said, "We know that the orangutan is the descendant of the extinct *Gigantopithecus* and *Sivapithecus,* both quite large, ape-like creatures, but I doubt very much if they are still alive." The good doctor suggested that perhaps our eyes and mind were playing tricks on us due to the storm conditions I described. I thanked him for his time and left. In my remaining time in southeast Asia, I discovered there were other legends of similar creatures in many of the small villages in northern Thailand. It puzzled me how a large creature like the frequently seen Thai hairy wildman could just vanish without a trace? Once again, the answer may lie in the theory of parallel realities.

It's been almost forty years since that night at the Phimai ruins, but my memory is as clear to me as if it took place yesterday. I was surprised to learn that Phimai village is now a small city; the ruins are a national tourist attraction complete with a gift shop, paved roads, and even a McDonalds. I guess you can't stop progress, but what of the hairy wildman? It seems the creature is still talked about in legend, but hasn't been seen in more than twenty-five years. Perhaps encroaching human civilization scared it away, and the beast and its kin are still hiding somewhere deep in the hills . . . or perhaps they may have returned to their own world!

The Yeti of the Himalayas

Courtesy of the U.S. military, in 1971 I was able to visit India, Tibet, and Nepal—a country that seemed to me like another world. Nepal lies northeast of India and most of it is very mountainous. The northern part of the country contains eight of the world's ten highest mountains, including Mount Everest. Although a majority of the population practices Hinduism, the nation also has a strong Buddhist tradition. During the late sixties and early seventies, Nepal was quite isolated; most of the country very difficult to reach. Today it is quite the opposite: tour packages will take you to the most remote temples in the northeast mountains.

In August 1971, I spent five days in Nepal with a unit gathering "military intelligence" for the Southeast Asian war. Fortunately, I still had plenty of free time to explore. I was told the village we were staying in was a little more than a hundred kilometers northeast of Kathmandu, the country's largest city. In 2008, I obtained a detailed map of Nepal and to my surprise, no village was listed in that part of the country. The village I visited may still be too small and unnoteworthy to be on any map, or perhaps it had since been abandoned or destroyed. I remember seeing fewer than twenty small buildings in the center of town in addition to a Hindu temple.

While there, I was in constant amazement at how close I was to the Himalayas—the home of the Yeti. As an East Coast native, the mountains seemed impossibly high—the peaks disappeared above the haze and clouds. I thought perhaps this very village could have been part of the story in *Half Human*. The unit I was with would often hike through the Himalayan trails, so for the next five days, we hired a Sherpa to ensure we wouldn't get lost. This Sherpa became a friend to us for our short stay, and I'll never forget his name: Kamsadiak. "Kam" always had a smile on his face and was eager to make our stay as productive as possible. It is important that while in an isolated area like the mountains of Tibet and Nepal one seeks out a trustworthy guide. We would have dinner with Kam and his family every night and developed a close friendship. One night after dinner, I asked him about the Yeti and if he had ever encountered one in the mountains or heard any stories from other Sherpas. As I asked my question and waited for his response, Kam's face went from a smile to one that was very serious. Please remember that although he spoke English, Kam was not very fluent and to get precise details of the story he was about to tell was difficult.

THE SHADOW IN THE STORM

Kam said that the Yeti is more than a legend; he knows it exists because he and others have encountered the creature in the past. The Sherpa people stay away from paths in the mountains where a Yeti family is known to live. This is done not out of fear, but respect. They believe that the Yeti is an ancient spirit that takes physical form when it comes into our world. Just like the people of Thailand with the "wild-man," they believe that to look directly into its eyes would mean a premature death. Kam said he knows of at least one cave in the mountains that is home to a Yeti. When I asked him to take me to it, he quickly replied "NO!" Kam then told me of the encounter he had in 1956 with what he believed was a Yeti. The experience had a great impact on him—he claimed the creature saved his life.

Kam is a Sherpa; he makes a considerable amount of his income guiding people through the southeastern part of the Himalayas. Often, he would go into the mountains alone to find new paths and check that the most commonly used ones were still passable. A trip through this area is always dangerous; the weather can shift very quickly from a sunny day to a blinding snow squall. On one of his solitary journeys, a snowstorm began out of nowhere. Kam said the snow was coming down so heavily and the wind was so violent he had to cover his face. As he tried to make his way back to the village, the snow intensified and he was blinded in a complete whiteout.

The snow was accumulating quickly so Kam stopped in his tracks; he knew he could easily take a wrong step and fall hundreds of feet. As the wind intensified and the snow continued to fall, the temperature also began to quickly drop. He had two options: stay where he was and freeze to death or try to make his way down the trail and hope he didn't take a wrong step. Kam began to move in the direction he came, but the visibility was so poor he lost his orientation. Kam knew he was in serious trouble and thought of his family and what they would do without him. He stopped dead in his tracks ready to accept his fate when ahead of him, a large shadowy figure appeared. He said the figure was much taller than a man and stood upright. Although the figure was only about 20 feet from him, Kam could only make out a dark silhouette and he knew this was a Yeti; he thought for sure his death was near. As he watched, the creature stood motionless as if staring at him; then it seemed to wave its arms and make a gesture for Kam to follow.

The creature turned and walked very slowly; Kam followed, always keeping the same distance. The snow and wind continued to worsen but the figure led him to what appeared to be a cave. Kam walked into the cave for protection, but the creature did not follow. He looked in the cave and found primitive tools and the bones of a number of different animals, Kam knew this cave was a Yeti's home. A short time later the snow stopped and the sky cleared. The sun emerged from the remaining clouds and Kam left the cave. Looking at some of the nearby mountain peaks, he determined he was about 6 miles from the village on a back pass he had never previously used. Finally, Kam made his way back to a familiar trail and found his way home. He told his family and friends the story of how

that Yeti saved his life. Kam knew that if it weren't for the Yeti
that led him to shelter, he surely would have died that day.

There is no doubt in my mind that Kam's story was true
and that he did indeed encounter the so-called Abominable
Snowman of the Himalayas. I asked if he had seen anything more recently, found any tracks, or heard sounds. He
replied, "For years we would find their tracks in the snow
and hear the echoes of their cries calling to each other in
the night, but we do not hear them anymore." Kam and his
people believe the Yeti left the area because of the trouble
men brought to the mountains. They also believe that the
creatures are still somewhere hiding in the highest areas
of the mountains patiently waiting for man to disappear so
they might come down once again and claim the world.

The Texas Bigfoot Cattle Rustler

The year 1972 found me back in the United States and living
in the Austin, Texas, area. At the time, I was attending the
University of Texas studying astronomy and was still a member of the military. While driving to class one day, a news
story on the radio caught my attention concerning a Bigfoot
sighting in the Bandera Hills, about 50 miles northwest of
San Antonio. The story was quite brief but mentioned that
cattlemen and ranchers had seen a 9-foot-tall hairy creature
in broad daylight. The creature came down from the hills,
hoisted a cow onto its shoulders, and ran back into the hills.
I thought this was quite fantastic: a cow weighs quite a bit
so I thought to myself that if this story was true, then it

must have been Super Sasquatch! After class, I called the sheriff's office in Bandera; the officer (a deputy) who took my call was very cooperative and willing to share information. He informed me that a similar creature was also seen in the Medina Lake region walking by the reservoir. I explained to the officer that I was a science student at UT and would like to come out to investigate the sighting and get more detailed information. The deputy said he would be happy to show me the sighting location and possibly let me interview some witnesses.

I drove to Bandera the next weekend feeling a little worried as I walked into the sheriff's office. I was from New York and knew Texans were quite clannish back then. So when the sheriff came out and asked me "Where [are] you from, boy?" I replied in my best Texan accent, "San Antonio, sir." The sheriff then shook my hand and said "You just let the deputy over there know what you want." To make a long story short, I was taken to the sighting area in the patrol car and introduced to a number of cattlemen who saw the creature. The descriptions were all the same: a creature that was very large, with black hair all over its body. They also said that it walked upright like a man but must have been 8 feet tall and weighed more than 600 pounds.

I listened as multiple witnesses described how the creature grabbed a cow, hoisted it over its shoulders, and ran away with it. Such a feat was incredible to even imagine. One cattleman told me he ran inside to get his rifle, jumped in his jeep, and drove in the direction that the creature was last seen, but it was gone. "There is no way that thing could have got[ten] away," he said. "It just vanished." A similar incident that took place a few days before this one was in the afternoon; none of the witnesses had any doubt about the creature they saw that day: it was not a bear, a wild cat, a coyote, or anything they had ever seen. I also learned other nearby ranchers also saw the creature on their property as far back as two years ago. One person actually took a shot at it and the beast brushed its shoulder in slight annoyance and continued to walk away unaffected. As I was wrapping things up, my escorting deputy got a call on his radio to visit a location about 5 miles north; someone had found footprints!

We arrived at the location: a home with a great deal of acreage and about two dozen horses. The property owner was a forty-year-old man who lived there with his wife and two sons, ages fourteen and sixteen. The man said the horses in the barn started making noise during the previous night's storm, something they only did when a predator approached. The man grabbed his rifle and told his wife and children to stay inside. The rain was coming down quite heavily as he went outside. He looked around and heard a grunting sound coming from the barn area. He then projected his high-beam flashlight to where he heard the noise and was shocked to see a large figure running up the hill, away from his farm. The creature was moving so fast he lost it in the darkness in a matter of seconds. He cautiously walked to the barn where the horses were still panicked; it took several minutes to calm them down but they seemed fine. In the first light of morning, the man and his sons walked over to where he saw the creature vanish and found several prints in the still-soft mud. To preserve them, the man instructed his sons to place a box over each one.

We walked to the barn and he showed us the prints: they were huge! Whatever this thing was, it sure earned its "Bigfoot" name. The deputy returned to his car and radioed for assistance. Two hours later, another officer arrived with plaster and we proceeded to make a cast of the footprints. The deputy gave me one to take home—I still have it in my study today. I wanted to stay in the area for two more days and one of the ranchers kindly introduced me to a family that lived in a new development called the Flying L Ranch. The family graciously put me up while I continued my investigation. I spent most of my time there staking out the back roads and hills but never saw or heard anything. As far as I know, the creature never returned to that part of Bandera County, and still remains an unsolved mystery in the case files at the sheriff's office.

Although most Bigfoot sightings come from credible sources, some seem really questionable. For example, in 1992 I received a call from a Connecticut woman who said that a black helicopter landed in her yard and a Bigfoot jumped out, messed up the yard, and stole her clothes hanging on a line to dry. The creature then quickly climbed back into the helicopter and took off. As strange as it sounds, I've heard even weirder reports. Such tales are not this book's focus, but they *do* exist!

LAKE MONSTERS

According to the Global Lake Monster Database, lake monsters have been reported in two hundred and fifty land-locked bodies of freshwater around the world. Next to Bigfoot and his relatives, they are the second-most frequently reported creatures that seem to be from another reality. Many researchers would like to believe these creatures are actually dinosaurs that survived mass extinction and have been living and breeding in some of the lakes around the world. The problem with this theory is simple: where did these aquatic "dinosaurs" go during the ice age when most of these bodies of water were frozen or did not even exist? Despite thousands of hours of exploration, lake monsters seem to pop in and out of existence and no one has been able to prove their existence beyond a shadow of a doubt. They remain as elusive as Bigfoot, yet continue to be seen.

Perhaps there is another dimension very close to our own where marine dinosaurs did not become extinct and somehow occasionally find their way to our reality. Although I have investigated sightings of "Nessie" in Loch Ness, Scotland; "Ogopogo" in Lake Okanagan, British Columbia; and "Champ" in Lake Champlain, Vermont, I have never seen anything strange, but I have spoken with a great number of credible people who claim to have had sightings, some more than once. The creatures are all described as having a long neck, flippers, and several humps on its back. All of these lakes are quite large and remote, so it's easy to understand how a creature could stay hidden in one for a very long time. In 1983, however, I received a report from a witness who said he saw a "sea serpent" in Long Island Sound just off the coast of New Haven. I found out later that since 1873 there have been fourteen sightings of a similar creature off the coast of New England.[2]

New England Sea Serpents

A *New York Times* story dated July 31, 1875, reported that a "sea serpent" had been seen over the past two years from Sandy Hook and Cape Elizabeth in New Jersey to Cape Ann in Massachusetts. The same or similar "sea serpent" was also seen by ten people from a fishing ship just 10 miles off the coast of Portsmouth, New Hampshire. In every case, the creature was reported to be the size of a large boat with a neck stretching 12 feet out of the water. One encounter was reportedly so close to the boat, the men aboard said they could have struck the beast with an oar but did not to avoid drawing the beast's ire. Witnesses at Cape Elizabeth said the sea serpent had made twenty appearances in the harbor over the past two years. In one encounter, frightened people on a bridge threw stones at the creature, causing it to dive underwater and swim away.

Another story in the *New York Times* (from 1932) talks about a 40-foot creature that resembled a transparent sea serpent spotted in Sandy Hook, New Jersey—just 25 miles from Times Square. Frogmen and scientists were sent with cameras and equipment to verify its existence, but found

---

2. Source: *The Hartford Courant* and *The New York Times* from two stories dated 1873 and 1899 respectively.

nothing. Two days later, the sea serpent was spotted again, this time by a Mr. Buckley while on his boat in the Sandy Hook harbor. Buckley got so excited that he grabbed his gun and fired three bullets into the creature, causing it to cry in pain and dive underwater. The *Times* reporter speculated in the article that Buckley may have seen a giant water snake. Mr. Buckley later wrote a letter to the editor saying he was very familiar with snakes and this was not the case: the sea serpent had a long neck, two sharp fins, terrible claws and teeth, and a horn on its nose. When he shot the beast, it made a sound so horrible he wanted to run away.

A sea serpent of similar description was reported by the *New York Times* on August 1, 1933, in the waters of Long Island Sound, off the coast of Westport, Connecticut. At a party in the vicinity of Seymour's Rock, a group of people saw nine dark hump-like objects sticking out of the water about a quarter of a mile from the shore. The humps were moving slowly in a northeastern direction, and the witnesses reported that they had to strain their eyes in order to get a better look at them. As they watched, the objects suddenly began "churning" in the water at a rapid rate causing the water all around it to foam. The members of the party were convinced that they were looking at the famous sea serpent that had been seen so many times over the past fifty years. The people at the party estimated that the body they saw was very long, at least a hundred feet in length.

As they watched, a huge head and neck came out of the water and stood upright for at least two minutes. Two women in the party using binoculars said they could see the creature's eyes glowing red. The head and neck resubmerged and the creature swam away at great speed until they lost sight of it in the fog.

In 1983, I received a letter from a New Haven, Connecticut, resident who claimed to have seen a sea serpent in Long Island Sound. The individual did not give his name and there was no return address on the envelope. Perhaps this person felt foolish seeing such a cryptic animal in domestic waters. For years, the report was filed with a dozen others in my library; this is the first time I am publishing it.

> I heard you on a radio show and have read your column in the Greenwich Time *newspaper and I thought you would be interested in the sighting I had of a sea serpent right in Long Island Sound just off the coast of New Haven. Yes, a sea serpent. There is no doubt in my mind that what I saw was real and I prefer not to send you my name but want to report it to someone in case there are more people who saw it. I was out by the shore at about 5:30 in the morning, I do this quite often since it is peaceful at that time and you can see the sun low in the east illuminating the water. As I looked I saw this large body in the water and knew it was some kind of sea animal. My first impression was that it was a whale, but I realized it was more snake like. This creature was shiny black in color with a light green spotted neck. I saw it no more than 200 feet from me for at least thirty minutes. It started swimming back and forth in front of me and then started nudging a buoy around like it wanted to play. This was definitely not a hallucination, I looked for someone to see it with me, but no one was around. I would have given my right arm for a camera that day but it seemed like it was a show for my benefit. I was completely and absolutely frozen with wonder. All the hair on my arm*

*and neck stood up and chills ran down my spine. I then once
again ran frantically around looking for another person to see
this, but still found no one. When I went back to the water the
sea serpent was gone. This is not a hoax or the mutterings of a
lunatic since I still cannot believe what I saw. I have told very
few people this story and most of them just gave me a strange
look so I remained quiet until I heard you on the radio.*

The number of articles I was able to find in the *New York
Times* concerning sea serpents off the coast of New England
really surprised me. How could a creature this size live in such
crowded waters and not be captured or killed? The answer
once again is that this particular sea serpent's home may not
be in the waters off the coast of the northeast United States,
but in another dimension parallel to ours.

THE CHUPACABRA

While living in Texas, I heard stories of various animals being
attacked by some type of creature and drained of blood. The
most common types of domestic animal victim to this blood-
sucking creature were goats, sheep, dogs, and in some cases
cows. At first, killings were blamed on vampire bats that
would leave their nests in swarms and attack animals, killing
and draining them of blood. However, in all of the cases the
puncture was made by one animal that had canine-like teeth.
Since the puncture marks were mostly in the neck and the
wounds appeared like "vampire marks" some people thought
that the killings were actually due to human vampires or
some Satanic cult. At this time no one in the United States

had heard the word "chupacabra," Spanish meaning "goat-sucker"; *chupar* meaning "to suck" and *cabra* meaning "goat." Although the first documented attacks that made press were in 1995, it seems that the killings had been going on for much longer than that. There is a chance that I may have seen one of the creatures responsible for these bizarre animal killings during my Bigfoot investigations in central Texas.

I was driving the back roads with a friend just outside Medina Lake in autumn of 1972. It was about 10 PM and it was pitch dark; we were quite far from any major highway and there were no homes in the area. We pulled over to the side of a dirt path in a heavily wooded area. After killing the headlights and engine on my car, I began waiting to see if a Bigfoot would cross the road. We didn't know it at the time, but the car was closely parked to a large boulder at least 8 feet high. After about an hour, we were ready to give up and head for home when *BANG!*—something landed on the roof of the car! It jumped onto the hood and began running down the path.

I turned on the headlights and clicked on the brights and saw what appeared to be a large hairless dog with long hind legs. It ran down the path, stopped, and turned around as if to look at the light. It was then that we noticed it had a very long snout and its eyes glowed red reflected in the headlights. I must admit: this was a little unsettling. The creature turned around, resumed running away, and was soon lost in the darkness. My friend and I got out of the car to inspect the roof and found a large dent in it. I would estimate this animal was the size of a large German shepherd and must have weighed at least 80 pounds to do the damage it did. It must have been on top of the boulder and jumped off, landing on our car.

At first my friend thought we had seen a cougar, but then guessed it looked like a coyote with mange. I told him that it didn't look like any animal I had ever seen, and it sure wasn't a coyote—I encountered them many times in my night explorations in the Texas hills. It wasn't until early 2009 after seeing an amazing video taken by a deputy sheriff in Texas that I realized we may have had an encounter with a chupacabra! The story made the press on August 12, 2008; I will present a synopsis below.

Texas Deputy Sheriff Captures a Chupacabra On Video

For eight years, Officer Brandon Reidel patrolled DeWitt County, southwest of San Antonio. In all of his time, the only strange things he ever encountered were some of the criminals he arrested.[3] That all changed when Reidel had a new experience—chasing a chupacabra in broad daylight in his patrol car! Officer Reidel was lucky enough to record the creature running from him. The footage showed the animal in question appearing at first to be a hairless dog or coyote. Upon closer examination, the creature's front legs were much shorter than the hind legs, and the way it ran seemed quite strange . . . very different compared to any type of known animal. The creature had a very long snout and fit the description of what has been

---

3. Source: "Chupacabra Caught on Video." Six o'clock news. KENS, San Antonio. August 11, 2008.

called the Texas Chupacabra. Last year, a similar creature was found dead near the town of Cuero, and although DNA testing could not completely confirm it was a coyote, scientists in Texas believe it may be a rare mutant version or a wild dog. After looking at the photographs of the dead animal and seeing the video from the police car, I knew it was what I saw that night in Texas. Was it a dog? A mutant coyote? Or the Chupacabra?

I was originally going to end this chapter with the Chupacabra, but in the winter of 2009 I received an interesting letter from a person who had sightings of creature-like entities in the Pine Bush area. Pine Bush is located on the west side of the Hudson and, just like the rest of the valley, is the location of many reported encounters with UFOs, strange beings, and monsters. This is not the first letter I received concerning paranormal activity in that area, but it is one I would like to include in this chapter.

THE CREATURES OF PINE BUSH

"To start with, I lived in the Hudson Valley area for only twenty-two years of my life. My story is a bit strange, so be patient. I have recently become aware of things written that have brought me back to think about the strange occurrences and things that happened when I was growing up there. I have told some people about these things, but certain experiences were never told to anyone because I was often left alone as a child and felt my parents would be criticized for neglect for never being around at the time of these occurrences.

"When I was seven years old, we moved from a home my grandfather built in Walden, to Pine Bush, next to an extremely horrible old chicken farm. I say this because my home in Walden was filled with great experiences with lots of friends and community life. Pine Bush became a nightmare to me. It was lonely and also the start of the weirdest stuff (which I kept mostly to myself) starting with blue lights that came through my bedroom window. Some nights, I saw little hairy creatures with big round eyes mulling around outside near my pet's feeding bowls. They were bipedal and had hands with fingers that they kept flicking almost nervously. They seemed to be huddling like a football team and talking with one another and then they came around the other side of the house to peer at me through the window. There were always about ten of them. Three or four at a time would put their heads and hands against the window trying to see inside. My dog, an incessant barker, hid under the slip-covered chair I was sitting in, without a sound. I sat in front of the TV watching snow static on it until my parents came home at 2 AM. I was in deep shock, because I could not speak or move for about ten minutes after their return. They explained that they had no idea it was that late and they had been to Saugerties (a town quite a way's up the river) visiting friends. I burst into tears and asked that they never leave me alone like that again. I did not tell them what happened.

"Coming back from bike riding late one evening, I was stopped dead in my tracks when it seemed out of nowhere, a tall, brown-haired creature appeared standing up right in the road. Terrified, I stopped and waited about twenty minutes until the road was dark and I couldn't see the creature anymore. Then, in total darkness, I built up my momentum downhill and raced along the ditch without stopping, determined that I was fast enough to breeze by anything that might still be there. I made it home that night and didn't tell anyone since they would probably tell me it was just a bear. I knew it wasn't a bear because it walked like a person and was much larger.

"After letting the dog out one night, she would not come back but kept barking at the edge of the woods behind the garage. I walked to where she was and yelled at her to come. As I walked closer and closer I was suddenly stopped dead in my tracks by the loudest screeching yell I had ever heard. It was deafening and my body grew rigid with fear. It echoed through the night air and was unlike anything I'd ever heard. I fled back to the house and eventually the dog came back. About a month later, I heard the same screech one night at my girlfriend's house on Red Oaks Mill Road. We were inside her home listening to music when we heard it. We froze. Her father told us that it was a wild cat. Years later, my dog chased a bobcat up a tree and I heard it scream and believe me—it didn't sound anything like the screeching creature I heard."

REALM OF THE
EARTH SPIRITS

Many researchers have discovered that a high percentage of paranormal events takes place around sacred ground, including cemeteries, Native American burial grounds, and ancient sites in which megalithic structures can be found such as in Egypt, Central America, South America, England, and Ireland. However, you really don't need to go to South America or travel across the world—many ancient sacred sites are located right here in the United States. For example, a large number of mysterious stone chambers and megaliths can be found in New York and other New England states. Some researchers, including myself, believe they were constructed by an ancient people who explored the east coast of North America centuries before Columbus. I first presented my research on this topic in my book *Celtic Mysteries: Windows to Another Dimension in America's Northeast*. If you would like more information, I suggest you read it or contact the New England Antiquities Research Association (NEARA) (refer to the appendix for contact information).

The stone chambers were not constructed randomly; they are located on magnetic anomalies and it seems that they aligned with the same energy ley lines (hypothetical tracks on which monuments and megaliths are built with supposedly mystical energy) that run through many similar structures in Ireland and Scotland. A great deal of paranormal phenomena has been reported in and around these stone chambers and standing stones. In this chapter, I present some of the most recent cases and an experience that I and a small group had when we spent the entire night at one of the locations. It is my opinion that the chambers and standing stones found in the United States and Europe were built as markers to identify an area where a portal, doorway, window, wormhole (or whatever terminology you want to use) exists. My research on these stone structures and the paranormal activity that surrounds them began in 1982 while investigating the UFO sightings of the Hudson River Valley.

THE STONE CHAMBERS

If you take a drive through the back roads of Putnam County, you're bound to see one of these stone chambers hiding behind a bush or masked by wild flowers. Called colonial root cellars for many years, no one knows for sure who built them or what purpose they serve. There are at least seventy chambers in southern New York, and in 1984 I made a connection between them and the ancient Druids. As a result, some archeologists now consider the possibility that the chambers were built by Celtic explorers who came to the northeastern part of the North American continent more than two thousand years ago. Evidence comes in the form of an ancient type of script called Ogham (Ogam), which has been found at three chamber sites. The writing on the chamber walls give dedication to the Celtic festival of Beltane and to the goddess of the moon. At two chamber sites, I found carvings in a conical-shaped limestone rock that showed without a doubt the constellation of the Pleiades. What connection does this constellation have with ancient Druids? I should briefly explain: the Pleiades are not their own constellation; they are a part of the Taurus constellation. Also called the "Seven Sisters," the Pleiades has an eerie shape in the sky that resembles a ghostly, glittering little dipper of stars. The Druids believed that when the Pleiades was directly overhead at midnight, otherworldly spirits were at their strongest and the distance between their reality and ours was at a minimum. This celestial placement of the Seven Sisters takes place during a short period of the year: October 25 through November 5. Even in our modern calendar, this ancient Druid holy day is still celebrated—we call it "Halloween." The Druids may have actually witnessed an increase in paranormal activity at this time: many of their legends tell of strange lights and encounters with mysterious beings. The descriptions that have been passed down sound a great deal like our UFOs and aliens of today.

In Putnam County, the standing stones and the chambers are very similar to those in Ireland where a great deal of UFO and other forms of paranormal phenomena has also been reported. Stonehenge is also one of these mystical sites and has had its share of UFO reports. My study of the stone chambers in North America finally led me to Europe where there are so many sites that had paranormal events attached to them that I could choose only a few to visit since my time and money were limited. The site that I found the most interesting was Newgrange: it had an aura of mystery, and being there felt like I was standing in front of a tunnel that connected to another world.

The Magic Stones of Newgrange

In the early nineties, I explored many ancient megalithic sites in Ireland but of all the wonders I saw, Newgrange has my vote as the most impressive. Archeologists have dated the site as being more than five thousand years old, making it older than the Great Pyramids of Egypt and Stonehenge. Researchers all agree that Newgrange was used not only as a tomb, but also for ceremonial and religious rituals. There is some speculation it was dedicated to Dagda (the sun god of pre-Christian Ireland) because an opening at the entrance aligns with the sun on the winter solstice. Over many centuries, the tomb has been raided by grave robbers, but in 860 AD the remaining contents were removed by Viking raiders.

The actual mound (the tumulus) is egg-shaped, and some of the local UFO enthusiasts there believe the tomb was fashioned after a flying saucer. Originally, there were thirty-five standing stones but only twelve remain today. Visitors who touch the stones have claimed everything from miraculous healings to fantastic visions. When I put my hands on each stone, all I felt was a slight tingling in my fingers. The most striking thing I found about the Newgrange site is its precise astronomical alignment with the winter solstice. On this day (the shortest of the year), a shaft of sunlight enters through a large opening above the entrance. The beam of sunlight illuminates a basin at the end of a tunnel and lights up a series of spirals carved into the rock.

During my short stay, I was able to talk to several people who have witnessed, videotaped, and seen globes of silver lights bouncing around the stones during the day and night. The descriptions of the lights seem to have a striking resemblance to the spook lights of North America. I was not surprised: Newgrange lies on the same magnetic lines of force that pass though the Hudson Valley.

Having the New York stone chambers (also paranormal hotspots), in my backyard has allowed me to study them in great detail—it's like having my own version of Newgrange just thirty minutes away. As of the writing of this book, reports of people who visited these locations encountering beings and forces from different realities are still coming to me. The following story is from a local resident of Kent Cliffs, New York, who was attacked by an invisible assailant while inside one of the stone chambers. The witness prefers not to give his name, but graciously gave me permission to use his story with the hope that it will help solve the mystery.

Struck By an Unseen Force

"I was walking down Highway 301 in the late part of the summer of this year (1992), when I passed by the stone chamber on the road. I knew these things have been there for a long time and heard many stories about them. Some think they were built by Vikings or Druids, while others think they were built by the Indians or colonial farmers. To tell you the truth, I never thought much about them and at the time really didn't care. Well, if you're walking by them at night, they look real spooky. I know many people who won't even walk in front of them when it is dark. Anyway, it was about eleven at night and it was very dark, the sky was clear but there was no moon. I walked by the chamber on the opposite side of the road and noticed a faint red glow coming from the inside. This glow was so faint that I could barely see it with my eyes. I also heard a faint sound that was like a hum, sort of like an electrical generator was being used inside to produce electricity to make the light. So I crossed the street and entered what was then (before the road was widened) a short section of woods and entered the chamber. As soon as I walked in, the noise stopped and I could not see the red—it was all dark inside. I looked around and felt very uneasy like someone or something was watching me. You know the feeling . . . like when you're in a dark cellar with someone and you can't see them, but you know someone is there and you are not alone.

"I wasn't in there for more than thirty seconds when this force hits me. It was as if someone pushed me; I fell to the ground expecting to see someone standing there, but I saw no one at all! I was on the ground wondering what to do next, still feeling as if there was someone in there with me. I slowly got up to my feet and was struck again, this time in the face—it felt like a hand. There was some unseen force striking me every time I tried to get up, so I decide to stay down and not move. I looked toward the opening and saw the figure of a man standing there. He was wearing a white robe and had long black hair and a beard. His hair was very curly and hung over his shoulders. The thing that really scared me—almost to death—was when I looked into his eyes. His eyes seemed very dark, but they also glowed. The center of his pupils looked red. He just stood there looking at me; when my eyes met his, I could feel a tingling up and down my spine. He then raised his hand and pointed his finger to me and the message was clear; I was not welcome and should leave and never return. Although it was dark I could see him plainly. I don't understand this, but it seemed that he was surrounded by a soft white glow. The figure then dissolved into a cloud of mist that was then drawn into a nearby rock just as if there was a vacuum there. The entire incident lasted about three or four minutes. I then got up and ran out the entrance and never went back. Sometimes at night I would wake up in a cold sweat with my heart pounding because I could still see the image of this guy's eyes starring at me. I always feel that he is waiting for me somewhere in the dark ready to take me to another place as some kind of prisoner."

Beings of this type have been reported in several of the other chambers close to that area. Sometimes the entity in the white robe is accompanied by several Viking-looking figures; sometimes they are seen with small dwarves in hooded robes. Are they ghosts, ultra-terrestrials, or aliens? Sometimes, the reports include the "grays," which are often reported in UFO abduction cases as well as alien reptilian creatures I believe may be Djinn.

Reports of encounters are too numerous to dismiss and those who make them are usually more than eager to erase the encounter from their memories permanently. Recently, I heard of a new case near a standing megalithic stone located on the New York State University—Purchase campus. The witness claims that one night while putting his hand on the stone, several hooded entities appeared out of nowhere and surrounded him. The beings circled him for several minutes and then vanished into a vapor. The witness told me he could not see their faces, and their hands were covered in the robes. They were no more than 4 feet tall and he thought they were more animal than human by the way they moved. As they circled him, he could hear a faint, unanimous chant. He did not understand the words, but he compared the sounds to a growl.

The Beings From Another Dimension

The account below is from a person who has become a close friend of mine over the years. She changed her name to Golden Hawk after having a spiritual awakening at a sacred place called Hawk Rock. "Goldie" (as we call her) is a spiritual teacher and hosts a radio show, *Another Reality*. She would often visit the chambers by herself and on occasion would bring others. Her favorite chamber is one we call the "Mother Earth" chamber or the "Womb" since it is oval in shape and goes slightly underground. Goldie and several others had an incredible experience with hooded beings illuminated under some type of ball of light one night in that chamber. Goldie's account appears in her own words.

"It was August 12, 2007, at about midnight when we arrived at the chamber that I call the 'womb.' With me was
my friend Alana, her brother, and a friend. I had been to this
chamber a number of times over the years at night with different people so I knew how to get there in the dark and
felt comfortable walking into the woods in the dark. I was
trying to get as much time inside the chamber since every
time I went I felt more open up to this incredible energy.
Our purpose for the trip that night was to observe a meteor shower we heard was taking place. What was different
about this trip is that we got lost trying to find the chamber in the dark. We had lights, but got lost and this caused
quite a great deal of tension. The strange thing is that we
finally found it after walking by it several times. Alana finally found it in a place we had already definitely looked. It
had rained recently: the stream in front of the chamber was
not trickling—it was flowing fast and deep. We spent a very
long time looking for the chamber . . . it was as if the energy
was shifting back and forth causing us to lose direction. We
were searching for the chamber for a long time and passed it
no more than 20 feet and did not see the 'womb,' it was like
the chamber was invisible for a time.

"There was something almost eerie in how Alana saw the
chamber in the dark without a light. The night was cloudless
and there was a moon in the sky. We entered the chamber
and started a meditation. I said to everybody that we would
not leave until daylight because it was so dark and wet outside. Alana's brother started to complain that he was cold
and tired so we started huddling together and everything got

quiet. Then, there was a vibration-like buzzing sound and I looked at Alana and said 'Do you hear something?' She said yes. The two boys stayed inside while Alana and I went out side the chamber. We saw this white light, very bright at the top of the hill to the right of the chamber. It was hard to tell if the light was in the air or on the ground because we were looking through woods, but it was illuminating the trees.

"The light was a whitish-blue and very bright—like a spotlight. The light was only about a hundred feet from us and at this time we saw only a light. My first impression was someone was in the woods with us and that worried me, but then I thought, 'Well, there's a meteor shower tonight and they must have come here to see it also.' I remember thinking it was strange they had such a bright light on, expecting to see the meteor shower. As I looked more closely, there were figures illuminated by the light that seemed to have hoods on their heads and the light appeared to be above them.

"The light seemed to be round or a rectangle, but I could not tell for sure. We still heard the buzzing sound; it was very intense. We stood there looking at these beings and my first feeling was that I needed to protect everyone with us because there were strange people out in the night with us. We called the boys out, pointed out the light and beings, and told them to stay quiet. I suddenly got a strong urge to leave. After some discussion, the plan was to walk right past them to get to the path that led to the car without paying any attention to who or what they were. We neared the beings and started to pass them on the right. I was too afraid to look and told the others to not look; to stay focused and talk loudly as if they were unafraid and didn't care if they were there. Basically, I told them to not show fear. I didn't try to sneak past these strangers; I wanted them to know we wanted no trouble and were leaving.

"There were three beings with a light above them doing something with their hands. They seemed very busy with something that I could not see. They were all wearing black hoods and were at least 7 feet tall. As we passed, I caught a side glance; they had a scary presence. I did not see any faces, just the hoods. We were then walking arm and arm and I was trying to be strong and focus on one thing: to get to the car safe and sound. We walked by them and it was a little tricky because we had to walk through the stream so we got wet. The beings were silent; the only sound was us. I told everyone beforehand I wanted to let these beings know we were aware of their presence, and we were not afraid. The beings paid no attention to us as we walked by them. The ground was well lit from the light so we had no trouble seeing. We made it to the path by 3:30 AM and didn't look back. The feeling I got was that they were not friendly beings. I thought this because we reacted to them and they didn't do anything. I also got the impression that we saw them but they could not see us. We finally made it back to the car and I was surprised the sun was starting to rise—I didn't think we spent that much time in the chamber."

It is possible that whatever Golden Hawk and her companions saw that night was interdimensional and not fully integrated with our universe. This could be why the hooded beings appeared not to be able to see them . . . or was it that they considered their task of great importance and the humans were of little interest?

The Cursed House

The Hudson Valley of New York is full of "haunted" places: some are real and some are not. I documented a great deal of paranormal activity around the locations that contain chambers and standing stones. I also discovered the locations in which these structures were constructed have strong magnetic anomalies. I always wondered what it would be like to live in a house located near a chamber. Although there are several of these "haunted" stone structures with homes on the same property, there is one farmhouse built right on top of a chamber, and the builders used it as part of the foundation and cellar.

The house was built in 1826 and located in Putnam County, in the town of Kent Cliffs. Since the property is now vacant and the owner is hoping to rent or sell it, I will not give its location. This house has had a number of people occupy it over the past twenty years, and all have been scared or forced out after seeing apparitions and the feeling that something evil was walking through the rooms at night. In two cases, the personalities of the people who lived there changed and one incident resulted in the breakup of a couple that had been happily married for fifteen years.

While the house was still empty in 2004, I spent a night in it with my camera and the last of my ultraviolet film. Throughout the night, I had a feeling that something was watching me from the dark rooms, most likely wondering what I was doing there. I didn't get any sleep that night, and although I heard what sounded like bangs and footsteps throughout the dark hours, unfortunately the entity didn't think I was worth an appearance or manifestation. I had ten frames of film left and only one had something on it: an ectoplasm-like blob that should not have shown up on the film—the rest of the frames were blank (clear) indicating there was no UV light striking the film. The house's owner promised to keep me informed of any strange happenings taking place. On more than one occasion, he tried to have the house blessed by a Christian priest, a rabbi, and even a Buddhist monk from the nearby Chuang Yen Monastery, but nothing worked.[1] If the chamber and house is the home of a Trickster (Djinni by any other name) then it will not leave until it wants to. The age-old rituals of exorcism performed by the Catholic Church will just not work when it comes to this type of entity.

The Sleeping Dragon

The Chuang Yen Monastery was built in a central point surrounded by stone chambers. Under the Buddha Hall is a large rock that looks like a sleeping dragon. It makes up the foundation of the building and is referred to by the monks as "The Dragon Rock." According to their beliefs, this rock channels up energy into the Great Buddha and allows the energy to flow through all who visit and mediate. Some people who visit the Buddha Hall for the first time experience headaches and nausea while others have seen visions or felt a spiritual

---

1. The Chuang Yen Monastery is a Chinese Buddhist temple/monastery in Putnam County, New York, near the town of Lake Carmel. Its Great Buddha Hall houses the largest Buddha statue in the United States.

awakening of one form or another. I asked one of the monks, "If the energy is so pure, why does it have a negative effect on some?" He asked me in return if I felt that way, I replied no, I always felt good and at peace when I visited. He said, "It's because your energy centers in your body are unobstructed and [energy] flows through you. Many who visit for the first time are clogged up and it backs up causing headaches; one must learn to open up before attempting to commune with the Buddha." Perhaps like the Dragon Rock, the chambers were also designed to harness earth energy—people who visit them experience the same sensations as those who mediate in the Great Buddha Hall.

Hawk Rock

Hawk Rock is located deep in the woods of a New York City watershed in Putnam County, and it is perhaps one of the most mystical places and best kept secrets in North America. The rock was once Native American sacred ground and there is no coincidence that it is found in the same area in which Golden Hawk had her experience. There are three other chambers at this location, and it seems that the builders, just like the Native Americans, knew the land was a gateway to the gods and earth spirits.

The rock itself is about 25 feet tall and a perching hawk is carved on one side. There is no doubt about its shape; the rock doesn't just resemble this bird of prey, it looks *exactly* like it. Whoever carved Hawk Rock definitely had a bird in mind—you can even see layers of feathers in the wing. The stone was cut and shaped at angles that could only have been done by intelligent beings; it was not formed naturally. The difference in appearance between each side of the rock is amazing: the hawk figure can only be seen on the rock's eastern side. Alongside of the great bird, just below the wing is a smooth area that has three carvings: a sun, long-tailed bird (no longer found in the area), and a turtle. All three are Native American symbols that represent the heavens (sun), sky (bird), and earth (turtle).

Some local residents claim the carvings were done by Boy Scouts decades ago, but I spoke with a Native American shaman who indicated the symbols have been there for as long as any of his people can remember. He found it amusing that those who are not descendants of the tribes in New York continue to take credit for all the amazing things ancient Native Americans did. Some historians and researchers in New York feel that the carvings (petroglyphs) could be more than six thousand years old.

If you ever get the chance to visit this site, you will see it was intended to be used as a ritual area to perhaps communicate with beings from another reality. I and many others have made frequent visits to Hawk Rock; when you enter the sacred area, you can actually feel the energy shift. There is a feeling of peace and goodness and all negative thoughts seem to dissolve from your mind. You have a strong feeling of being under a protective zone that isolates you from the harsh reality of our modern world.

During my investigations of the stone chambers and other megaliths structures in New York and New England, I became good friends with a Native American Algonquian shaman whose non-native name was "Charlie." Charlie told me that the stone chambers are very old and built by people who came across the sea, but Hawk Rock is much older and was carved by his ancestors. During his life, I visited Charlie many times and learned the locations of sacred ground once kept secret by the Native Americans of New York. Charlie told me that Hawk Rock and the stone chambers are not the only sacred things found in the watershed area; it is also the location of burial grounds of an ancient people and the home of a Trickster.

Who or What Is a Trickster?

The Trickster is a spirit found in mythologies all around the world capable of shape-shifting into animals or humans. The Algonquian people believe the Trickster is a creator, destroyer, giver, and taker and will always try to trick unsuspecting humans just to have fun with them. Neither good nor evil, the Trickster has no moral or social values and is constantly at the mercy of his passions. Almost every indigenous tribe believes the Trickster has some divine traits and a few actually worship him as a god. The animal shapes he likes to take on most are the coyote, wolf, hawk, and owl. Whatever he may be, the Trickster seems to be a survivor that uses his wits to adapt to changing times. Even in modern times, the Trickster is believed to appear in many guises and continues to outwit the shaman and the people of the twenty-first century who live on the land he protects. Perhaps the shaman was correct in indicating the aliens and hooded beings as well as the strange sounds, animals, and

UFOs seen at Hawk Rock are nothing more than the Trickster having fun and scaring people off his land. Native legends of the Trickster remind me of the Islamic tales of the Djinn—perhaps they are one and the same.

Was It a Trickster?

When I began my research, few people knew about Hawk Rock and the stone chambers.[2] As a result of my efforts to spread the word, quite a few people have been visiting these sites in warm weather hoping to touch another world. It has become a favorite location for the local Wicca population, which conducts their rituals during the most magical times of the year. On May 1, 2007, I received a call from two people who had an encounter with a creature from another reality at Hawk Rock. The two witnesses whose real first names are Jeff and Liz gave me permission to use their story (I am withholding their last names for privacy purposes). I arranged to interview them both at Jeff's home in Kent Cliffs, New York, one week after their experience. Their story appears below.

Jeff had read about the stone chambers and Hawk Rock in an article I wrote for the local newspaper. He and Liz decided to try finding the place and picked a warm, mild day in May. Although they made a number of wrong turns, after several hours they finally came upon the sacred rock at about two in the afternoon. Jeff said, "As we walked through the perimeter of giant boulders, you could feel the atmosphere

---

2. My research into the stone chambers and other megalithic structures began in late 1982.

change and despite us being tired and hungry we both felt quite energized." Liz added that when they walked into the "sacred area" she felt a presence as if someone or something was watching them. Together the couple walked over to the perching giant stone hawk to admire its craftsmanship.

Jeff and Liz placed a blanket on top of a large flat stone that faced the giant rock bird and began to eat lunch. After about fifteen minutes they heard a loud sound, like a human screaming. Startled, they both jumped to their feet thinking that some crazy person was in the thick wooded hill above them. Then the couple heard another sound off to the right. It sounded the same, but now there were two sources of the noise and they seemed to be signaling each other. Jeff and Liz felt surrounded. The screaming then changed to a series of grunts, then growls. The sound no longer seemed human but from some type of animal. The couple then heard something big moving in the woods and saw a dark mass no more than a hundred feet away from them. At first they thought it was a bear, but noticed that it was walking upright like a man. The creature stopped, and although it was partially hidden by the thick brush, they could see it looking straight at them. Terrified, they left their belongings behind and ran to the trail. They could still hear the creature's cries in the woods as they made their way back to the car. The experience was so unsettling they never went back to Hawk Rock again.

Over the past ten years, I have received several emails, letters, and calls from people who saw a similar creature in Hawk Rock's vicinity. There were also reports of globes of light circling the petroglyphic bird and sightings of alien-like beings with red eyes that glowed in the dark. On two of my many solitary trips to that area, I have also heard strange sounds and Celtic flute music that seemed to come from everywhere in the woods. I often asked myself, were the sounds flowing in from another reality, or was it just a Trickster having fun?

Night Out at Hawk Rock

A number of people I have worked with on past paranormal investigations had been planning to camp out at Hawk Rock for several years just to see what would happen. We finally agreed the all-night vigil would take place in August 2008. The group, which was originally to consist of nine, were people from many backgrounds and expertise. They included Francine Vale, a healer and spiritual teacher; Paul Greco, an artist and founder of the UFO Roundtable in Yonkers, New York; Golden Hawk, whom I mentioned earlier; her friend Alana; Rosemary Ellen Guiley, a well-known paranormal author and researcher; Scott, a musician; Nadine, a very talented artist and her husband, Ted; Donna Savino, a member of the New England Antiquities Research Association (NEARA); and myself, the leader of this group and resident scientist.

I decided to divide the exploration of Hawk Rock into three parts: the first would be a meeting at my home where we would discuss both the history and paranormal events of that area, the second would be a day trip to Hawk Rock, and the third would be our spending the night under the stars near the great bird. The first meeting took place in July at my home in Connecticut. All of us in the group discussed what they expected to accomplish at Hawk Rock; the general agreement was to document some type of contact experience. We planned a day trip the first weekend in August, weather permitting. The Saturday of the day trip came and we couldn't have asked for better weather to begin our hike to Hawk Rock. While walking through the woods and passing by two stone chambers, Golden Hawk (whose story is presented earlier) began to reminisce about her experience with the hooded beings at the Mother Earth ("the Womb") chamber. The journey to Hawk Rock took about an hour or so, and I could tell that several members of the group were quite tired because the day was warm and the insects were biting.

As we reached the end of the trail and entered the sacred circle, I pointed out the many boulders pushed down from the north by giant glaciers during the last Ice Age. For some group members, this was their first trip to Hawk Rock, and as we passed through the line of carved stones that indicated the entrance into sacred ground, everyone experienced a definite shift not only in temperature, but also in temperament. The cooler temperature made us all feel very good, and the fatigue was gone as if some unknown force was flowing through giving us a second wind. Everyone also noticed the flies and other insects were no longer bothering us! As we continued walking, several group members commented that the trees and plants here were different than those in the rest of the woods. There were tall pines with many brown needles on the ground that gave the area a surreal appearance.

Just below and to the east of the perching stone hawk was a large outcrop of rock about 5 feet above the ground. This rock was flattened on top and was large enough to fit all nine of us comfortably. We relaxed for a while, ate our lunch, and talked about how peaceful it felt. After lunch, Francine led us through a meditation in which some members of the group said they saw images and had vision-like dreams. Paul then photographed the area and was able to image bright globes of light invisible to the naked eye. The globes Paul photographed were very bright and more than the usual orb images that appear in many digital photographs. These bright globes appeared only around Hawk Rock and in the location where others have reported seeing the spirit of a Native American shaman.

Our group stayed for about two hours. Then we slowly made our way back through the woods to the cars. On the return hike, all the members of the group, myself included, continued to comment how good—almost euphoric—we felt. In a way, we had our own private experiences that day, but they were not going to prepare us for our next objective: the overnight stay.

We agreed that the 23rd of August would be a good night to sleep out at Hawk Rock; my only concern was with the weather. The northeastern part of the United States is notorious for spontaneous midsummer thunderstorms, and I didn't want us getting trapped in the woods since that particular area is noted for multiple lightning strikes. As we got closer to the date in question, Francine and Paul were not able to make it, but the rest of us were ready and eager to go. We arrived in the parking area about six in the evening and began our long trip into the woods. As we got closer to Hawk Rock, Donna and Nadine strongly felt that something was following us but keeping its distance. We arrived at Hawk Rock just before sunset and began preparing for a long night.

The seven of us set up our sleeping bags on the flat meditation rock and although we had flashlights, a candle was lit and the group began to relax and talk. As darkness fell, we were all quite surprised how noisy it was with insects and other sounds that came from the surrounding woods. By eleven o'clock, it was so dark that we could not see beyond our candlelight illuminating the side of the great hawk like a living apparition from another world. A short time later, I got the group together and decided to do a meditation that Charlie (the Native American shaman) had taught me to connect with our spirit animals. Although I don't believe in rituals of any nature, it seemed a good way to get everyone in the mood and open our minds to act as a possible conduit to connect with the intelligence Nadine and Donna felt was watching us.

We finished the meditation, and as if in response, a startling sound came from the woods. I will never forget it: at first it sounded like a human trying to imitate an animal, perhaps a coyote. Donna asked what it was, thinking at first it was an animal, but another member of our group said it was human. We thought there was someone out in the woods watching us, having a laugh at our expense. However, the sound continued and shifted into more of an animal noise. It's very hard to describe, but we realized that this was not a human and not any animal that we were familiar with. It was almost like a cry, but it seemed to be directed toward us. Rosemary and I thought it could be a shape-shifter because its vocalizations went from human to something not human. The sound came from the north side of the ridge, but the foliage was so thick that even with our flashlights we could not see what was causing it.

Some of the members of our group became fearful and the sound stopped, as if in response. Needless to say, no one was able to sleep . . . but more was yet to come.

Things remained quiet until about two in the morning. Shortly after, while all of us were lying down on the rock, a barely visible object or force passed over us. Most of us saw it; as this thing passed overhead, the sky became distorted; like when one looks through heat waves coming off a car or roof on a hot summer day. In the woods, several of us saw what appeared to be tiny red lights that disappeared and reappeared. To me they looked like eyes, but to Rosemary they looked like small individual lights. At about three in the morning, I sat up and Donna said something to me. It seemed my eyes closed for a second and the next thing I knew it was five in the morning and members of the group were calling my name! I really can't say what happened, but I seemed to have lost consciousness for about two hours and experienced no passage of time. You might say that perhaps I fell asleep, but the answer to that would be absolutely not: due to severe knee injuries acquired during my time in the military, I was in a great deal of pain sitting on the hard, damp rock. We packed our gear at the break of dawn to the

202 REALM OF THE EARTH SPIRITS

tune of two owls in the still-dark woods. We had a long trek
through the woods back to our cars.

We discussed what had taken place on the way to the
parking area and decided to stop at a diner in Carmel. I was
happy to hear that Rosemary and Scott were able to tape the
sound we heard; at least there was some evidence that could
be analyzed. While eating, three crows landed on the railing
outside our window and just perched there, staring at us.
As I watched them, I thought of Charlie's many stories of
the Trickster that could take different shapes to play with
one's mind. One of the crows had an injured leg, but they all
stood almost motionless and stared into the window. They
stayed and observed us until we left; it was a very strange
sight.

FOLLOW-UP

To summarize, we could not identify the sound that we recorded that night, despite input from various wildlife experts.
The people on a website about owling thought it may have
been an unusual call of a barred owl, but I consulted an owl
expert who once worked for the Audubon society: he told me
it was not an owl—it sounded more human.[3] He made the
suggestion that perhaps someone was playing a trick on us.
All of us present that night will never forget the sound—it
was no trick—at least not a human one! As for the red lights

---

3. The Audubon Society's mission is to conserve and restore natural
   ecosystems, focusing on birds, other wildlife, and their habitats for
   the benefit of humanity and the earth's biological diversity.

in the woods and the invisible thing that passed over us, we also have no explanation. The Native American Medicine Council of Litchfield, Connecticut, told me we heard a shape-shifter, and the red lights were evil spirits that only came out in the dark and could not approach the sacred rock. The Council believed the invisible force was a good spirit that protected the sacred grounds and knew we had good intentions and allowed us to stay under its protection. All the members of our group are eager to once again return to Hawk Rock and spend the night, but this time we plan to bring various types of equipment and instruments so that any manifestations can be fully documented.

PSYCHIC POWERS: REALITY, HOAX, OR DELUSION?

The number of practicing psychics in the United States is staggering. I can drive up and down the major streets in any town of New York and Connecticut and see a sign saying "Psychic Readings," "Palm Readings," or "Tarot Card Readings." Like any profession in the service industry, there are good practitioners and bad ones. Over a ten-year period, I conducted a part-time investigation and visited thirty-six psychics across the northeastern United States. My goal during this investigation was to observe the range of abilities in professional practicing psychics. In one month, I actually had three readings from three well-known psychics, and although they were correct in some aspects of my personal life and history, most of the information differed between them and was only partially correct.

Each "professional" psychic claims to have a specialty: some channel spirit guides (or, in rare cases, aliens from another star system), while others are hired to find lost items. Most of the practicing psychics I have talked to are mediums—individuals who claim the ability to contact spirits and those who have passed over. This is a popular specialty and some well-known mediums who have shown a track record of accuracy made it big with book sales and their own radio and television shows.

During my thirty-plus years in researching the paranormal, I have encountered a number of psychics who have extraordinary abilities, but there is an equal number who have not impressed me at all. My investigation of the psychic world has been published in a number of Connecticut newspapers over the years. In one of these publications, I was compared to Harry Houdini, who, in an attempt to prove whether or not life exists after death, paid many visits to psychics ("mediums" as they were called) in the early twentieth century.

Houdini never found any proof that the self-professed mediums of his day were in contact with the next world. He exposed some famous mediums as frauds and received many death threats from unstable individuals and cult groups as a result. I fashioned part of my investigation on Houdini's work but did so with less passion than the great magician and escape artist. The great Houdini investigated the psychics and mediums of the early twentieth century with too much emotion and no objectivity, so I decided to be objective and let the data from the research determine my conclusions—not my personal feelings. To get a better understanding of my investigation in this area, I would like to share with my readers the great Houdini's exposé of the psychics of his day.

HOUDINI AND THE PSYCHICS

Harry Houdini was a world-famous magician and for his time, he did a number of amazing feats, some of which have never been duplicated to this day.[1] When his mother died, he nearly lost the will to live and wanted to know if she was still alive in another form or truly gone forever. He desperately hoped that his mother could send him a message assuring Houdini she was alright. In an attempt to communicate with his mother, Houdini started visiting psychics and mediums around the world, but he was not successful in his efforts. According to his diary, the great magician and escape artist did not find a single genuine psychic. From there on, he made it his personal mission to expose fakes so they could not prey upon those who were similarly emotionally distraught after losing a loved one.

Houdini was a master of illusion and using this knowledge was able to expose fakery during a séance. To his dismay, Houdini found the psychics of his time so unscrupulous that he was shocked that they would manipulate grieving people out of their hard-earned money. He also discovered that most of these so-called mediums were using cheap parlor tricks and illusions to deceive their victims into believing that contact with the other side had been achieved. Houdini went to psychic after psychic and found them all to be frauds. Their deception made him so angry that he began a crusade

---

1. Harry Houdini (March 24, 1874–October 31, 1926) was born Ehrich Weisz, and is considered by many today to be the greatest escape artist and stage magician of the twentieth century.

to expose charlatans who would prey upon the naïve and grieving to make easy money. At first, he focused his attention on well-known mediums and joined in their séances. In the middle of the session or manifestation, Houdini would jump to his feet and reveal the tricky. Of course, this resulted in the medium losing every client and Houdini making many enemies. Houdini's crusade was so successful, psychics all over the world were worried he would expose them next. Because of this, Houdini had to resort to disguises—most mediums would not allow him to join their sessions. When I discovered this about Houdini, it seemed very familiar—it is exactly what happened to me. To this day, I am no longer invited to any channeling sessions or group psychic readings by most, if not all, well-known psychics in New England.

I should reiterate: my goal is to find the truth, not to discredit anyone. It is interesting to note that although Houdini's standards for proof were much higher than mine, we did get similar results. While Houdini was very successful in his crusade to expose fake psychics, deep in his heart he always wished for one authentic medium to come forward and prove his or her ability to communicate with the dead to him beyond a shadow of a doubt.

PICKING UP WHERE HOUDINI LEFT OFF

I began a study in 1997 lasting to 2007 to determine if the many people out there who claim to be psychics actually have this ability and if they do, to what extent. When choosing a psychic, one must be careful—some are in fierce competition with each other and will claim extraordinary abilities to get your business. To start out, it is best to talk to people who've had experiences with the psychic to see what he or she has to say and if the professional possesses the specialty you seek. Before your visit, ask for references; a few are willing to give you names and phone numbers of past clients. I found the average cost to see a psychic was anywhere between fifty and two hundred dollars an hour; some well-known individuals charge more than a thousand dollars! Some psychics charge more than a professional therapist. Perhaps I should have become a psychic rather than an educator, but alas, I was always better at teaching science than trying to predict the future or contact the dead.

Of the thirty-six psychics tested, only three convinced me of any psychic abilities beyond a shadow of a doubt; the remaining thirty-three I have to label as inconclusive. My testing success rate represents only 8 percent of the total number of those in my study, but it may not necessarily represent the true percentage on a global scale. On occasion, I would go to a session with fabricated information strongly placed in my mind. In more than one case, the psychic was able to read the information from my thoughts. This convinced me that some may be telepathic and are not getting their information from the other side, but from their clients' minds. In most cases, the psychic may not know he or she is telepathic and would instead assume information is coming from a "spirit guide." After one session with a well-known Connecticut psychic, I told her the information she related to me was totally accurate but made up in my mind. I told her the accuracy of the fabricated information she related was amazing. This psychic now informs people she is telepathic and to ensure the accuracy of the information coming from the other side, she has her clients meditate before the reading to try and clear their thoughts.

A Real Psychic

I met a psychic named Loretta Chaney during my investigation; Loretta was able to give me information about my father who passed away in 1995. The things she told me were so accurate, I was very surprised. Amazingly, some of the information was very personal and unknown to me at the time; I was able to confirm the information later. Loretta has dozens of testimonies and letters from a variety of people she's helped. One of the things that impressed me most about Loretta is that she keeps a low profile. Loretta is not looking for publicity; and she is not trying to sell books and doesn't have her own television or radio show. Loretta is very selective about her clients and will only use her abilities if she believes she can help the person. Loretta and her husband, Scott, work as a team doing not only psychic readings but also healing. The following letter is one of many testimonies that give credit to Loretta's amazing abilities. It involves a young girl named Chrissy who was murdered by a person she met in an Internet chat room. In a touching session with Chrissy's mother, Shelley, Loretta was able to contact her from the other side.

A letter from Shelley to Loretta

"Five months after my niece Christina died, I attended a Body, Mind and Spirit Expo where Loretta Chaney was lecturing on the subject of life after death. During her lecture, Loretta did brief readings for some of the people in the audience, including myself. But as Loretta began to 'tune in' on my niece for me, she suddenly stopped and said that she wanted to talk to me about my niece after the lecture. At the time, Loretta didn't know who I was or that my niece was named Christina ('Chrissy' as she's called in this letter). I later learned that when Loretta had first heard of Christina's death on television and learned that she lived nearby, she prayed and asked God to bring her parents to her in the hope that she could be of some help to them. Chrissy's primary parent most of her life was me. For that reason, I believe God brought me to Loretta.

"When I caught up with Loretta after the lecture, she immediately felt compelled to do a reading for me. Her very first words were, 'Chrissy is telling me that you always wanted her to call you Mom, but she never did.' That blew me away immediately: only Chrissy and I knew that very personal fact. Loretta asked me not to respond, just to listen, because she said Chrissy was talking very fast and she wanted to concentrate on what Chrissy was saying. Loretta gave me details on how Chrissy died that matched the official police and FBI report. The media was reporting the wrong information so the public, including Loretta, did not know the real truth.

"Through Loretta, Chrissy described my deepest emotions and thoughts. For example, I had been going to the crime scene and going over the crime itself obsessively. Chrissy asked me to stop that behavior because it was affecting both of us in a negative way. Chrissy had a wonderful sense of humor and could make anyone laugh. Loretta was able to let that identifying sense of humor come through and at several points she used mannerisms only Chrissy would. Loretta described in detail artwork of Chrissy's I had framed after she died . . . no one knew about that. Loretta described activities I did while Chrissy was missing. She also described meaningful activities Chrissy and I did before she died. There was so much detail in this reading, I was convinced I was talking to Chrissy. By the time Loretta was done, I was in awe. I was now a definite believer that there is life after death, which took a huge weight off of my physical and emotional being. I was able to continue with my grieving process in a much healthier way.

"However, six months after the reading, I was at an emotional low point again. I was blaming myself for not getting involved in Chrissy's life the first three years after her birth, which are so critical and key in a child's basic, overall development. I felt that maybe if I had gotten involved with her life, she would not have made the fatal decision to meet her Internet contact at the mall. I was beating myself up mercilessly and while I was at this low point, Loretta called me on the phone to see how I was doing! Several minutes into our conversation, Loretta said that she felt Chrissy's presence around me. She told me Chrissy wanted to speak with me again. Through Loretta, Chrissy told me to stop worrying about her. (I was worrying if she was OK and in a safe place.) She said that she was fine and very happy. Chrissy also told me to stop worrying about not being with her in the first three years of her life. She explained I wasn't supposed to be there then. My not coming into her life when she was three years old was as it was supposed to be.

"Then Loretta told me details of the surrounding area where I was standing in my house. Remember, we were talking on the phone and Loretta had never been to my home. This part of the impromptu telephone reading was validation from Chrissy that she was and is always with me when I need her. Chrissy, through Loretta, told me that my prayers and others' prayers are strengthening her, and my actions on this earth are helping her where she is now. This information was an invaluable gift to me because it means I can still take care of Chrissy even now with my actions here on Earth. A primary need of a mother is to be able to take care of her child. Chrissy, through Loretta, gave me back my will to live and to be productive in society again because I now realize that through prayer and helping others, I am helping Chrissy too."

I could present letter after letter just like the one above that give testimony to Loretta's incredible ability, but I think the point has been made. The number of practicing fake psychics is like an overcast sky blocking out the sun on a warm day, but Loretta is a break in those clouds and has allowed the light to shine on this skeptic's face making me believe that although very few psychics are on the level, some are legit. If only the great Houdini was around today, I feel his view on the subject would have been considerably less negative after meeting

Loretta. Loretta and her husband became very good friends of mine and often assist me in my paranormal investigations.

Psychic Channeling of Angels

Some people who do psychic readings claim to channel "higher beings." My research has convinced me that some of these individuals are channeling nothing more than their own imaginations. Many enjoy having an audience and being the center of attention and some like to have a following because it makes them feel very important. Although I have sat through a good number of channeling sessions, the one I will present is from a woman in New York who claims to channel the archangel Gabriel. There must be at least a hundred psychics in the New York area alone who claim to channel this angel . . . Gabriel must be a busy guy! Speaking through the psychic, Gabriel asked the small group if anyone had any questions. I raised my hand and asked a number of basic scientific questions and all I got were very long answers filled with spiritual interpretations, none factually correct. Finally, although seemingly getting very annoyed, "Gabriel" allowed me to ask one more question. I asked a simple one; out of the blue I said; "What's the capital of North Dakota?" Well, Gabriel didn't know the answer to that one either and it seemed strange to me that an archangel couldn't answer questions my sixth-grade science class could. The channeling of angels, extraterrestrials, and other beings is very complex and more of a contact experience. My investigations into this phenomenon will be covered in a future book.

THE STRANGE CASE OF JOHN GRAY

Sometime back in 1979, a number of people involved in paranormal research told me of a very interesting man named John Gray who lived in Greenfield Hills, Connecticut. It wasn't until 1982 that I finally gave him a call and said that I wanted to meet with him. It was quite difficult understanding John—over the past several years he had suffered two strokes that left his vocal cords partially paralyzed. Despite this handicap, however, I was able to understand every word he said. It felt as if our communication was taking place on a higher level . . . perhaps telepathy was being used.

I made an appointment to visit his home that weekend and had four days to prepare but something unusual took place. In the days preceding my meeting with John, I felt a presence as if something was trying to probe my mind. Looking back, I compare the feeling to the Pink Floyd lyrics "There's someone in my head bu it's not me!" At night, I had vivid dreams of meeting an old man with a white beard in some mountain temple. Every time, he would walk over to me and touch my arm and then I would wake up. This dream recurred over three nights and by the third time, I knew it was not just a dream; someone was trying to contact me, perhaps using psychic projection and remote viewing.

Saturday, our meeting day, was still a couple of days away so I spent some time trying to get background information on John Gray. The only bit of information I found on Mr. Gray was a Fairfield, Connecticut, police report made in 1981 concerning prowlers on his property; other than that he seemed a blank slate. Then I got a lucky break: a reporter for a local newspaper, *The Fairfield Citizen* recognized the name and found a story written about John Gray in 1970.[2] It seems the paper selected Mr. Gray as Citizen of the Week for his past accomplishments in science and the arts. It's important I present at least part of this story because it will show that although John Gray made some very incredible claims, he was not crazy or mentally unstable. He was a very credible man who had the respect and admiration of many.

An Accomplished Gentleman

Mr. Gray was a Briton who lived in Canada for many years before coming to the United States. He was an expert engraver, artist, engineer, philosopher, and inventor—truly a Renaissance man. Mr. Gray was not just a dabbler in many pursuits; he was very well trained in all areas of his expertise. Over the years, he has contributed cutting-edge technologies to industries in a number of fields. I found it very extraordinary that a single human being could achieve all of this in one lifetime. From 1945 to 1970, John was a consultant for the American Bank Note Company, the largest firm of its type in the world. There, John worked as the only engraver who made embossed dies, a highly specialized skill. In 1945, Mr. Gray engraved a picture of King George V of England later placed in a British palace. Queen Mary sent John a letter congratu-

---

2. This reporter once did a story on me, so I called him for a favor; he had considerable connections in the Fairfield and Bridgeport areas of Connecticut.

lating him on his excellent work and remarkable likeness of the image.

During World War II, John established the John Gray Company in which he manufactured critical equipment for the English armed forces. He made range finders for the Royal Navy and invented a barrel gauge locator for anti-aircraft guns that improved the efficiency of shooting down German aircraft. This device was considered one of the keys in English victory during the Battle of Britain. Another of John's crowning inventions was a periscope that could be used in tanks. This allowed soliders to stay in the protective armor of the vehicle and safely spot their targets. This device is still in use today by the United States and its allies in Iraq.

My Visit

My first visit with John Gray was in the summer of 1982; at the time his wife had just passed away and his granddaughter was taking care of him. I arrived at his home in the late morning on a warm August day, knocked on the door, and was greeted by his granddaughter. She led me into the living room where her grandfather was waiting and introduced me. John was sitting in a chair with his back to me but as he got up and turned around, I was shocked—this was the man who had appeared in my dreams! John had two strokes over the past year and although he was able to get around quite well, his speech was greatly affected. As we sat, John opened up with a strange revelation: "I am not the original soul in this body; I walked into it in 1935." I was taken by surprise—John was claiming to be a walk-in. According to a Hindu belief, a walk-in is a person whose original soul has departed the body and been replaced with a new soul. It supposedly takes place when the human body is injured, ill, near death, or when a person loses the will to live. The soul agrees to leave the body and a new one is placed into it by a higher being, usually angelic in nature. Deep emotional trauma and suicidal desires are said to be suitable settings for a walk-in.

After entering the body, the walk-in may behave differently and have a totally new personality. She or he may speak in an unknown language, respond to a different name, be disoriented, or have a greater spiritual awareness. In popular New Age writings, the walk-in exists to carry out a task in the physical plane. This mission may involve one or large numbers of people, and it usually entails the teachings of wisdom and matters of spirituality. The "new" soul inside the body may claim he or she is an angel, or an ascended being; some claim to be extraterrestrials here to save the world. Many walk-ins claim heightened psychic sensitivity and may become healers or ministers. In John Gray's case, the walk-in soul is a great Tibetan master who lived more than a thousand years ago and now has come to the physical plane to teach a number of apprentices the secret arts to battle forces of evil. Although John seemed to be a man of peace, this would explain his contributions during World War II that helped the allies be victorious.

In Islamic belief, a walk-in is not a human spirit but an evil Djinni who has come into our world to get revenge on a man or woman who injured it or the Djinni's family.[3] It is also believed that a Djinni will walk into the body of a recently married young man so it can experience the physical pleasures of intercourse with his wife. The possession of the human body is not forced; the person must consent and for allowing use of a physical body, the Djinni may offer a wish as payment. However, there are stories in which the Djinni never gives up the body or commits murder. When the original soul finds itself back in the body, he or she may wake up in a mental hospital or on trial for a crime he or she didn't commit. Sometime during their research, paranormal investigators may encounter people who claim to be walk-ins, but what bothers me about this is the simple fact that if you are a walk-in, would you be so eager to advertise it?

Anyway, after hearing John's tale, I didn't know what to make of it. The claim was fantastic and this was the first time I had actually met a walk-in face to face. I asked John if it was he who had probed my mind and visited me in my dreams. He said, "Yes. I had to know your true intentions . . . they are pure or else you would not be here now." John said he was often visited by UFOs and showed me a number of photos he had taken. He also claimed that a secret government agency in league with organized crime has been

---

3. In Islamic folklore, a D*jinni* (also genie or *Jinni*) is a fiery supernatural creature in possession of free will. Djinn are mentioned in the Qur'an, where an entire surah is named after them (Al-Jinn). They can be either good or evil. In some cases, evil genies are said to lead humans astray. The translation of the word *Djinn* into English means "to hide, conceal or remain hidden."

trying to get him to agree to work with them. John said that on more than one occasion, a powerful evil master came into his bedroom at night and tried to kill him, but he was able to drive it away. According to John, he was able to win the battle and vanquish the dark force, but it left him in the weakened state that I now find him.

John claimed to have extraordinary powers, so I asked for a demonstration. John replied that he had the ability to levitate things and showed me a photo of a pie plate floating above a table. I replied to him that anyone can take a photo and fake it, if he had this power then he ought to prove it to me. I was sitting across from him on the couch with the windows open behind me. John seemed a little upset that I would make such a demand, but as I looked at his face he then smiled and the pupils in his blue eyes turned to pinpoints, then he waved his hand and behind me there was a *crash!* All three windows slammed shut at once with great force and the sound made me jump out of my seat. I asked John, "Did you do that?" He replied, "Yes I did. Enough demonstrations for the moment; there will be plenty of time for that later." Of course I wanted to see more, and thought that perhaps it was just a freak accident. John seemed to be reading my mind and said, "There are no such thing as accidents and coincidences."

John claimed to be part of an ancient secret society called the "Brotherhood of Mahatmas," the spiritual guides of mankind and the guardians of the secrets of the cosmos with the Master Djwhal Khul as his teacher.[4] As mentioned earlier, John was a talented artist; he took me into his workshop and unveiled two paintings: one of Jesus and the other of Babaji, an Ascended Indian Master. The oil paintings were incredible and the detail was so life-like they appeared to be high-resolution photographs. As we walked back into the living room, John told me he had selected me to go to India and study under Babaji who has incarnated many times over thousands of years. He said this is Babaji's final time on Earth, and I must go and see him because he is going to leave soon. John then showed me photos taken by a student of his in India of a young-looking man levitating off the ground in the lotus meditation position in front of a crowd of people. There was a long letter that started out saying, "BABAJI IS REAL!" I guess this student had some doubts before his trip. John said that he would pay my way and all expenses if I would agree to study with the master Babaji for five years.

According to Hindu mysticism, Babaji is one of the representatives of God-the-Father. From time to time, he incarnates on the Earth as a teacher for the sake of helping people. One of his incarnations took place at the end of the nineteenth

---

4. According to legend, Djwhal Khul is a Tibetan Master of ancient knowledge. His teachings have been channeled through many mediums from the nineteenth century to the present. I could find no record of this person ever existing, but he seems to play an important part in the formation of a new world order and helping people ascend to the next spiritual level.

century; it was described by Paramahansa Yogananda.[5] Yogananda describes in particular how Babaji easily dematerialized and materialized several times in front of his students; he also performed the materialization of objects out of thin air. According to the followers of Babaji, his last incarnation was from 1970 to 1984, again in northern India. He walked into a young man's body and lived in it for fourteen years.

John asked me once again if I would be willing to go to India. I had recently started a new position teaching science so I politely declined his offer. John seemed disappointed but said it was my decision to make. I asked John if it would be possible to get copies of his notes and photographs, and he said, "No, but someday you will get most of it." He excused himself; he was tired so I left for the day. I visited John several more times before I moved out of the area.

Did John have psychic powers? Well, it sure seemed like it; he was able to get thoughts out of my mind and insert vivid images. John passed over sometime in the early nineties. I had no idea he had left this world until one day when I got a call from a friend. He said he got lost in the back roads of Fairfield, Connecticut, while driving and suddenly got the urge to turn down a lonely road. He came upon a house that had a sign outside that said "Estate Sale." He then said that I came into his mind and he swore he heard the voice of a man say, "Stop and get it for Phil . . . you will know when you are there." He got out of the car and was "directed" to a small

---

5. Paramahansa Yogananda (January 5, 1893–March 7, 1952) was an Indian yogi and guru who introduced many Westerners to the teachings of meditation through his book, *Autobiography of a Yogi*.

box of papers and photographs. He purchased them from a woman and then left and found his way back to the highway. Two days later, he gave me a call and said, "Phil, I have something for you, but don't ask me how I know." I went to his home the following weekend, he gave me a packet and said, "I heard a voice say this was for you." I opened it up and could not believe my eyes—it was John Gray's notes, drawings, and a number of photographs. I always wondered if John was a real walk-in or was it just the imagination of an ill old man trying to escape reality. One day while shopping at the mall in Danbury, Connecticut, I saw a sign outside a hair stylist shop saying "Walk-Ins Welcome" and it made me stop, wonder, and finally smile. As for Babaji, well, I never went to India but whoever he was, he would show up again in my life in another form (a bizarre incident, presented in the chapter Messages from Beyond).

METAL BENDING

Using the mind to bend spoons and other metals is a controversial subject. It began in the 1970s, when Uri Geller held spoons in his hand and seemed to bend them by psychic means. Many magicians have come forward and claimed that Geller's metal bending ability is nothing but a trick, and they have been able to duplicate the feat. During my investigation of a "haunted home," all the spoons and forks in a kitchen drawer were found bent the morning after my visit. Was it the result of an angry ghost or a hoax? Whatever the cause, the people who lived there didn't think it was funny—they had to buy a considerable amount of new silverware. I have seen spoon bending before, and although I accept the idea that it can be done with trickery and without psychic powers, perhaps in rare cases a trick is not involved.

In the mid 1980s, John G. Fuller and I worked on a number of projects for FOX Television.[6] One particular show we did was on psychic metal bending. The producers rented out a church hall in Weston, Connecticut, and invited a number of the townspeople and their families to participate in an experiment for the show. If I remember correctly, there were twenty-five adults and ten children whose ages ranged from six to ten years old with an equal number of boys and girls. Most of the people who participated to my knowledge had no interest in psychic phenomenon, and most agreed to take part in the experiment because they wanted to be on television. A spoon was passed out to everyone, and as they held it in one hand between two fingers with my direction everyone yelled out, "BEND, BEND, BEND!"

I didn't know what to expect, and I think the producers of the show probably would have been upset if nothing happened, but it did. Most of the spoons in the adult's hands did not bend, in two there was a slight bend near the handle—but it was a different story with the children. Four of the spoons held by the children ages six, seven, and nine bent right before my eyes as if they were rubber. To make things

6. John G. Fuller, Jr. (1913–1990) was a New England–based author of several nonfiction books and newspaper articles, mainly focusing on themes of extraterrestrials and the supernatural. For many years, he was a regular columnist for the *Saturday Review* magazine and *Reader's Digest*.

more incredible, two of the spoons continued to bend as they were all placed on the table. There is no way that these young children could have bent their spoons by trickery. This experiment convinced me and those present that what is called psychokinesis is possible.

Why did the children's spoons bend and not the adults'? To answer this question for myself, I thought of the *Star Wars* movies. In Episode V, Luke Skywalker's ship sank in the swamp and he attempted to levitate it using the Force. Luke found the task too difficult and failed. Then, using his power and knowledge of the Force, Yoda raised the ship out of the swamp and onto the land with little difficulty. Luke exclaimed, "I don't believe it!" Yoda replied, "That's why you failed." Perhaps in order to tap into our psychic powers, we must have no hidden agendas and most importantly, we must believe!

ENTITIES FROM
AN UNSEEN WORLD

In the early eighties, I would often attend UFO conferences, most of which were sponsored by the Mutual UFO Network (MUFON).[1] It was a good way to hear about research being done in the field. However, when a case bordering on the extreme paranormal was presented, it was always considered as not being scientific and therefore without place in the UFO community and its research. I will never forget the MUFON conference held at MIT sometime in 1982 when one of the speakers (I can't remember who specifically) asked if there were any questions. An audience member asked, "Where are the UFOs from and why are they here?" The speaker answered, "I really don't know. That's the million-dollar question." At that moment another spectator raised his hand and stood up, and in an accent that sounded Jamaican said, "We

---

1. The Mutual UFO Network (MUFON) is a civilian organization dedicated to the collection of UFO reports. It is now regarded as the world's largest organization of this type.

really all know where they are from and what they are!" While looking at everyone in the audience he yelled at the top of his lungs, "THEY ARE DEMONS FROM HELL, MAN!" The speaker responded, "Well, there is no proof of that, but we do respect your opinion. Thank you." This individual became very agitated and accused UFO investigators of being in league with the Devil. After several minutes of a heated exchange, security was called to escort the gentleman out of the building.

SO WHAT ARE DEMONS?

I have asked this question to a number of people who research and investigate the paranormal, including self-proclaimed exorcists, and not one can give me a definite answer. We get the word "demonstrate" from the word "demon"; in medieval times, it was thought that they were advanced beings with great power. Demons were called upon to teach the sciences, tell the future, and reveal locations of buried treasure. In modern society, the word "demon" is often associated with something very horrible and evil and in the service of the Devil. The redefinition was the result of the Roman Catholic Church's efforts to scare people and steer them away from occult practices. These days, people are still afraid of demons and will often blame them for the bad things that happen in life. Some even believe that inanimate objects like statues and mirrors could be cursed and, if placed in a home, will connect with demonic forces that could cause physical and psychological harm. I know of one person who collects these "cursed objects" and stores them in his home to keep them out of the world.

Some say demons are angels who went bad and instead of dwelling in hell are actually roaming the world looking for human victims. To get a better understanding of these non-human entities, especially angels, one must erase from the mind the typical image of wings and a cherub-like face. Angels are beings in the universe that do not have physical bodies—they are highly evolved and have great power. The names of angels often appear in cases of UFO contacts and channeling. Some of these channels and contactees claim UFO beings called the "Nordics" are responsible for our angel myths. Nords are described as tall, light-skinned, and blonde. Angels have their own society and seem to be bound by a higher law. It is often said angels lack free will; meaning the extent to which they can interact with the physical universe is very limited.

Personally, I do not believe angels interact with humans by channeling. I do not believe fallen angels are the demons many paranormal investigators and exorcists fear. I do not believe that angels can possess a human being or strike one in anger. We are told in a number of ancient writings that there are good and bad angels, but once again both seem bound by the same strict laws that govern the universe. Angels seem so far above humans on the evolutionary scale, there isn't a clear reason for them bothering with us. It seems implausible that a being of such intellect would want to torment humans by moving things around in a home or possessing a person to have fun or vent anger. However, there is another class of being that has been totally ignored by the Western world; this entity will do all the nasty things mentioned above and more: the Djinn.

ENTER THE DJINN

The Djinn were briefly mentioned in *Interdimensional Universe* and since its publication, I have received numerous emails from people who were interested to either learn more or confirm whether they have had an encounter with one. The only reference we have of the Djinn is in the Qur'an (Koran) and Sunnah of Islam. The Djinn were created before humans and lived on Earth in a parallel dimension. Their home is so close to ours that at times they are able to clearly see us, but we perceive them as only dark shadows. This could explain the many and continually escalating reports of the so-called "shadow people."

The word *Djinn* (sometimes *Jinn*) comes from the Arabic word meaning "hidden" or "concealed" and, although I don't believe that they are actively hiding from us, they are nevertheless invisible. The Djinn are referred to as "God's other people" in the Qur'an and according to legend, once lived in this world while it was still a paradise. Instead of following the laws of God, the Djinn turned to greed and slowly started to destroy the planet and make war upon themselves and other intelligent beings. As punishment, the Djinn were taken out of this world; they were relocated to another reality where they could do little harm. Earth was then healed and cleansed and a new being was allowed to live in this world; God and the angels called this new being "man." According to the Qur'an (surah 15: 26–27) God made the angels from light, man from the clay in the earth and the Djinn from smokeless fire.[2] Like humans, Djinn are born with free will and may choose the path of good or evil. They have emotions, can marry, and raise children. Their life span is much longer than a human's and the older a Djinni is, the more knowledge and power it acquires. What clearly distinguishes the Djinn from mankind are their powers and abilities: most Djinn can manipulate matter into any form they wish. They have the ability to fly, disappear, reappear, and shape-shift. It may be that the myths of Native American shape shifters and Tricksters are really Djinn.

The ability to influence humans and control animals is another power of the Djinn. In most cases, the person has to invite the Djinn into their life by asking them for favors (wishes) and the Djinn will ask for payment. The Djinn seem to be able to ingest physical food and absorb energy as nourishment; in some cases they may attach themselves to a person and induce fear just to feed upon them. It must be considered that the Djinn are a chief component in most paranormal manifestations, and according to the Qur'an, they delight in having fun with humans by conjuring a variety of things to induce fear. The world of the Djinn is both sinister and interesting; by acknowledging their existence, what we call the paranormal will make more sense. As mentioned earlier, to the Islamic people, Djinn are very real and are not to be taken lightly. In March 2009 I received a letter from a woman born in Turkey who had read *Interdimensional Universe* and wanted to report information she had on these beings.

---

2. Noor Foundation-International, various translators (1977).

Hi Phil,

I was born and lived in Istanbul, Turkey, until I was nine years old, then my family immigrated to Canada. I am currently 51. As you may know, almost all of the Turkish population is Muslim (Secular). My generation of Turks is quite modern, nothing like the Arabic countries. The reason why I feel I must give you this information is because growing up knowing about the Koran and beliefs of the other life forms are quite intact in my mind and there is no doubt of the existence of the Djinn in the Muslim countries. So, even though I was skeptical, I accepted this fact because it was written in the Koran as a FACT. I just want to add that I am not religious at all. I have not read your entire new book Interdimensional Universe *but have gathered enough information about your definition of the Djinn to say that it is exactly as you have described and defined Djinn. In Turkish, it is call CIN.*

In 1996, while I was living in Istanbul, my husband (we were engaged at the time) and about six of his friends went on a business trip to a city called Rize along the shores of the eastern part of the Black Sea. One of his friends was originally from that city, so they visited his family. The friend also had a brother that was quite religious and lived in a village up in the mountains. They knew that he had special abilities and went to visit him.

That night as the men were all gathered at this brother's house, my husband—who had been driving—was tired and went to the bedroom to sleep. He did not close the bedroom door and was trying to get warm in his bed (even though it was summer, the village was located up in the mountains so it was very cold). They have very thick bed covers in Turkey made of lamb's wool and my husband had pulled this thick cover over his head trying to warm himself up, but he was not asleep when this amazing incident took place.

His friends coaxed the brother to call upon the Djinn, because they knew that he was capable of doing this, they wanted to see for themselves, they still did not believe it could happen. ALL OF THIS was happening while my husband was in the bedroom, he was able to hear it all, and as I said he had his bedroom door open to let some of the heat from the fireplace in. This man was reluctant to call upon the Cin (Djinn) because he said they did not like to be bothered. But, after some coaxing, he agreed.

Apparently, he chanted some Arabic prayers, as you know the Koran can only be read out loud in Arabic (in its original language). Then from the windows, these glowing orbs entered the room. The light they gave off was so bright that my husband, who at this time was really frightened, said it penetrated through the thick comforter he had thrown over his head. These light forms were round in shape (orbs), and they came right through the glass window without breaking it. The Djinn were very agitated and angry that they had been called forth. They spoke and asked why they were called. I don't know the exact conversation, but they advised these men that they lacked faith and they should get closer to God. All this time, my husband was too afraid to get out of his bed. The Djinn got angrier and started to turn the lights on and off, banging the doors and finally left. Everyone was shocked. A couple of minutes later the phone rang, it was the man's neighbor calling to say that the

Cin (Djinn) were over at his place and that he should come over to get rid of them; apparently this had happened before. The really weird thing was that one of the guys was missing, as if all this was not enough. With all the commotion, they thought that he was spooked and hid somewhere. They found him hours later soaked with sweat on the house balcony. The Djinn had taken him and brought him back as payback. This man said that they took him to where they lived, by a brook. This poor man was so scared he could hardly talk. When my husband came back home after this incident, he was so exhausted that he slept for days and would not tell me what happened because he did not want to frighten me.

I spoke to his friends afterward, and they were all amazed at what happened that night.

Isn't this incredible? I have researched the Djinn on Turkish internet sites. These beings can be called upon in various ways. There are sacred books, but I am too afraid to go further because in the Koran it is also mentioned that it is dangerous and sinful to delve into the world of these beings. As you have written in your book, the consequences of going too deep is dangerous. This is the common theme I have received from all of my research. If you need my help in your research, please let me know.

Name withheld

Having encountered the Djinn before, I know how dangerous they can be and people—whether an exorcist, paranormal investigator or priest who thinks they can control situations when these beings are involved—are only fooling themselves. The following case is the report of an individual who, for a good part of his life, has encountered some type of interdimensional intelligence that may be a Djinni. I will refer to him as "Bill" as he would like his real name and location kept out of the public eye. Bill is an intelligent person with a respectable background in science; his logic and understanding of the universe has always made him question everything. However, Bill was not prepared for what was to happen in his life as he crossed paths with a force that was not part of his reality. His story is indeed fantastic and, in my opinion, Bill has encountered the Djinn on many occasions and on more than one level.

Bill's Story

"My first encounters with interdimensional intelligent beings occurred on October 14, 2004, at three in the afternoon while lying in bed at my Caribbean island home watching TV. I felt some small rapid movements, like cicada-sized creatures scurrying and making ticklish vibrations inside the mattress below my head. The vibrations continued for ten minutes until I checked them out by poking around the underside of the box-spring. Unable to locate any animal (the house was well-exterminated), I tried again to relax, but the movements continued beneath me whenever I lay down. Later, a friend sat there and confirmed feeling the movements without my having asked or mentioning them to him. Without warning, something like flying 'metallic bees' shot at us from the bed and made a beeping noise. Then they vanished.

"A half hour after the first mattress critters reappeared, I got up to go to the bathroom to sit on the toilet and smoke a cigarette. As I tried lighting the cigarette, the foot mat around the toilet base suddenly shot up into the air, knocking the lighter, cigarette, and magazine out of my hands. Quickly, I inspected the mat and found nothing attached to it like puppet strings that might account for the sudden levitation. Then I stood up to look out the small window in the private toilet, but saw no one outside. At that time I started hearing voices outside the front door and observed small groups of hazy half-visible people speaking.

"These were the first two major events that convinced me invisible entities exist, and I was especially shaken by the flying mat—the first supernatural event I had ever witnessed or given any credence to. From that point on, I checked and rechecked my observations to see which events might be in my imagination.

"Like any critical observer, I wondered whether these 'phenomena' might just be products of my imagination so I tried to stick to actual physical evidence. However, the flying bath mat had convinced me that some abnormal yet indisputable force was at work in and around my house. I continued to wonder how many subsequent events could be called mere products of an overactive imagination or 'thought control' as many subsequent occurrences lacked a concrete physical quality and became more subtle, expressed as visual, auditory, olfactory, or psychic phenomena. Fortunately, many incidents were confirmed by other people visiting my house. Here, I will stick to the occurrences that seemed to have no ordinary explanation.

"The voices I heard outside the house were ordinary human voices saying things I could barely make out, but during a two-year period I saw semi-transparent humans talking in the same voice. The two near-invisible or cloudy human forms I saw most were a fifty-ish man and a woman dressed in white. These voices were usually outside my house, usually at the front door or west-end near an empty lot forested with bamboo and other tropical vegetation. They first appeared inside the house, apparently studying my home security system panel. When I moved toward them, they quickly retreated and were nowhere to be seen. All the voices I heard and visages I saw consistently involved these two beings.

"On October 16, I began seeing more activity and detecting a presence in the house. I often used the alarm system of the house to detect opening doors or movements. Upon closing a sliding glass door, securing the 'empty' room that I had thoroughly checked, a slider was opened causing the alarm to go off. I immediately ran through the same door and searched outside, but saw no one in the open areas around the house. I continued through the adjacent overgrown lots, sensing presences, but saw no one. After half an hour, I felt I had the entities cornered in a dense, dark forest. I began speaking to them and challenging them to come forward. After taunting them in this way, a rock was thrown at me from the forest!

"I always looked for human movements inside and outside the house, but did not see these when doors were opened. On the large living room sliding doors, I discovered three extremely fine wires fixed with scotch tape near one of the upper-corner magnetized door-break sensor. These wires appeared far too small to be highly magnetized to by-pass the entry-sensor, except under very high-tech conditions I could not understand. The semi-visible nature of the other intruders was usually in the form of mongoose-sized creatures scurrying at estimated speeds at least triple those of the fastest mouse we can barely see through the corner of an eye. These creatures could shape-shift to fully human-size 'cloudy' forms best seen through their reflection on the silver recording side of a compact disk or the night-setting in older rearview car mirrors. These uses indicated that detection by bent light or infrared-sensitive reflection illuminated the forms. Some of the invisible human forms appeared so frequently I gave them names according to their faces' resemblances to movie actors or their activities, such as the one that had a beard and was dressed in a rubberized body apron; he wore expensive infrared/UV goggles and I called him 'Silent Bob.'

"On October 17, the evidence showing the presence of the characters in various forms around the house and elsewhere while driving around the island continued to grow. They usually assumed three forms, shape-shifting at will between them: human shape, mongoose-like, and insect-like. None appeared to fly, but were able to mount trellises, arches, etc. Their speed was three to four times that of an animal's, making the mongoose forms barely detectable except as trailing images. Dogs could easily detect their presence and neighbors' pets barked loudly when they entered their yards from the beach. On one occasion, two dogs I was taking for a drive to the beach entered the backseat and went wild sniffing, barking, and pawing at something under the passenger seat. On a different occasion while parked downtown, I saw a phenomenally fast 'mongoose' whip from beneath the car into the floor well as I exited a store. I looked under the passenger seat again and beheld the most horrific face I had ever seen— it looked satanic! I had no stick or sprays on hand to prod it into moving and was too terrified to move my hand near it, although ordinarily I gladly interacted with the disincarnate humanoids. I re-entered the store to look for someone who might look like a wise shaman or witch-doctor to witness the entity in the car, but no patrons impressed me as such.

"A few times I witnessed drawings and cloth or paper 'sculptures' made cleverly on the outside sliding glass doors so quickly no ordinary human could have made them. The art was very expressive and seemed to be used for a psychological terror effect. They would start with cute harmless rocking-horse-like figures, then remake into a terrifying, tortured beast with head and neck craning skyward in an agonizing contortion. There were also a number of occasions when I left the open kitchen area of the house, but still had a clear view of its access. I would return to the kitchen a few minutes later only to find origami figures of birds or horses cut out of magazines that had not been there moments before; the figures could only have been made extremely quickly. I was often driven out of the house by panic-causing electromagnetic forces dependent upon the house-current; I cut it off and noticed that the disturbance could recur in areas of house where there was current.

"One night I thought I saw a four-foot-square generator-like metal machine on the roof—it was like nothing I have ever seen before. It made perfect sense that this UFO-type unit was responsible for the electrical disturbances, possibly controlled remotely or by the invisibles. I tried like hell, but never caught sight of any humanoid figures on my roof, though I certainly heard them walking and carrying heavy equipment; there were unmistakable loud sounds of feet on the roof. I had a ladder set to quickly climb to the roof, but never saw footprints or other evidence. One painted metal antenna-like piece, five inches in length, protruded from the cupola above the living room of which I have little recall or explanation. I never did figure out where they could tap into light fixtures, or other 110V power sources, but they undeniably received their stationary electric power from these lines—again, because the higher-energy activities ceased when I turned off a section of house-current.

"One morning when I woke up, I found a twelve-millimeter circular scar on my upper arm without any pain, signs of burning, or inflammation. Similar to a body-art tattoo, the scar remained unchanged after two years and dermatologists were unable to explain how a permanent scar could be formed overnight without effects. About sixty degrees of the circle is unscarred, as though it might have served as a flap for implants or other invasive procedures. Additionally, a permanent bluish 'bruise' of broken blood vessels remains on one ankle that doctors could not explain. While I had these strange marks, it was more difficult to lift my legs while walking, similar to the effort one makes during a centrifugal ride at an amusement park. Doctors have noticed the varicosities present only in this small area, atypical of any circulatory condition.

"One cloudy and still afternoon, low clouds suddenly darkened over my yard and strong winds blew through the house for ten minutes without warning, although the neighboring property had no wind at all. I can say after fifteen years living at the house that this was a complete atmospheric anomaly. On many occasions when the beings seemed close, I could feel the 'whoosh' of breeze created by their super-rapid movements. When I sensed their presence outside my sliding glass doors and cracked the door open, there were strong rushes of air (outside the air was totally still) into the house as curtains flew.

"To rid myself of the beings, I often 'tricked' the beasts into following me into a room where I'd quickly slam the door to trap them. This method appeared to cease disturbances for a short period, although their shape-shifting abilities between human and small animal forms allowed them to escape through cracks eventually.

"Finally, I need to emphasize the deep and all-consuming interactive nature with the aliens: these events spanned an uninterrupted period up to six weeks long. If I were challenged to summon their company today, I could easily do so. On only a few occasions have I seen unexplainable things happen, such as a household item thrown to the floor a few feet away when I had left the room for a minute. During the periods of contact on the islands, East and West Coasts, the beings appeared to have a definite agenda to remove me from my home through harassment. On the other isolated occasions they had no agenda except to cause movements, electrical sparks and disturbance to domestic pets. One of my cats in particular is disturbed by invisible movements a few times a week in the same part of the house. Under ordinary circumstances, I lack the energy or motivation to pursue the entities as I did on their long-term visitations. Their detection and strong interactions require great concentration and dedication to the exclusion of all else. I usually cannot devote so much time to anomalies research. I have a family life, an investment business, and I travel frequently between residences on both coasts. Nevertheless, I would at any time or place be able to resume contact and reproduce these experiences at any location and with just a couple hours to prepare. At some point I would also like to see whether the entities are present at sea, in the air, or on foreign soil.

"It was an all-consuming and exhausting process to keep up with the interactions and study them as best I could, armed only with ordinary household equipment and materials. I have never had my wits and my scientific education put to practical test with such breadth and intensity."

As of this book's writing, Bill has had no further contacts to speak of and has moved from his home in the islands. It seems Bill may have lived close to a Djinni or a family of Djinn that wanted him gone.

SHADOW PEOPLE AND THE DJINN

Shadow people are silhouettes of human and non-human forms that are seen mostly at night and are the most common form of nighttime visitation. Sightings of the so-called shadow people have been with us for centuries, but it is only in the past ten years that reports seem to be increasing. Shadow people are not hindered by walls, but on occasion they seem to maneuver to avoid physical objects. There have been many shadow forms reported: some big, some small while others wear a hood or a hat. Shadow people can appear surrounded by a black mist or vapor and have been reported to move in a crouching position as if stalking a prey. There are quite a number of reports where shadow people have appeared at the foot of a person's bed, usually between two and four in the morning, either just standing there or pointing at the person. Most of the time there is no communication and the facial features are dark and distorted, but on occasion glowing red eyes have been seen. A shadow being's makeup seems to be dense since the beam from a flashlight is absorbed into their bodies, but if something is thrown at them they seem to flinch, even though the object passes right through them. Just before the appearance of a shadow person, the experiencer wakes up in the middle of the night with a feeling of stark terror. As they glance into the darkened room, a shadowy human figure floats through the doorway and positions itself at the foot of the bed. The apparition stays there for a while causing terror in the witnesses, then either disappears or floats out of the room usually leaving through the ceiling or under the bed. Also, sometimes before these entities are seen, the person will have a bad feeling, as if something is not right during the day. As they go to sleep, they have terrible nightmares and are awaken by the bed vibrating or even bouncing up and down on the floor. The shadow person will then float into the room or materialize out of nowhere. In many cases, the experience will repeat several times a month.

It seems to me these shadow beings or people are actually an intelligence located in a parallel universe or dimension. As they press up against the membrane that separates the two realities, we perceive them as a shadow image. No one really knows the true motives behind these visitations, but many victims feel as though they are being spied on. It is my opinion that these shadow people are actually Djinn trying to cross the barrier from their world into ours—we should pay very close attention to all these reports.

An Encounter With a Shadow Being

I have seen a number of photos of shadow people over the years, but to me they just look like vague shadows; some are just like the shadow of a person being photographed indoors with a flash. The best image I've seen is from a man who, after numerous UFO sightings and alien visitations, was able to get a shadow person on his security camera in his home. This person also has psychic abilities and is one of those rare individuals who may be partially connected to the dimension of the Djinn. After hearing a series of banging noises on his door, he was able to get the culprit on video. The shadowy figure moved off-camera and was not seen again. The feeling of many paranormal investigators is that the image is a hoax because it is too clear. Again, we see the strange researcher mentality that all clear photos must be fakes, and blurry photos real. Not one of these investigators who labeled the image as being fake ever interviewed the witnesses, but I and Rosemary Ellen Guiley both conducted lengthy interviews with this person. We are both in agreement that the witness is credible and the image of the shadow person from the home security camera is real.

PHANTOMS OF
TIME AND SPACE

Ghost hunting has become a popular pastime in the United States; unfortunately, most doing it are unfamiliar with paranormal investigation. The question of whether ghosts really exist or not is an academic one; people report seeing *something*. Are there spirits that refuse to pass over to the other side, or are we actually viewing the past and—perhaps on rare occasions—the future? One of the many theories of the new theoretical physics is that all points in time coexist together at the same area of space but with a different quantum signature. This difference in frequency would be enough to separate points of time even a nanosecond apart. To make matters more complex, the theory suggests that all periods in time are in motion and constantly changing, but we have no awareness of it.

I have investigated many hauntings and the appearance of human apparitions. Some may be disembodied spirits while others could be explained as the past or future merging together with the present for a brief moment. In Putnam Valley,

New York, near and around the stone chambers I mentioned in the chapter Realm of the Earth Spirits, people have reported seeing soldiers in uniform from the Revolutionary War entering and exiting the stone structures and in the basements of some of the nearby homes. My research showed that some of the stone structures and the homes were used to house soldiers during that time period. I would like to present one case that illustrates this point. It involves a twenty-first-century man who seemingly had a conversation with an eighteenth-century person while crossing a frozen reservoir one cold winter evening. The account is presented below in the witness' own words.

WHEN THE EIGHTEENTH CENTURY MET THE TWENTY-FIRST CENTURY

"It was February 2006 and at about seven or so, I decided to take a walk out in the cold night air after dinner. I live near the reservoir in Kent Cliffs and in February, it's frozen solid and safe for walking. I took a flashlight with me and headed out. The night was clear with a bright moon and the stars were flickering in the sky; it was quite beautiful despite the eight-degrees-above-zero temperature. I shined the light ahead of me and saw someone walking toward me; it was still in the distance so all I saw was a shape. As it approached, it looked like the air around it was distorted, like looking through heat waves. As the figure got closer, it became clearer and that's when I noticed it was a man, but he was dressed in strange clothes. He had long hair in a pigtail and was wearing old clothes, like from the eighteenth century. What I thought was really strange was that he wasn't wearing a coat and didn't seem to be affected by the cold. We got closer to each other and he started looking at me like I was out of place. We both stopped and I said, "How you doing?" He replied, "Good day, sir. Are you a resident of this town?" I said, "Yeah I am. Where do you live? Are you going to a costume party?" He replied, "Excuse me sir, *you* are the one in a costume, not me." I asked him how he could be walking on the ice on this cold winter night without a coat. He looked at me very strangely and asked me what I meant, saying that this was not a body of frozen water, but a field and it was a warm July night. He looked at me like I was some kind of freak, ran away, and vanished into the dark. I was convinced I saw a ghost."

Although my files contain several reports of witnesses having conversations with people who are out of time, so to speak, I find the report above one of the most interesting. In the eighteenth century, there was no reservoir at that location—there *was* a large, flat, open area. It seems that the witness above did not see a ghost but was in the right place at the right time when the past and present merged.

THE INDIAN GHOST OF NINHAM MOUNTAIN

Ninham Mountain, located in Kent, New York, is a place where a great deal of paranormal phenomenon has been reported. To the Native Americans, it was sacred ground and the home of earth spirits. It was named after the last great Sachem (chief) of the Wappinger, Daniel Ninham. During the American Revolution, sachem Daniel Ninham and his people joined Ethan Allen and fought in New York, Pennsylvania, and New Jersey against the British and Iroquois. Ninham was a fine warrior, and rose to the rank of captain. On August 30 and 31, 1778, Ninham's men, along with a company of patriots, fought British troops at the Battle of Tibbet's Brook. Ninham, his son, and forty of his men died during the battle. They were buried where they fell, a place now known as Indian Field. Local legend says that Ninham's spirit can still be seen walking up and down the trails protecting the mountain that bears his name. I have been on the mountain many times, and on more than one occasion have heard Native American drums that seem to have no source of origin. I have also collected several reports from people who, while hiking, claim to have encountered the spirit of the great sachem.

The Ghost of Daniel Ninham

The case involves several middle-aged people who decided to hike up the trail to the top of the mountain on a brisk February day. As they approached the mountaintop, a tall man with long hair clad in buckskins appeared out of nowhere. His skin was dark and he appeared to be Native American. He was tall in stature and wore deerskin boots. His hair was tied in a ponytail and his eyes were very dark. He approached the hikers and greeted them. He then said that he had just returned from the top of the mountain and would greatly appreciate it if they did not touch anything. When asked who he was, the stranger simply replied, "I am the keeper of the mountain and servant of the spirits who live here." The man passed them and the hikers continued to walk, discussing how strange the man looked. When they turned around to get another look at him, he had disappeared. According to the hikers, there was no way that he could have moved out of their line of sight so quickly—one can see up and down the trail for a considerable distance. The hikers thought the entire incident was strange but proceeded to the top of the mountain.

As they approached the top, they noticed large amounts of snow piled over one particular location; it was as if it had just snowed over that area and nowhere else. The group was amazed how white it looked, like fresh snow, but there was not a cloud in the sky. As they approached the snow, they noticed a crater; around it was what they described as Native Indian symbols of nature drawn into it. There was a turtle, bird, shooting star, and a figure of a warrior all deeply carved and filled with a red substance they thought might be blood, but they weren't sure. The red substance made them worry; they thought someone was performing a ritual so they decided to leave the mountain. As they walked down the trail, they looked to the right and out of nowhere, the strange Indian appeared again. He walked across the path, stopped and looked at them. He then said, "I am very sad that those who have followed me have not kept with the old ways. I have tried for many years to restore the power of this sacred place, but now I am tired and cannot continue, for my power is also failing and the Great Spirit is asking me to move on." The man then started to walk to the left side of the trail and, according to the witnesses, simply vanished into thin air. The description of the man matched that of

Daniel Ninham . . . is his spirit still protecting the mountain? This is not the first case in which hikers and hunters have reported seeing this apparition roaming the trails along the mountain. In 2008, a Ms. Sonya Sartori photographed an image of what may be the spirit of Daniel Ninham himself. Sonya's account is presented below in her own words from a written statement given to me in the fall of that year.

The Spirit of Ninham Mountain Captured in a Photograph (Sonya's Account)

"I read a book called *Hauntings of the Hudson River Valley* by Vincent T. Dacquino that had a chapter about Chief Daniel Ninham of the Wappinger tribe. The book mentions the stone chambers and spirits that protect Ninham Mountain. My son and his wife told me about their hike up the mountain and the tall fire tower at the top. They said the view was incredible and I should hike up to see for myself. It was a warm sunny October day and the leaves were a vibrant color so my daughter and I decided to take our dog for a walk up the Ninham Mountain trail. When we parked our car at the halfway point of the mountain, I noticed a stone chamber on the right side of the parking lot. I wanted to take photos, so my daughter said to hurry up to keep up with her. Well needless to say, I was lagging way behind her.

"Walking up the dirt road alone, with my daughter way up ahead of me, I felt a sad feeling I couldn't shake—it felt like I was being watched. Perhaps I felt sad because I read the story about Daniel Ninham's fight for this sacred mountain that belonged to his people and the loss. I decided to pile two rocks, one on top of another, on the side of the road and said, 'This is a symbol of my respect for you and this mountain. I am sorry that you died trying to keep your land.'

"When I reached the top of the mountain, other hikers were around the fire tower talking, eating, and admiring the beauty all around. I decided to start snapping photos of the area with my digital camera to show my father when I got back home. I looked all around when I took the photos to make sure no one else would be in the frame. When we started to walk back down the mountain I snapped more pictures of my daughter and some of the woods. As soon as we got back to the parking lot, I took more photos of the stone chamber.

"When we got back home, I loaded the photos on my computer and saw these amazing orbs in the chamber at the parking lot, and when I viewed the other photos of my daughter, I saw a figure against a tree in the background. When I zoomed in on the figure, I could see a face. I asked my friends and relatives what they thought, and they said it looked like a tan face with sunglasses or black paint over its eyes. When I took these photos I swear no one was near that tree at the time, and my daughter will also swear that no one was there at that particular time."

Shortly after the photo was taken, Sonya emailed me the image. The photo was so interesting that the next day I went up to the mountain with Rosemary Ellen Guiley (introduced in an earlier chapter) to find the exact location where the photograph was taken. We found the tree but could not find any explanation as to what caused the figure on the digital

254 PHANTOMS OF TIME AND SPACE

image. We even took a number of images ourselves from the same angle and time but got nothing. It's interesting to note that Sonya gave thanks to the spirits of the mountain and was then able to capture the image digitally. Was something responding to her good intentions? Was it the spirit of the mountain, the ghost of Daniel Ninham, or a being from a parallel dimension?

The Invisible Entities of the Mountain

In the fall of 2003, right around Halloween, I decided to go up to Ninham in the evening with my trusty 35mm camera and black-and-white infrared film. I was hoping to capture something on film because hunters and hikers had reported a multitude of paranormal events over the past ten years. It was dark as I walked up the trail and all seemed very quiet, . . . maybe a little too quiet. Then I noticed a faint ring of red lights that seemed to be bobbing up and down, coming down the trail and heading right for me. The lights were no more than 2 feet off the ground and perhaps the size of a baseball. I stopped dead in my tracks waiting for this thing to approach me and I thought, "Wow, I just got here and I am about to have a sighting of something!" Well, as the lights approached me I was able to identify them: they were a lit red collar on the neck of a dog and not far behind him was his master. I talked to the man and asked him why his dog was wearing a collar with red lights. He said that he was out coon hunting and this was the only way he could keep track of his dog to make sure he didn't shoot him. We went our separate ways, but I had a hard time believing this guy was out hunting raccoons in the dark; it was a little strange for someone to be doing this in New York.

I decided the first location to set my camera up would be in front of the stone chamber located just off the trail. I considered this a good place to start since there were reports of glowing figures and balls of light seen going in and out of the entrance. I placed my camera on a tripod and in conjunction with the infrared film, attached a Wratten 25A filter to the lens. This would ensure I would get only the red end of the spectrum. Attached to the camera body was a special lens that focused to a number of infrared wavelengths. Using a cable shutter release, I began taking a number of time exposures. Some were short, while others were several minutes long. After each frame I recorded my data because if something *did* show up, accurate information would be essential to identify the image with the exact time and location. I had a thirty-six exposure roll and took photos at a number of locations. Although it was still only October, the air was quite cold and it took me a good six hours to accomplish my task. I still had my own darkroom at the time, so the next day I developed the photos. The entire roll was blank, except for two frames taken in front of the stone chamber showing a bright infrared source apparently doing maneuvers in front of the camera lens.

Any light source moving across an open shutter would create a streak on the frame; whatever made the images only appeared on two of six exposures taken at the chamber entrance (they were consecutive shots). The source was not visible to my eye, though then again, why should it be since the object only emitted infrared light. I was very happy with the images obtained that night, since it proved to me these strange globes of light may be around us more often than we realize, but we very rarely perceive them since they are invisible to the naked eye. Over the next several years, I tried to duplicate my success with the hope of getting better images, but didn't. However, I was not the only one getting photos of the phantoms of Ninham. In the years to follow, I received fifteen photos from my readers who were able to capture images of unusual lights (both day and night) inside or in close proximity to the stone chamber.

WAS IT AN IMAGE OF THE PAST OR ANOTHER REALITY?

With the rise of digital photography, there has been a marked increase in paranormal photography. I must admit the reason for this eludes me; perhaps it's because people are taking more photos since they no longer have to pay expensive processing fees. Some skeptics believe the answer to this question is because digital images are much easier to fake.

In 1978, before the use of digital photography, I obtained a number of photographs with negatives of what is considered by many researchers to be the best paranormal photos ever taken. All the images on the twenty-four exposure roll show one reality disappearing and another taking its place. One of the most interesting frames shows flowers in the foreground in focus (the intention of the photographer) then more flowers behind out of focus (as it should be). What's amazing is that another image appears very clearly, behind the out-of-focus flowers that, according to the laws of physics, should also be out of focus but isn't. The image in this particular photograph shows what has been identified as a Babylonian bull and a winged man that some paranormal researchers think is an angel. A microscopic examination of the negatives proved that this was not a double exposure and, despite a lengthy investigation that included working with the company that processed the film, there is no indication that the negatives were faked. The photographers were two teenage girls taking photos of flowers on Block Island (off the east coast of New England), and until the film was developed, the girls had no idea what was on it because they saw nothing unusual in person. The negatives and prints were also sent to Kodak labs where technicians could find no explanation for how the images got there. It still remains a mystery and it may be one of those rare occasions when images of the past merge with our present.

MESSAGES FROM BEYOND

Throughout history, human beings have been fascinated with the idea of communicating with another plane of reality. Before the great boom in electronics, people went to mediums and used instruments such as Ouija boards in an attempt to contact the spirits of loved ones who had passed over. The case for "contacting the dead" using these methods is very weak and the product of an eager, possibly over-active imagination. The majority of individuals who attempt spirit communication want to believe their loved ones are still with them; they want to believe there is a life after the death of the physical body; they want to believe there is more to existence than education, working, and raising a family, but these peoples' desires exceed their common sense, in my opinion. One of the simplest and cheapest tools to attempt contact is the Ouija board. Many users of the board claim success, but just as many will say that it doesn't work and the Ouija is nothing more than a game.

OUIJA BOARD CONTACTS

A Ouija board, also known as a Talking Spirit Board, is a flat board with letters and other symbols painted on it. For decades, it was used by many people from all walks of life to contact the dead. Although its popularity peaked at the latter part of the nineteenth century, it is still manufactured (these days by Parker Brothers, who has trademarked the term "Ouija") and used today in attempts to contact ghosts and spirits. In the late twentieth and early twenty-first centuries, it has also been used to contact "demonic" entities and, in some cases, extraterrestrials. For however long its lifespan, the Ouija board hasn't changed very much; it still consists of a highly polished board with numbers and letters printed on it and a planchette, or indicator, which can mover freely across the board with a minimal of friction.[1] A very similar device is described in the Greek historical account of the philosopher Pythagoras of Samos in 540 BC and was used to communicate with the gods and spirits of nature.

In the late 1800s, mystics claimed that in order for the board to work correctly, it had to made out of wood from a weeping willow tree; the letters must be painted in red; and, most importantly, the board had to be blessed by a priest sprinkling holy water while reciting the Lord's Prayer. Today, the boards are made out of everything from pressed wood to plastic, and in today's world, I am doubtful Parker Brothers

---

1. The planchette is usually heart-shaped, but other shapes are also found. In very early boards, a small drinking glass turned upside down was used, and the boards were lubricated with lard or some type of oil.

calls in the services of a Catholic Priest to bless the boards as they roll off the production line.

In the twenty-first century, the use of the Ouija board is controversial; some claim usage is very dangerous because it can avail one to "evil" spirits (Djinn?) from other planes of existence. I have investigated a great number of cases where a series of paranormal events began to take place after the use of a Ouija board; terrifying events that in some cases, never went away. I do know for sure that well-noted author and close friend the late John G. Fuller used a Ouija board while doing research for his 1976 book *The Ghost of Flight 401*. Although skeptical, John claimed to have gotten amazing results when the board was used with a psychic he had worked with in the past.

I have also used a Ouija board in investigations of supposedly haunted houses. In a séance-like setting, the pointer moved so rapidly it actually surprised me. While my hands were on the pointer with another person, I said, "At the count of three, take your hands off." To my surprise, the pointer continued to move for about two seconds on its own. We repeated this several times and I was convinced that an outside force was pushing it during the session. I and everyone else present during this session had no negative experiences from use of the board, but others have. The case that illustrates this concerns a young man by the name of Bruce, his sister, friends, and a multitude of paranormal experiences that began after he and his friends decided to "play" with a Ouija board one night.

Night Terror (Bruce's Story)

"I was born in England and came to the United States when I was fifteen years old. At seventeen, I went back to England to spend time with my family who owned a pub. One day in 1977, in the early evening, a friend of mine made a Ouija board from a mirror and drew letters on it with a marker and used lard to make it slippery. We then found an old shot glass, turned it upside down, and used it as a pointer. It took awhile for us to get it started, but we asked some questions, at first it moved very slowly. Then as time went on, the indicator started moving so fast we had to have somebody write down the letters so that we could keep up with it. It was giving us quite a great deal of information and it seemed like there were different personalities communicating with us. Sometimes it spelled out words in modern English and then a new entity would take over and start spelling out words in old English.

"After awhile, whoever was communicating with us would use the extra lard to make patterns and draw a face. Sometimes, when we asked a question that it didn't want to answer, the shot glass would tip over on its side and stay there until we changed the subject. It drew a face I thought at the time looked like the *Creature from the Black Lagoon*. When I think about it today, it was more like that of a reptilian extraterrestrial with huge eyes, scaly skin, and a small mouth. My sister took some photos of it and they didn't come out, but strangely, every other photo she took did. We tried using the board again the next day and once again used the lard as a lubricant. A short time into the session it drew a picture of a solar system that looked like ours, and they said that they were from another planet that was on the other side of the sun that we didn't know about. They told my sister and her husband that in Kent (England) there was a natural time window, and if they went there that weekend the aliens would appear to them. In the days that followed, my sister's husband started acting very strange and finally had a nervous breakdown so they never went. After that, my sister never wanted to talk about what happened, and she stopped using the board to get messages.

"My friend and I continued to use the Ouija for several weeks, but weird stuff started happening around the apartment every time we used it. We heard strange sounds that came from nowhere and things fell off of shelves and sometimes flew across the room. This started to take place every time we used the homemade Ouija. During one session, it got so violent that my friend got scared and said that she wanted to stop. I picked up a bible that was next to me and placed it close to the board; when I did the words KILL spelled out. Then it said GET RID OF BIBLE, KILL. This went on for ten minutes, and I finally said that I wasn't going to put the bible away. As I picked the bible up, it flew out of my hands and smacked against the wall. The bible hit the wall with such a force that we just sat there startled for at least several minutes without a sound and just stared at each other. It was clear that whoever we were communicating with meant business and didn't want that bible around. Then the glass that we used as a pointer emitted a bluish white spark and shattered in my hands into a thousand different pieces.

"Things started happening after that night: it was a two-room apartment and my roommate told me that I was stiff on the bed one night and bouncing up and down as if something was shaking me. We often would wake up in the middle of the night or walk into the house after being away and smell a strong scent of burning sulfur of which we could not find the source. There was always a presence in the house that seemed evil; I told my friend not to leave me alone in the dark because whatever this thing was, it was after me and wanted to get me alone.

"Weird things continued to happen for a few days. Then one night in the early morning hours, my friend and I woke up at the same moment and saw a green circle of light moving across the room. When we saw it, a feeling of terror grew in both of us and I felt that if the light moved to the center of the room something was going to open up and it was going to be very bad for the both of us. I then got out of bed and turned on the lights and said, 'I don't want to do this anymore, I will not use the board again and look into this stuff anymore, leave me alone.' After I said this, the green light vanished and that was it, nothing happened for six months until I moved back to America. While in the United States I experienced what could be called dimensional contacts."

I would like to stop Bruce's story here since most of what took place after he came to the United States did not involve a Ouija board but was a series of dimensional alien contacts. It could be that the use of the board opened or created a conduit for these entities to continue contacting him. His further experiences will be presented in my next book, which details my investigations into the contact phenomenon.

ELECTRONIC VOICE PHENOMENA (EVP)

When I see people on a television paranormal reality show walking around a cemetery with a portable digital recorder asking, "Is there any one here who wants to talk with us," I can't help but laugh. Even if it was possible to communicate with those who have passed over, do these people really believe that the spirit of a deceased person would be hanging around the place where their body is buried? Over the centuries, many have tried to communicate with the dead with no success. Recently, a number of researchers have claimed to have received voice communication on their recorders and modified radios, but the evidence is weak at best. I must mention again that UFO investigators (including myself) have recorded messages, strange noises, and voices on tape recorders while conducting interviews with UFO witnesses decades before ghost hunters. Electronic voice phenomena was more frequent if the person was a contactee or had claimed alien abduction. UFO investigators and ghost hunters alike have to consider that taped anomalies on recordings may not be from the dead, but from intelligent beings from another reality playing a favorite game called "Fool the Human."

Human attempts from this physical reality to contact another realm of existence go back hundreds of centuries to the oracles of ancient Greece and Rome. Druid priests believed there was one special night of the year in which the past, present, and future coexisted, and it was possible only at this time to talk with those who had died and yet to be born. They also believed that doorways opened up to another reality where spirits would enter our world and interact with humans. Likewise, it was also thought possible to journey into their reality, but this was considered to be extremely dangerous. Today, we still acknowledge this special day of the ancient Celts and call it Halloween. According to my research, a peak in paranormal reports takes place on or around this day—is it just a coincidence, or are portals opening up at this time?

There are unconfirmed stories that Thomas Edison was working on a communication device to contact the dead. However, most Edison experts would contest this point and say the story about the genius trying to contact the spirit world is only a myth.[2] In 1899, while experimenting with a large electromagnetic generator (now called the Tesla coil), the great self-taught scientist Nikola Tesla claims that—after the device was turned off—to have heard a series of clear dots and dashes on his radio monitoring equipment. He said that the signals "were of a clear order that could not be traced to any known source."[3] Had Tesla's coil produced enough electromagnetic energy to create a small wormhole on the quantum level allowing beings in another dimension to send a message?

While on board his yacht in the Mediterranean in summer 1921, the inventor of the wireless telegraph Guglielmo Marconi claimed to have detected "unidentifiable radio signals" he said sounded like voices and strange sounds in the dis-

---

2. Cheney, Margaret, *Tesla: Man Out of Time* (Upper Saddle River, NJ: Prentice Hall, 1981).

3. Kenneth Corum, "Nikola Tesla and the Planetary Radio Signals," http://www.teslasociety.com/mars.pdf (Tesla Society Publications).

tant static.[4,5] He also said some of the sounds he heard were very similar to the same type of signals Tesla had detected in 1899. Stranger still, Marconi was very surprised when he heard dots and dashes he was able to decode as the Morse letter "S," the exact duplicate of the first radio transmission that was sent over the English Channel from South Foreland, England, to Wimereux, France, on December 12, 1901. He speculated that somebody was trying to communicate by sending his message back to him. Since no one was using the frequencies Marconi was experimenting with at the time, there would be no explanation for what he heard. Marconi was respected by his peers as being a down- to-earth person so no one doubted his claim; it remains a mystery.

Later, in the mid-twentieth century, a number of radio astronomers speculated that Marconi may have received extraterrestrial signals. However, it is much easier for me to believe part of his first radio transmission leaked into a parallel dimension where it was picked up by intelligent beings and then sent back twenty years later. Why wait twenty years to acknowledge the signal? Perhaps time flows at a different rate in this other reality and a period of twenty years between Marconi's experiment and when he picked up the unknown signals was only minutes in this other dimension.

---

4. "The Marconi Wireless Telegraph System," *Scientific American* 23 (November, 1907).

5. "Macroni Testing His Mars Signals," *The New York Times* (29 January, 1920).

Modern Technology and EVP

Electronic voice phenomena (EVP) refers to an inaudible voice (or voices) being successfully recorded on tape recorders or heard on some type of communication device like a radio receiver. Also, we have to consider EVP being heard on computers, television sets, and telephones. I have experienced EVP a number of times while recording a telephone interview. When you play the tape back and hear something your physical auditory system did not hear, it can send a chill up your spine!

The voices that are picked up give some type of message and very rarely can an actual conversation take place. People experimenting with EVP think the voices originate from the spiritual plane and are actually messages from discarnate people who have "passed over." I don't agree with this theory; it seems more reasonable to me that the voices are coming from another nearby dimension in our physical reality. It could also be that in some cases, entities in this other reality (Djinn perhaps?) are using identities of deceased humans to gain trust and establish communication with our world.

Back in the early seventies, I used a tape recorder with magnetic heads to record interviews and on more than one occasion, picked up voices and sounds that were not audible in the room. It seems the magnetic properties of those now-outdated recorders seemed more suitable for picking up EVP than new digital recorders of today. The digital recorders can pick up some sounds, but the voices are not clear and sound more electronic.

THE "GHOST BOX"

The most popular equipment for receiving EVP by radio is the "ghost box." Basically, it is an AM receiver set to rapidly scan up and down the commercial bands from about 550 to 1640 kilocycles. According to the paranormal researchers who have used this device, it creates audio bits and white noise that ghosts and/or spirits can manipulate into formed words. I have my doubts about this explanation and the truth of the matter is that no one really knows how the ghost box works.

I have used several versions of this device belonging to paranormal researcher Rosemary Ellen Guiley and have had mixed results: although you can hear words quite clearly, who or what ever is communicating seems to be able to answer one question only and very briefly. For example, when the researcher asked the question, "Is anyone out there?" the answer came back, "Spirit bodies." When another question was asked, the paranormal researcher didn't receive any more answers. On one occasion, the question, "Can you see?" was answered with, "It's too dark." When using the ghost box, the main problem is that only a very small percentage of questions answered actually make sense. Although the responses are clear, they are usually short; most skeptics feel it's just a coincidental mixing of words formed when the receiver is scanned through this crowded radio band.

Is It Real?

The question of whether or not these transmissions are from some type of spirit or dimensional entity is difficult to answer. My personal response would be: I believe so, but it would take a great deal of evidence to completely convince me of its origin. The voices on the radio seem to be coming from somewhere and, in rare cases, they are apparently responding to questions but usually only one question receives an acceptable answer. The only recording of EVP I've heard that gave answers to several questions was done by Rosemary Ellen Guiley in the basement of the Lincoln Theater in Decatur, Illinois. Some EVP recordings made from the ghost box have intrigued me so greatly that I used my background in science and technology to try to understand what had taken place.

The biggest question about the ghost box I have is *who* is coming through the devices and why are their messages only two or three words long? Some people feel that EVP are from demons, fallen angels . . . some even think they have received messages from extraterrestrials. Most of the paranormal community believes the voices are from ghosts, or the spirits of people who crossed over to the *"other side."* Although I can't discount any of these theories, I personally do not agree with them. It is my opinion that the voices are coming from beings from another dimension: they are not human and have never been human. The EVP messages received are for the most part non-threatening, but at times the "communicator" on the other side can become malevolent and just plain nasty without cause or warning.

My Analysis

The ghost box operates by scanning through an entire band with the EVP being received over a number of adjacent frequencies in the AM, FM, and upper and lower sidebands. This means the EVP is not on any particular channel; it is a signal with a very wide bandwidth. In my mind, this is what makes it so unusual. In order for the device to work and pick up a "spirit voice," a strong standard signal is required, so the more crowded the band with radio stations, the better chance of getting EVP. It seems the EVP part of the signal is so weak that it needs a stronger standard AM signal to piggyback itself on in order to be heard. The piggyback effect is simple to understand since one weaker radio signal on the same frequency rides on another stronger one to reach the receiver. I have seen the same effect in amateur radio when a signal that normally would be much too weak to hear will piggyback itself on a stronger and closer signal and be heard. By throwing a "dead carrier" (transmitting a signal with no modulation), you can actually hear stations in the background hundreds and even thousands of miles away riding in with the carrier wave. This is what seems to be happening with the voices on the ghost box; they are riding (or piggybacking) on standard AM radio station transmissions to the receiver. This seems to be done by design, indicating intelligence with a purpose.

To check this theory, I took a number of EVP recordings obtained from a ghost box and ran them through an oscilloscope. I discovered there were two basic signals in the transmission: the first is the standard AM radio station signal erratically modulated due to the band sweeping. The second signal was aligned with the first and could be separated by changing the sweeping rate. After this was done, the signal showed two independent transmissions that had continuous modulation very similar to an FM source.

Light and radio signals will follow the curvature of space so theoretically, these messages should not be able to reach our reality from another dimension. Also, what makes matters so puzzling is that the questions are asked by voice using no transmitting equipment at all. Is it possible that whoever is responding can hear us but we can't hear them? The only way an electromagnetic wave is going to pass through the barriers of alternate dimensions is through a wormhole or perhaps a very strong magnetic field that can actually bend space and allow the signal to reach a hidden reality.

It should also be noted that, despite optimal conditions, sometimes the ghost box doesn't work at all. The person operating the device seems to play an important part in its success since some people never get any results while others frequently do. Is it possible that the psychic makeup and attitude of the individual operating the ghost box is an important component to its success? We have to consider the possibility that the intelligence on the other side may only want to communicate with certain people. There is a considerable amount of research and analysis that still must be done in this area, but the one conclusion that I have reached is that the ghost box, although limited in its performance, does work.

Building Your Own Ghost Box

I always encourage my readers to experiment and report any findings to me. Constructing a ghost box is inexpensive and quite simple; you really don't need a background in electronics to put one together. There are a number of individuals who build ghost boxes and sell them, but they are quite expensive. Most devices use simple AM radios modified by cutting and connecting a number of wires together.

The older the radio the better, but RadioShack makes an AM radio that is very easy to convert into a sweeping band AM ghost box. RadioShack model 12-820 is the easiest to convert: all you have to do is remove the four screws in the back exposing the circuit. You will see quite a few gray wires, but the bundle you want will be on your left. Carefully cut the third gray wire from the left of the red wire; this wire is the mute or squelch and will cause your receiver to scan up and down the band. The next thing you might want to do is set up an external speaker so the sound will be clearer and louder. It's that simple! You now have a working ghost box to possibly receive EVP transmissions from another realm of reality.

Improving the EVP From the Ghost Box

My analysis indicates that the signal from the EVP is actually "piggybacking" on a standard AM signal, however since this is a very noisy part of the radio spectrum, it usually results in the EVP signal being distorted and very difficult to hear. Since a carrier signal of some sort is required, it would make sense to try a different part of the AM band. The long wave section of the electromagnetic spectrum between 100 and 400 KHz is very quiet, but the problem is that we need to generate an unmodulated signal in order for the EVP to be received. The solution would be to transmit what is called a "dead carrier," a signal with no voice modulation. The dead carrier would have to transmit over a very wide band area; this can be accomplished by a modified radio frequency (RF) signal generator. I believe such a generator would produce a clear EVP signal that might result in the ability to eavesdrop on the intelligence at the other end. This improvement may also result in our ability to have clearer and longer EVP conversations not limited to just a few words.

My attempts to suggest this method of improving radio EVP reception to those building versions of the ghost box have been ignored. It seems that some people are actually making a large profit by selling ghost boxes that are nothing more than very cheap AM radios that sweep the commercial bandwidth. In using any EVP device, remember that if you don't get any results, it doesn't mean that the system isn't working; it just indicates that whatever it is causing the EVP does not want to communicate. You must remember—conversation is a two-way street!

DIRECT COMMUNICATION WITH ANOTHER PLANE OF EXISTENCE

In rare cases, "alien" intelligence from another reality may choose to communicate directly with you. This kind of contact does not require a ghost box, voice recorder, or any other technological device—it is bizarre and will often take a person by surprise. I believe this happened to me on at least one occasion after I had my last meeting with Mr. John Gray (see the chapter Psychic Powers . . .). The contact was not only face to face, but also over the telephone. Although it took place quite a few years ago, I have never published the story because it has taken me a very long time to accept that the experience was indeed some type of communication from an alternate dimension.

A Message From Babaji

I was at the Port Chester, New York, train station on the platform waiting for the train to go north to Stamford, Connecticut. It was early summer of 1983, mid-afternoon, and as I looked up and down the ramp, I noticed I was alone, unusual for that time of the day. I then felt a little dizzy and closed my eyes for less than a second. When I opened my eyes and looked around, a strange little person approached me from the left. My first thought was, "Where the heck did this person come from?" As this person came closer, I could tell she was an elderly woman about 4 feet tall dressed in a white one-piece dress wearing a pith helmet similar to the ones worn by people on safari in Africa. As she approached, I continued to notice how strange and out of place this person appeared. She was heading in my direction, and I knew this person was going to stop to talk with me. The first words out of her mouth were in an accent that I could not identify: "Mr. Imbrogno, I have a message for you from Babaji. He wants you to know that this earth is in very grave danger from those forces that call themselves the fallen angels." Her skin was pale white and she had a great amount of makeup on her face to give it color. I think what made this little lady look so creepy was the amount of bright red lipstick she had on; it gave her face a clown-like appearance. I was quite surprised and asked her how she knew my name. She replied, "My friend from outer space told me you would be here and I must also tell you the message from Babaji: he said it is very important that you go to India and study with him." I tried asking more questions, but she would not answer.

I then asked where she came from since there was no one else on the platform and it looked like she appeared out of nowhere. She replied, "My friend, who is not of this world, made me appear here. I must tell you, Mr. Imbrogno, I am also not part of this world, but I used to be." She told me her name was Freda and she used to live in Connecticut before she "ascended to a higher plane." Freda then said, "I am only here for a very short time and have to go now." She then started to walk away from me and at that exact moment I heard the train approaching. I looked the other way and then looked back to ask her more questions, but she was gone. There was no way this person could have moved out of my sight in that short period of time!

I boarded the train and tried to rationalize what had just taken place: there was no way this "Freda" could have known who I was and have personal information like my whereabouts that day. The story does not end here: two days later I received a telephone call from a woman who said her name was Freda and that we met at the train station. We talked for about fifteen minutes and she repeated the same message word for word from our conversation on the train platform. I then asked her where she was calling from and she quickly mentioned something about the Greenwich Senior Citizen Center. Then, I heard a great deal of static and the connection was broken. Two days later, I paid a visit to the senior center in Greenwich, Connecticut, and asked for Freda—I was shocked when a staff supervisor told me that Freda used to live there but had passed away almost six years ago. The news really caught me by surprise and made me feel like I was in a *Twilight Zone* episode. Did I really have contact with a person from the other side? Luckily, I taped my phone conversation with Freda, but only recently played it for paranormal researchers who have come to visit me simply because it is just too incredible to accept.

2012 AND BEYOND

There has been a great deal of media coverage about the so-called doomsday prophecy of December 21, 2012, but what does it all really mean? For those of you who are unfamiliar, this prediction is based on the Mayan calendar and like any record that keeps time, it has a beginning and end. On the Mayan calendar, day one began on August 11, 3114 BC and the last page, so to speak, takes place in the year 2012 AD, on December 21, to be exact. Just because the calendar ends, does not mean life on this planet will cease to exist or that the world will be destroyed. The end of the old calendar can also be interpreted as the beginning of a new era, so we may start to see conditions on Earth change both geologically and socially very quickly after 2012. There are in fact a number of significant astronomical events that will take place at this time. In my point of view, these events have to be more than a series of unrelated coincidences.

The first major event concerns our sun. Our star is not perfectly stable; its energy output changes over a twenty-two-year cycle. For eleven years we see a very quiet sun with few sun spots and minimal solar flares. For the next eleven years, we see a very active sun with many spots and enormous eruptions taking place on its surface. According to research done by scientists at the Max Planck Institute in Germany, there is a direct correlation between the solar cycle and climatic conditions on Earth.[1] As of the publication of this book, we are in a solar maximum, or active sun. For some unknown reason, the sun has been abnormally quiet and this concerns scientists at the National Oceanic Atmospheric Administration (NOAA). In the years 2011 and 2012, our sun will be at the peak in this cycle; atmospheric and solar scientists fear we may be experiencing the cam before the storm.[2] It is thought that the sun is starting to build up energy for a number of massive solar flares that could be devastating for our tiny planet.

When the solar maximum cycle peaks in 2012, Earth will be subjected to much more solar radiation that it has received in the past decade. This will definitely have a direct effect on the magnetosphere of Earth and cause an increase in electrical energy being generated on the magnetic lines of force and ley lines surrounding the planet. It will also result in power blackouts, problems with satellite transmissions, and more spectacular views of the Northern and Southern Lights (Aurora Borealis and Australis). A good analogy of this effect would be pumping high voltage into a small ca-

1. Friedrich M., Remmele S., Kromer B., Hofmann, J. "The 12,460-year Hohenheim Oak and Pine Tree-Ring Chronology from Central Europe" *Radiocarbon* 46 (2004): 1111–1122.

2. National Academy of Sciences (NAS), January 2009.

ble. Since the great number of electrons cannot pass freely through the small cable, the result would be a considerable amount of energy built in the form of heat and an intense magnetic field. Applied to Earth, this phenomenon will cause the magnetic nodes on our planet, as well as other magnetic anomalies, to intensify.[3]

Also in 2012, our sun and planets will align with the galactic equator, subjecting Earth to an increase in radiation from the central black hole of the Milky Way. This also means our solar system will experience a great deal more gravity and radiation, which in turn will affect atmospheric and geological forces, and perhaps the rotation and revolution of our planet. Some geophysical scientists believe this may result in our planet wobbling more in its orbit and a shift on its axis resulting in a change of direction where the poles line up with the celestial sphere.[4] Last but not least, it is predicted that Venus will cross the disk of the sun in the summer of 2012 so our sister planet will be directly aligned with Earth.

So what does all this have to do with the paranormal? I believe that most of what we label as a "paranormal event" filters into our world from a number of parallel dimensions. A supercharging of Earth's magnetic field could cause the barriers of these parallel realities to either break down or fold on each other resulting in both realities merging for an

---

3. A magnetic node is a crossing or twisting of magnetic lines of force.
4. Pole shift is not to be confused with magnetic reversal, which is the periodic reversal of Earth's magnetic field.

unknown period of time. Such a merger would allow forces and perhaps living creatures of two or more realities to inter-twine. An easy way to understand this is to imagine a hotel with adjoining rooms. Normally, the door is locked and you can't see the adjacent room's occupant(s). However, you may hear some activity on occasion but the information you have about your neighbor(s) is limited. Now imagine there is no door or that it is partially open; the amount of information about who is staying there has increased considerably. Not only can you hear them clearly, but as they pass by the door, you can see them.

It is very possible this has taken place a number of times in the past giving rise to our legends of dragons, dwarves, fairies, trolls, and Djinn. These creatures of mythology (and sometimes our nightmares) can be found in the legends of many cultures across the world, and the truth of their real-ity may be more then we are willing to admit. As we enter a new beginning in 2012, human beings may experience a considerable increase in UFO sightings, psychic contact, and other types of paranormal phenomena. I believe every-one can sense the change taking place in our world. It is my belief that we should not fear the coming of 2012, but look at it as a new start for the inhabitants of Earth. When this time arrives, everyone's life will be filled with wonder and awe because another reality will be merging with our own; human consciousness will be greatly expanded!

A BRIEF ANALYSIS

Over the years I have accumulated a great deal of data regarding all aspects of the paranormal. If you are a researcher
and let the reports and case investigations sit in a binder,
then it really doesn't do any good at all. Luckily, on many of
the investigations I also collected the exact date and weather
conditions at the time of the report. Some of the analysis
presented in this chapter is based on 854 reports of paranormal events from my files; many cases go back a number of decades or even further. In this study I excluded UFO
reports, because if they were also included, the number of
raw cases would go into the thousands. This is because I
have a very large data bank concerning the sightings that
took place during the 1982–1999 flap in the Hudson River
Valley. The total number of UFO reports overshadows other
paranormal events, and so I have been left them out. I personally investigated many of these 854 cases. Some occurred
before my time, requiring a considerable amount of research
in magazines and newspapers archives. In some cases, I was

able to personally interview original witnesses, their families, and friends.

I tried to make the following graphs as accurate and clear as possible so the reader will be able to see patterns among the case studies. This pattern is apparent when the month, time of day, phase of the moon, and weather conditions are taken into consideration. In one of my previous books analyzing the UFO-Contact situation, I included a number of charts and graphs and received a few negative responses from self-proclaimed "scientific researchers" complaining the data was not presented "scientifically"; and at too simplistic a level. I'd like to remind these people that the actual time and funds needed to do this type of work is considerable; 99 percent of all paranormal-UFO investigators do research on a part-time basis while juggling a full-time job and family matters. There is very little money from royalties and lectures to fund in-depth, full-time study, so real science in this field is at a minimum. Also, this publication is not a paper for *Scientific American*; my goal was to make my findings as clear as possible for all who read this book. I feel that my work and the efforts of many others over the years, (although team efforts are somewhat not cohesive at times) are preparing the plot upon which the foundation of a new science will be built.

CHART 1: BREAKDOWN OF TYPE OF CASE

This study is based on 854 cases that have either been placed in a specific category or in one that closely represents the type of phenomena.

AP: This includes all types of apparitions.

NL: Nocturnal globes of light: includes spook light (I have also included globes of light seen in the daytime)

CRE: Strange creatures, Bigfoot, lake monsters, ECT

US: Unusual sound: Voices, growls, howling, electronic, music and a host of others

EP: Electromagnetic phenomena: Glows, unknown effects on cars, radios, and other technologies

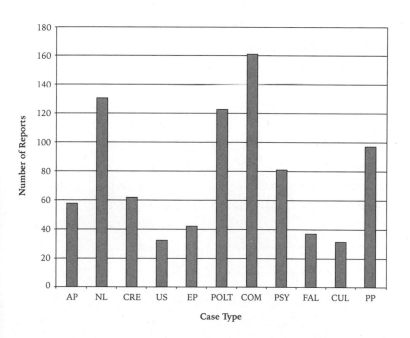

POLT: Poltergeist, the moving or bending of physical objects, and people without explanation

COM: Communications, dreams, channeling, drawings, automatic writing, Ouija boards, and ghost box communications

PSY: Psychic phenomena: increase in abilities of those who claim to be psychic, or not be psychic. Can take the form of a wide variety of events from precognitive dreams to out-of-body experiences

FAL: Falls from the sky

CUL: Cult-related activity

PP: Paranormal photography: imaging the unseen

CHART 2: MONTH AND FREQUENCY OF EVENT

The greatest numbers of reports are made in October. Interesting, given this is also the time of the year that many cultures claim a parallel world of spirits is close to ours.

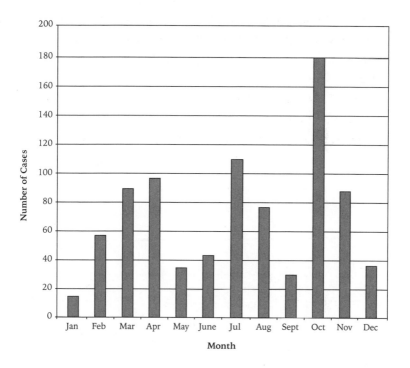

CHART 3: TIME OF DAY

I only had the accurate event times from 620 cases. The study is based on a 24-hour clock with one in the morning represented as 1 and one in the afternoon as 13. All times were rounded off to the nearest hour.

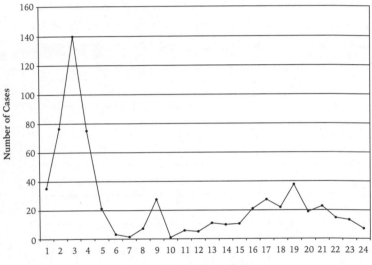

Time: 24-Hour Clock

CHART 4: LUNAR PHASE

Is there a relationship between a paranormal event and the phase of the moon? It seems likely, but it does not take place on full or new moon; instead, two to three days after each. Although the time period from full moon to full moon is 29.53 days, in this graph 1 represents new moon, 15 represents full moon, and 30 represents the time just before new moon. To know the lunar phase, I needed to have the exact day of the month and year. I could only do this for 614 cases. Arrows indicate locations of new and full lunar phase.

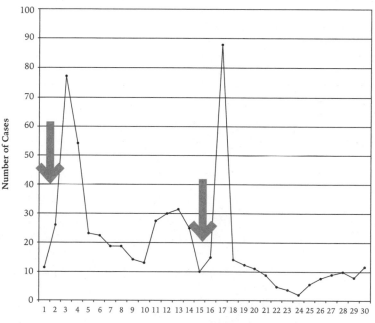

Phase of the Moon

CHART 5: WEATHER CONDITIONS AT THE TIME OF THE PARANORMAL EVENT

I have to admit, this was a difficult one since I could only use data in which I was able to gather the relevant information. It is based on 230 cases.

T Storm: During a thunderstorm

AT Storm: Within 24 hours before or after a severe thunderstorm

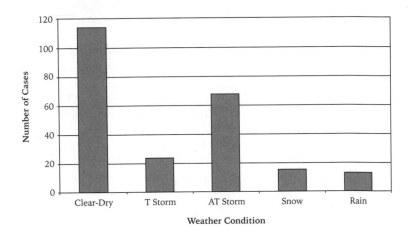

FOR FURTHER READING

Carter, Reverend Michael J. S. *Alien Scriptures*. Sun Lakes,
AZ: Blue Star Productions, 2005.

Casteel, Sean, and Timothy Green Beckley. *Our Alien Planet:
This Eerie Earth*. Uniondale, NY: Global Communications,
2005.

Friedman, Stanton T. *Flying Saucers and Science*. Franklin
Lakes, NJ: New Page Books, 2008

Guiley, Rosemary Ellen. *Atlas of the Mysterious in North
America*. New York: Facts on File, 1995.

Hansen, George P. *The Trickster and the Paranormal*. Blooming-
ton, IN: Xlibris Corporation, 2001.

Hynek, Dr. J. Allen, Philip J. Imbrogno, and Bob Pratt. *Night
Siege: The Hudson Valley UFO Sightings*, 2nd edition. St.
Paul, MN: Llewellyn, 1998.

Imbrogno, Philip J. *Celtic Mysteries; Windows to Another Dimension in America's Northeast*. New York: Cosimo Books,
2005.

————. *Interdimensional Universe; The New Science of UFOs, Paranormal Phenomena and Otherdimensional Beings*. Woodbury, MN: Llewellyn, 2008.

Joseph, Frank. *Unearthing Ancient America*. Franklin Lakes: New Page Books, 2009.

Richardson, Judith. *Possessions: The History and Uses of Hauntings in the Hudson Valley*. Cambridge, MA: Harvard University Press, 2003.

APPENDIX

A list of organizations and people you may want to contact for further information.

Philip Imbrogno
C/O Llewellyn Worldwide
2143 Wooddale Drive, Dept. 978-0-7387-1881-1
Woodbury, MN 55125-2989
Bel1313@yahoo.com

Loretta Chaney
Psychic Readings
203-730-0060
Lchaney22@msn.com

Joan Cara
Psychic
TRS Professional
44 East 32nd Street, Suite 44
New York, NY 10016
psychicjoan2@aol.com

Louis
Psychic
212-631-3577
Mysticpath2002@yahoo.com

Eddie Conner
"Soul Intuitive" (Psychic Readings)
eddie4soulaware@aol.com
http://www.eddieconner.com

New England Antiquities Research Association
Polly Midgley, State Coordinator for New York
P.O. Box 307 4G1
Scarborough, NY 10510
polmidge@optonline.net
Researches the stone chambers in the northeast United States.

Paul Greco and Francine Vale
UFO Roundtable
Yonkers Public Library (Will Library)
Yonkers, NY 10710
uforoundtable@gmail.com
http://ufos.meetup.com/237/

Another Reality
Hosted by Golden Hawk
goldenhawkfeather@yahoo.com
A radio show concerning spiritual matters and the paranormal.
Email Goldie to get show times and dates.

The Bigfoot Field Researchers Organization

CONTACT@BFRO.NET

Phone (949) 278-6403

FAX (949) 682-4809

Great database for you Bigfoot fans

Lake Monster Database

http://www.lakedragons.livingdinos.com/

Rosemary Ellen Guiley

Paranormal researcher/author

http://www.visionaryliving.com/

From Rosemary's site you can navigate to just about anyplace in the world of the paranormal!

International Fortean Organization

INFO

P.O. Box 50088

Baltimore, MD 21211

http://www.forteans.com

BIBLIOGRAPHY AND CITATIONS

A large percentage of this book's material comes from my own experiences and case files. However, I used the following references below to check facts and correlate data.

THE NEW SCIENCE

Alumni Newsletter of the Massachusetts Institute of Technology (December 2005).

Hawking, Stephen. *The Universe in a Nutshell*. New York: Bantam, 2001.

Susskind, Leonard. *The Anthropic Landscape of String Theory* (MIT Lecture, 2003).

———. *The Black Hole War*. New York: Little Brown Publishing, 2008.

Tegmark, Max. "Measuring Space and Time from the Big Bang to Black Holes." *Science Magazine* 296 (2002): 1427–1433.

————. "Parallel Universes." *Scientific American* (February 2001): 68–75.

————. *Parallel Universes: Science and the Ultimate Reality*. Boston: Cambridge University Press, 2003.

OUT OF NOWHERE

Clarke, Ronald W. *Benjamin Franklin: A Biography*. New York: Random House, 1983.

Fort, Charles. *The Book of the Damned*. New York Press, 1919

————. *Lo!* New York Press, 1931.

————. *New Lands*. New York Press, 1923. Today there are various publishers for the collected work of Charles Fort. His work now falls under public domain.

Mitchell, John. *Phenomena: A Book of Wonders*. New York: Pantheon Books, 1973.

New York Times, archives 1820-1983: http://www.nytimes .com/ref/membercenter/nytarchive.html

Viemeister, Peter E. *The Lightning Book*. Boston: MIT Press, 1972.

HIGH STRANGENESS

The Holy Qur'an (Koran). Translated by Various. Noor Foundation-International, 1977, 15:26–27, 7:27, 55:15, 10:39, 27:39–40.

THE GHOSTS OF THE LOST MINES

Casteel, Sean, and Timothy Green Beckley. "History of the Joplin Lights." *Our Alien Planet: This Eerie Earth*. Uniondale, New York: Global Communications, 2005.

Crystall, Ellen. *Silent Invasion*. New York: Saint Martin's Press, 1991.

Dallas Morning News, July 4, 1982.

Fort Worth Star-Telegram, August 3, 1980.

Imbrogno, Philip. "The Lost Mines of Putnam County, New York." *Earth Magazine* (May 1992).

The News Times (November 30 1895); found in the Danbury Library, Danbury, CT.

Putnam County Historical Society, Cold Spring, NY

Putnam County Records and Archives: Brewster, NY

The Southeast Museum: 67 Main Street, Brewster, NY (Maps and history and folklore of local mines).

CREATURES FROM A HIDDEN REALITY

"Wildman Spotted in Winsted" *The Republic-American Newspaper*, Waterbury, CT (August 23, 1895).

REALMS OF EARTH SPIRITS

Fell, Barry. *America B.C.* (revised ed.) New York: Times Books, 1989.

Imbrogno, Philip, and Marianne Horrigan. *Celtic Mysteries: Windows to Another Dimension in America's Northeast.* New York: Cosimo Books, 2005.

Various authors. *Hawk Rock and Other Megaliths in Putnam County.* Pound Ridge Museum, Pound Ridge, NY.

PSYCHIC POWERS: A REALITY, HOAX, OR DELUSION?

Houdini, Harry. *Houdini; A Magician Among the Spirits.* New York: Fredonia Books, reprinted 2002.

PHANTOMS OF TIME AND SPACE

Dacquino, Vincent T. *Hauntings of the Hudson River Valley.* Charleston, NC: The History Press, 2007.

Putnam County Historical Society records. *A Historical Account of Daniel Ninham,* 1897.

MESSAGES FROM BEYOND

Clark, Ronald William. *Edison: The Man Who Made the Future.* New York: Putnam Publishing, 1977.

Corliss, William R. *Mysterious Universe: The Sourcebook Project Books I and II.* Glen Arm, MD: Sourcebook Project, 1979.

Fuller, John G. *The Ghost of Flight 401.* New York: Berkley Press, 1983.

Tesla, Nikola. *Autobiography of Nikola Tesla.* Rockford, IL: BN Publishing, 2008.

2012 AND BEYOND

Kit Peak Solar Observatory Newsletter 72 (December 2002).

INDEX

GET MORE AT LLEWELLYN.COM

Visit us online to browse hundreds of our books and decks, plus sign up to receive our e-newsletters and exclusive online offers.

- • Free tarot readings • Spell-a-Day • Moon phases
- • Recipes, spells, and tips • Blogs • Encyclopedia
- • Author interviews, articles, and upcoming events

GET SOCIAL WITH LLEWELLYN

Find us on Facebook

www.Facebook.com/LlewellynBooks

Follow us on twitter™

www.Twitter.com/Llewellynbooks

GET BOOKS AT LLEWELLYN

LLEWELLYN ORDERING INFORMATION

Order online: Visit our website at www.llewellyn.com to select your books and place an order on our secure server.

Order by phone:
- • Call toll free within the U.S. at 1-877-NEW-WRLD (1-877-639-9753)
- • Call toll free within Canada at 1-866-NEW-WRLD (1-866-639-9753)
- • We accept VISA, MasterCard, and American Express

Order by mail:
Send the full price of your order (MN residents add 6.875% sales tax) in U.S. funds, plus postage and handling to: Llewellyn Worldwide, 2143 Wooddale Drive Woodbury, MN 55125-2989

POSTAGE AND HANDLING:

STANDARD: (U.S., Mexico & Canada)
(Please allow 2 business days)
$25.00 and under, add $4.00.
$25.01 and over, FREE SHIPPING.

INTERNATIONAL ORDERS (airmail only):
$16.00 for one book, plus $3.00 for each additional book.

Visit us online for more shipping options. Prices subject to change.

FREE CATALOG!

To order, call
1-877-
NEW-WRLD
ext. 8236
or visit our
website

NIGHT SIEGE

The Hudson Valley UFO Sightings

DR. J. ALLEN HYNEK, PHILIP J. IMBROGNO & BOB PRATT

In 1983, just a few miles north of New York City, hundreds of suburbanites were startled to see something hovering in the sky. They described it as a series of flashing lights that formed a "V," as big as a football field, moving slowly and silently.

It has been seen many times since then, yet the media has remained silent about it, as has the military, the FAA, and the nation's scientists. Now, in *Night Siege*, expert UFO investigators reveal the amazing evidence that cannot be denied and the more than 7,000 sightings that cannot be dismissed.

A classic in the field, *Night Siege* has been called one of the best researched and factual UFO books to date. This second edition is revised and expanded with sightings up to 1995.

978-1-56718-362-7
288 pp., 5³/₁₆ x 8   **$9.95**

TO ORDER, CALL 1-877-NEW-WRLD
Prices subject to change without notice
Order at Llewellyn.com 24 hours a day, 7 days a week!

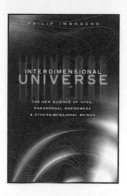

INTERDIMENSIONAL UNIVERSE
The New Science of UFOs, Paranormal Phenomena & Otherdimensional Beings
PHILIP IMBROGNO

Over the course of his thirty years of investigation into UFOs, including his own field research, photographic evidence, and meticulously compiled case studies, Philip Imbrogno has provided fascinating new insight into paranormal phenomena. In this book, he reveals for the first time the detailed experiences of prominent paranormal experts as well as his own firsthand experiences. Using the latest quantum theories, Imbrogno sheds new light on classic UFO cases, government cover-ups, and the hidden connections between UFOs and other unexplained phenomena—from crop circles and animal mutilations to angels and jinns (or genics).

Imbrogno's intimate knowledge spans the very early UFO activities to present-day sightings. He personally investigated four of the best-known UFO flaps of the modern era—Hudson Valley, Phoenix lights, the Belgium sightings, and the Gulf Breeze, Florida sightings—and shares information never released before, including photographic evidence that something very unusual is taking place on planet Earth.

978-0-7387-1347-2
312 pp., 5 $^3/_{16}$ x 8 $17.95

MESSAGES

The World's Most Documented Extraterrestrial Contact Story

STAN ROMANEK, WITH J. ALLAN DANELEK

We are not alone, and Stan Romanek can prove it.

From his first sighting of a UFO to chilling alien abductions, Romanek relives his personal journey as a conduit of extraterrestrial contact. But what's most shocking are the strange messages these unearthly visitors communicate to Romanek—authentic equations relating to space travel and planetary diagrams pinpointing what could be an auspicious date for the human race.

The national spotlight has followed Stan Romanek ever since the release of the "Peeping Tom" video of what he strongly attests is an actual extraterrestrial. Interviewed on *Larry King Live* and elsewhere, his true story of extraterrestrial contact is quite famous. More importantly, Romanek's gripping tale—augmented by video footage, photos, and physical evidence—is the most documented case of all time.

978-0-7387-1526-1
288 pp., 6 x 9 $16.95

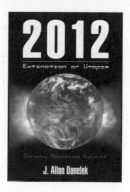

2012: EXTINCTION OR UTOPIA
Doomsday Prophecies Explored
J. ALLAN DANELEK

Is 2012 the end of the world as we know it?

From 2012 to global warming to worldwide epidemics, our society's fascination with doomsday is as strong as ever. Do any of these apocalyptic scenarios pose a real risk? Why does our modern culture embrace these bleak beliefs?

Divorcing hype from truth, J. Allan Danelek scrutinizes the ancient Mayans' 2012 end date, in addition to a wide array of doomsday beliefs from biblical prophesies to biological warfare. With piercing logic, he objectively explores each apocalyptic threat . . . and reveals startling insights about what kind of future—dire or dazzling—awaits humanity.

978-0-7387-1464-6
216 pp., 6 x 9   **$16.95**

UFOs: The Great Debate
*An Objective Look at Extraterrestrials, Government Cover-Ups,
and the Prospect of First Contact*
J. Allan Danelek

Do UFOs really exist? Are we alone in the universe? Is the government hiding
the truth from us? With his signature objective and balanced approach, J. Allan
Danelek explores the controversial questions surrounding extraterrestrials that
have raged for years.

This wide-ranging and captivating book begins with a historical overview of
the decades-long debate, followed by an incisive look at the case for and against
extraterrestrial intelligence. Danelek presents scientific evidence supporting
UFOs and other life-sustaining planets, examines hoaxes, and raises practical
objections based on radar findings and satellite observations. Next, he delves
into government conspiracies and cover-ups—including Roswell, alien visitation, and alien technology. There's also intriguing speculation about the alien
agenda—crop circles, alien abductions—and suggestions of possible scenarios,
both benign and malevolent, for first contact with an alien race.

978-0-7387-1383-0
264 pp., 6 x 9 $15.95

THE FOG

A Never Before Published Theory of the Bermuda Triangle Phenomenon

ROB MACGREGOR & BRUCE GERNON

Is there an explanation for the thousands of people who have disappeared in the Bermuda Triangle? What can we learn from Charles Lindbergh, Christopher Columbus, and Bruce Gernon—the coauthor of this book—who have survived their frightening encounters in this region?

The Fog presents Gernon's exciting new theory of the Bermuda Triangle, based upon his firsthand experiences, reports of other survivors, and scientific research. Gernon and MacGregor intelligently discuss how a meteorological phenomenon—electronic fog—may explain the bizarre occurrences in this region: equipment malfunctions, disorientation among pilots, and time distortions. They also explore the fascinating history of this infamous region and its potential link to Atlantis, UFO sightings, and a secret navy base on Andros Island.

Rob MacGregor has written several books on New Age topics and has won the Edgar Allan Poe award in mystery writing. Both Gernon and MacGregor live in South Florida, on the edge of the Bermuda Triangle. Bruce Gernon is a pilot who has flown extensively in the Caribbean. He has appeared in many documentaries about the Bermuda Triangle.

978-0-7387-0757-0
240 pp., 5 ³/₁₆ x 8 $12.95

THE UFO PHENOMENON
Fact, Fantasy and Disinformation
JOHN MICHAEL GREER

Do UFOs exist? Are the lights and strange craft in our skies aliens from other galaxies—or the product of fraud, delusion, or mistaken identity?

John Michael Greer, a respected authority on occult traditions, reveals the secret hidden at the center of the UFO labyrinth. This meticulously researched guide plunges into the thick of the controversy with an unexpected and compelling approach to the UFO mystery. Moving beyond the familiar debate between those who believe that UFOs are extraterrestrial in origin and those who believe UFOs do not exist at all, this unique work goes further to examine stranger and more rewarding topics—the nature of apparitions, the history of secret American aerospace technologies, the mythology of progress, and the role of popular culture in defining experienced reality.

978-0-7387-1319-9
264 pp., 6 x 9 $16.95

UFOS OVER TOPANGA CANYON
PRESTON DENNETT

The rural Californian community of Topanga Canyon is home to 8,000 close-knit residents, the Topanga State Park, and an unusual amount of strange activity going on in the sky.

Like Hudson Valley, New York, and Gulf Breeze, Florida, Topanga Canyon is considered a UFO hotspot, with sightings that began more than fifty years ago and continue to this day. Here is the first book to present the activity in the witnesses' own words.

Read new cases of unexplained lights, metallic ships, beams of light, face-to-face alien encounters, UFO healings, strange animal sightings, animal mutilations, and evidence of a government cover-up. There are even six cases involving missing time abductions, and a possible onboard UFO experience.

978-1-56718-221-7
312 pp., 5 $^3/_{16}$ x 8   **$12.95**

TO ORDER, CALL 1-877-NEW-WRLD
Prices subject to change without notice
Order at Llewellyn.com 24 hours a day, 7 days a week!

HAUNTING EXPERIENCES
Encounters with the Otherworldly
MICHELLE BELANGER

Working the graveyard shift at a haunted hotel, encountering a Voodoo spirit in New Orleans, helping the victim of an astral vampire attack . . . the supernatural has played a part in Michelle Belanger's life since the age of three. Yet she refuses to take the "unexplained" for granted, especially when the dead speak to her.

From haunted violins to dark fey, Belanger relives her thrilling experiences with haunted people, places, and things. Inspired to understand the shadowy truths about these paranormal mysteries, she examines each otherworldly encounter with a skeptical eye. What remains is a solid survey of the paranormal from a credible narrator, who also learns to accept her own gifts for spirit communication.

978-0-7387-1437-0
264 pp., 6 x 9 $15.95